The
History of
Switzerland

The
History of
Switzerland

JOHN WILSON

COSIMOCLASSICS

NEW YORK

The History of Switzerland
Cover © 2007 Cosimo, Inc.

For information, address:

Cosimo, P.O. Box 416
Old Chelsea Station
New York, NY 10113-0416

or visit our website at:
www.cosimobooks.com

The History of Switzerland was originally published in 1832.

Cover design by www.kerndesign.net

ISBN: 978-1-60206-117-0

Hagenbach, who could not conceal his hatred of the confederates, seized every opportunity of outrage against the whole people, or its individual leaders. He increased the tolls, invaded the rights of Swiss owners of land whose property lay in the new Burgundian territory, and supported with his influence every enemy of Switzerland.

——from Chapter IX: "From the First Alliance with France to the Death of Charles the Bold of Burgundy"

CHRONOLOGICAL TABLE

OF

SUBJECTS

IN THE

HISTORY OF SWITZERLAND.

CHAPTER I.

INTRODUCTORY DESCRIPTION OF THE COUNTRY, ITS NATURAL
FEATURES AND BOUNDARIES. — ORIGIN AND CHARACTER OF
ITS EARLIEST KNOWN INHABITANTS. — SUBJECTION TO ROME.
— CONDITION OF PROVINCIAL SERVITUDE. — HISTORICAL OB-
SCURITY, AND VARIETIES OF RACE AND LANGUAGE, RESULT-
ING FROM THE INROADS OF BARBARIANS. B. C. 110—A. D.
500.

A 4

CHAP. II.

MIXED POPULATION IN THE CENTRAL AND SOUTHERN PARTS
OF EUROPE. — GRADUAL DEVELOPEMENT OF THE FEUDAL
SYSTEM. — JUDICIAL AND ECCLESIASTICAL POLITY. — DE-
GRADATION AND EXTINCTION OF THE CLASS OF COMMON
FREEMEN. — FOUNDATION OF TOWNS CREATES A THIRD
ESTATE IN THE GERMAN EMPIRE.

CHAP. III.

STRUGGLE BETWIXT THE PAPAL AND IMPERIAL POWER FOR
SUPREMACY. — CHARACTERS OF HENRY IV. AND OF HILDE-
BRAND, AFTERWARDS POPE GREGORY VII. — THE CRUSADES.
— THE DYNASTY OF ZÆRINGEN IN HELVETIA.

CHAP. IV.

TIMES OF RUDOLPH OF HAPSBURG.

CHAP. VI.

FROM THE REVOLUTION OF ZURICH TO THE LEAGUE WITH APPENZELL.

CHAP. VII.

FROM THE COUNCIL OF CONSTANCE TO THE BATTLE OF ARBEDO.

CHAP. VIII.

WAR OF THE CONFEDERATES WITH ZURICH.

CHAP. XII.

COMPETITION OF THE GREAT EUROPEAN POWERS FOR THE
ALLIANCE OF THE CONFEDERATES, AND THE ASSISTANCE OF
THEIR TROOPS. —— SYSTEM OF FOREIGN ENLISTMENTS INTRO-
DUCED, AND PLAUSIBLY JUSTIFIED. —— ITALIAN EXPEDITIONS.
—— PERPETUAL PEACE WITH FRANCE.

CHAP. XIII.

FALL OF THE SWISS FROM MILITARY PRE-EMINENCE ASCRIB-
ABLE TO THE CHANGES IN THE ART OF MODERN WARFARE.
— PREDISPOSING CAUSES, AND FIRST MOVEMENTS OF THE
REFORMATION.

CHAP. XIV.

STRUGGLES AND VICISSITUDES OF GOVERNMENT IN GENEVA. — ITS
ALLIANCES WITH THE CANTONS, AND EXTORTED INDEPEND-
ENCE OF SAVOY. — MORAL AND SOCIAL CHANGES PRODUCED
BY THE INFLUENCE OF CALVIN.

CHAP. XV.

FROM THE COMMENCEMENT OF THE THIRTY YEARS' WAR TO THE PEACE OF WESTPHALIA.

CHAP. XVI.

INSURRECTION OF THE PEASANTRY IN BERNE, LUCERNE, SOLEURE, AND BASLE.

CHAP. XVII.

RELIGIOUS WAR, AND WAR OF TOGGENBURG.

a

CHAP. XVIII.

COURSE OF EVENTS DURING THE EIGHTEENTH CENTURY.

CHAP. XIX.

DISTURBANCES AT GENEVA AND IN NEUFCHÂTEL.

CHAP. XX.

GENERAL VIEW OF THE STATE OF SWITZERLAND SHORTLY
BEFORE THE FRENCH REVOLUTION.

CHAP. XXI.

FROM THE FIRST YEARS OF THE FRENCH REVOLUTION TO THE
PEACE OF AMIENS.

CHAP. XXII.

FROM THE ACT OF MEDIATION TO THE PRESENT TIME.

HISTORY

OF

SWITZERLAND.

CHAPTER I.

ANCIENT HELVETIANS. — ROMANS AND BARBARIANS.

B. C. 110. — A. D. 500.

ASPECT OF THE COUNTRY. — ANCIENT INHABITANTS. — ALLY THEMSELVES WITH THE CIMBRI AND TEUTONES. — DEFEAT A ROMAN ARMY. — INVADE GAUL. — REPULSED BY JULIUS CÆSAR. — ROMAN CONQUEST OF RHÆTIA. — HELVETIC INSURRECTION UNDER VITELLIUS. — QUELLED BY AULUS CÆCINA. — JULIA ALPINULA. — HELVETIA SUBJECT TO ROME. — BARBARIAN INROADS ON THE EMPIRE. — SETTLEMENTS OF BURGUNDIANS, ALEMANNI, FRANKS, AND OSTROGOTHS. — DISTINCTIVE FEATURES OF FRENCH AND GERMAN SWITZERLAND.

A TRACT, however outwardly devoid of those advantages which are commonly viewed as the chief, if not sole elements of national greatness, will always take up a space in human history more extended than its visible strength and surface seem to claim for it, where " a petty population, without allies, munitions, or money, without state-craft, without military skill, save that which nature taught, could maintain itself in possession of its primitive rights and usages through all the European revolutions of five centuries."*

The land of which the history lies before us has been said to fight the battles of its inhabitants, and by

---

* Müller.

B

the very structure of the ground to screen them from
subjection, as well as to preclude them from conquest.
Its main features still remain the same as Strabo has
described them.—" Through the whole extent of the
Alpine chains," says that exact geographer, " there are
hilly platforms capable of cultivation — there are also
highly cultivated valleys ; yet the greater part of
the hill country, especially in its highest recesses,
is unfruitful, on account of the snow, and of the
severity of the climate. As its rude inhabitants felt the
want of all the productions of agriculture, they sometimes showed forbearance towards the cultivators of the
plains, in order to obtain from them the necessaries of
life. For these they exchanged resin, pitch, pine-wood,
honey, and cheese, of which they had enough and to
spare."*

Helvetia is placed nearly at the centre of Europe, and
may be considered (geographically speaking) as a corner
of Germany. The ancient name of the country was
derived from its first known inhabitants; the modern,
from the canton of Schwytz, the cradle of Swiss independence. It is bounded on the north by the lake of
Constance and the duchy of Baden, on the east by the
Tyrol, on the west by France, and on the south by
Italy. No other division of our quarter of the globe
presents a panorama so astonishing,—no other exhibits
so surprising a diversity of landscapes, ever interesting, and ever new in their features. Nowhere such
extremes meet as in Switzerland ; where eternal Alpine
snows are fringed by green and luxuriant pastures,—
where enormous icebergs rise above valleys breathing
aromatic scents, and blest with an Italian spring,
— and where the temperatures of each zone alternately
reign within two or three leagues. But not alone the
contrasts of nature claim our attention in these regions.
Those of man are equally remarkable ; from the life of
the Alpine shepherd, who preserves in his lonely valley
the simplicity of primitive times, to that of the inhabitant

* Strab. Geogr. iv. 6.

of towns, refined and softened by the manners and the language of France.

East and west, from the lofty central point of the St. Gothard, extend the Alps, in the form of a mighty crescent, embracing the north of Italy, and on every side environed by tremendous clefts and caverns, which ensnare the incautious traveller with a veil of greyish snow. Here is the horrid birthplace of the glacier and the avalanche; but hence, too, streams are welled forth by the genial warmth of nature to supply romantic lakes, and spread fertility over the face of the soil. Four principal rivers flow through Switzerland; the Rhine, the Rhone, the Ticino or Tessin, and the Inn. All of them originate in the high line of the Alps, and indicate by their course the main declivities of the country. The northern slope is watered by the Reuss and the Aar, which meet in the Rhine; the southern by the Ticino, the north-eastern by the Inn, and the south-western by the Rhone.

It would be useless to enquire how long the land was overshadowed by the foliage of impenetrable forests, and re-echoed only the roar of the bear and ure-ox, and the scream of the lammergeyer; or who were the first human stragglers, urged by love of freedom or solitude to seek a scanty subsistence there by hunting, fishing, or pasturage. The condition of the tracts between the Rhine, the Rhone, and the Jura, remains involved in almost entire obscurity till the appearance of the Helvetians, a race of Gallic Celts, whom some unknown accident had guided from the borders of the Rhine and the Main to those of the lake of Geneva. The toilsome cultivation of these regions, while it left but little time for martial enterprise, conduced with the pure mountain breezes to form a stout and hardy people, which divided itself into four districts, then, as in later ages, connected with each other by the feeble bands of a federal union.

It is probable that the Gallo-Celtic inhabitants of these regions, bordering so closely upon Italy, took part

in the great inroads of the Gauls on that country. But
their first ascertained military enterprise was conducted
in alliance with the Cimbri and Teutones, who roamed
from unknown regions in the east and the north; extended their conquests and ravages along the banks of
the Rhine, and even struck the already powerful Roman
commonwealth with terror. Whether few or many Helvetian tribes accompanied that expedition is a point which
cannot now be determined. What is evident, however,
is, that each of these tribes had full liberty of waging
wars, and allying itself with foreigners. Thus, the
Tigurini, for example, marched with the Cimbrians
nearly to the mouths of the Rhone. But when a Roman
army, under the consul Lucius Cassius, threatened their
rear, they suddenly wheeled round, apprehensive of
being cut off from their homes; and, led by their young
general Diviko, gave the Romans a complete defeat on
the banks of the Leman lake (lake of Geneva). The
consul, and his lieutenant Piso, were left dead on the
field. The conquerors only permitted the retreat of
the survivors after they had given hostages, and marched
under the yoke.

Long after Diviko's excursion with the northern
marauders, recollections of the fat pastures and rich domains of Gaul, of which a glimpse had been caught in
the course of that excursion, furnished all who had, and
many who had not, shared the adventure, with a theme
for the most highly coloured description. There the
vine and olive ripened under a warmer heaven, and the
winter's snows were all but unknown. The effect of
these reminiscences was enhanced by the accounts
brought by travellers from the left bank of the Rhine,
which produced their natural workings on a rude and
simple people, — a people highly irritable, daring, and
self-confident, — with whom prudent deliberation passed
for cowardice, and in whom successful excursions had
encouraged the propensity to predatory warfare. Their
pastoral habits adapted them for any wandering enterprise: those distinctions of rank which are described

as having existed among them marked out a military
order. The priestly power is apter to take root among
the more pacific cultivators of plains.

A leader of the former class stood forth among the
Helvetians in the person of Orgetorix, — a man of rank
and ambition. In peace, he could not gratify his appetite
for absolute power, and therefore built his hopes upon
warfare. Having secretly gained a number of adherents,
he came forward in a public assembly, and artfully persuaded the people to quit their rocky fastnesses, which
barely furnished food for themselves and their cattle, and
to march with him into the fair and fruitful territories
of Gaul, where little resistance was to be feared from
the effeminate inhabitants. The orator succeeded in exciting the rude appetites and passions of his hearers.
His proposal was received with acclamations. It was resolved to break up and emigrate, after the lapse of three
years, with their wives and families, cattle and possessions. The interval was to be used in making the
needful preparations. Before, however, the year of the
expedition had arrived, the despotic designs of Orgetorix
were discovered; and he was reduced to lay violent
hands on himself, in order to escape death at the
stake.

The resolution of the Helvetians must have been
based on deep conviction, since it suffered no alteration
from so ominous an outset. That retreat might henceforth cease to be thought of, they burned their habitations, and even their corn, reserving only three months'
provisions. Moreover, they succeeded in persuading
several neighbouring tribes to burn their towns and villages in like manner, and accompany them. Three hundred and sixty-eight thousand souls, of whom ninety-
two thousand were able-bodied warriors, are computed
to have marched out on this Gallic expedition.

The Roman province of Gaul was, at the point of time
before us, under the government of Julius Cæsar, — already no less eminent as a military leader than he became,
a few years afterwards, as a statesman. He was, at this

moment, aiming at the same power over his countrymen
as that to which Orgetorix had aspired among the Helvetians; but, unlike the latter, the Romans had become
ripe for subjection. Orgetorix, besides, was no Cæsar.
Without granting the passage desired by the Helvetians
through his province, he found means to put them off,
to gain time and collect reinforcements. He followed,
with his army, their march through the lands of the
Sequani and Ædui (inhabitants of the territory afterwards the Franche-Comté and duchy of Burgundy),
alleging as his reasons the danger caused to the province
under his charge by the descent of so warlike and enterprising a people, and the petitions for aid addressed to
him by the Ædui, who were annoyed by the Helvetian
inroad. In fact, however, any and every pretext for intervening in the affairs of Gaul was welcome to him.
He made no demonstration of hostility till the main in-
vading body had already crossed the Araris (Saône),
when, falling on the Tigurini, who alone had remained
on the left bank, he cut most of them to pieces, and dispersed the rest.*

Notwithstanding this unlooked-for catastrophe, the
Helvetians did not yet renounce the main scope of their
enterprise, and made overtures to treat with Cæsar. Old
Diviko was commissioned for this purpose, who did not
forget in recent defeat his former superiority. No treaty
could be brought to a conclusion, and Cæsar followed the
march of the invaders a fortnight longer. At length,
after a desperate and long-sustained conflict in the
neighbourhood of Bibracte (Autun), the superiority of
the Roman arms and discipline decided the day against
the stubborn courage of the Helvetians. Their strength
and spirit now completely broken, they submitted.

The terms imposed by Cæsar on the vanquished
invaders were, to return into their desolated country,
and rebuild their wilfully ruined habitations. For their
immediate provision, he supplied grain through the Allo-
broges (inhabitants of the territory extending from Ge-

neva to Grenoble, and from Vienne on the Rhone to the Alps in Savoy); and promised for the future that they should live under their own laws, under the specious denomination of allies of the Roman people. In order, however, to watch and overawe these new allies, a fortress was built at Noviodunum (Nyon), near the lake of Geneva. Several other garrisons were stationed throughout the country.

The Rhætians only, screened by their lakes and icebergs, might for a moment yet esteem themselves invincible, and form leagues with the natural allies of their tribe, who were scattered along the course of the Inn, throughout the vales of the present Tyrol, and in the plains included since in the circle of Swabia. They pursued a wild and reckless mode of life; plundered travellers, or broke suddenly forth in numerous hordes through their mountain-passes, and fell by surprise on the neighbouring towns of Italy.

Even during Cæsar's Gallic proconsulate, there are traces of the Roman arms being turned against the Rhætians; and so soon as Augustus had firmly secured his dominion over the empire, he endeavoured to confine within more narrow bounds, on the southward, a people whose incursions had by this time become formidable even to the plains of Upper Italy. Soon afterwards he sent against the Rhætians his two step-sons, — Drusus from Italy, Tiberius through Gaul, and by the lake of Constance. Only after an obstinate struggle, renewed with repeated efforts, were these vigorous assertors of their country's independence compelled beneath the universal empire of Rome. (15 B. C.) A part of their youth were afterwards embodied in the legions, and the subject land was occupied by permanent encampments.

We have seen that the Helvetians were at first flattered by the Romans with the title of allies, — a title of precarious value at any time, and which, in the present case, seems only to have been given till the land should be secured in subjection. This is rendered still more evident by the circumstance of an equestrian colony, even in Cæsar's time, having been founded at Noviodunum (Colonia Julia Equestris). Under Augustus, Munatius Plancus founded the Colonia Augusta Rauracorum; and the settlement at Vindonissa (Windisch) cannot be of much later date. The franchises conceded to these settlements, the grants of land and subsidies which (in order to encourage such establishments, and build them up as outworks of the Roman dominion,) were conferred upon the Roman soldiers and colonists who chose them for a permanent residence, prove nothing with regard to the general welfare of the country, and the condition of its primitive inhabitants. They, indeed, retained in part their simple forms of polity, which soon, however, became merged in the central administration; and even so early as the reign of Augustus, heavy poll and land taxes, hitherto unknown, were introduced in these regions.

When the weaker come in collision with the stronger, one precipitate step may easily plunge them in ruin. This was experienced by the Helvetians, on the occasion of the murder of the emperor Galba (A. D. 69); an event of which either the tidings did not immediately reach them, or found them disinclined to acknowledge Vitellius, — the candidate for the purple against Otho. This prevalent indisposition, or ignorance, was not at all corrected by the conduct of the twenty-first legion (surnamed *rapax*) * at Vindonissa, which, with rapacity suiting its surname, seized the pay set apart by the Helvetians for the garrison of the castle. The latter retaliated, by intercepting letters between the German and Pannonian armies, and by arresting a centurion with a company of soldiers. Their general, Aulus Cæcina, who was marching from the Rhine with his unbridled bands to meet Otho in Italy, sacked and destroyed the bathing-place on the Limmat (now Baden), which had grown, during long peace, to the importance of a municipal town. He called out reinforcements from Rhætia, to fall upon the rear of the

* Tacit. Hist. xi. 43.

native insurgents. These, without practice in arms, discipline, or tactics, were, in fact, without any of the conditions of success, and found themselves attacked by mountaineers like themselves,—the Rhætians. Assailed in flank by the legions under Cæcina; in rear by the cohorts coming up from Rhætia, as well as by the disciplined youth of Rhætia itself; they suffered a severe defeat. Borne down by the Thracian cohort, pursued and tracked to every retreat by the light German and Rhætian troops, many thousands were left dead upon the field, or made prisoners, and afterwards sold for slaves.

When the news of the lost battle reached Aventicum, amazement and distress prevailed. The ambassadors, who were instantly sent to appease the wrath of the conqueror, were received and addressed with harshness by Cæcina. He demanded, first of all, the execution of the principal man in the nation, Julius Alpinus. He referred the people for mercy to the emperor, who alone had power to mitigate their well-deserved chastisement. When the ambassadors brought this answer back to Aventicum, through fear of Cæcina's wrath, no one dared to discuss the sentence. Julia Alpinula only, daughter of Julius Alpinus, and a priestess of the goddess Aventia, dared a filial effort for the rescue of her parent. She hastened to the embittered foe's encampment, threw herself at the general's feet, and, with all the persuasive powers of youth and innocence, entreated for the life of her father. Cæcina ordered his instant execution. Fifteen hundred years since the occurrence, the following sepulchral inscription was discovered in the ruins of Aventicum:—

"*Julia Alpinula hic jaceo; infelicis patris infelix proles. Deæ Aventiæ sacerdos, exorare patris necem non potui: male mori in fatis illi erat. Vixi annos* xxiii."

(I lie here, Julia Alpinula; unhappy child of an unhappy parent. Priestess of the goddess Aventia, my prayers could not avert the death of my father: fate had decreed him a lamentable end. I lived twenty-three years.)

The Helvetian envoys made their appearance before Vitellius, anxious, yet scarce hoping, to avert the last extremities. Audience at length being given, the infuriated soldiers brandished weapons of death before their eyes, and demanded loudly the total extirpation of a race which had laid presumptuous hands on Roman warriors. Vitellius himself knitted his heavy brows, and muttered menaces. The spokesman of the Helvetians, Claudius Cossus, stood pale as death before him, offered no excuse of the facts, but only depicted, in the liveliest hues, the misery of his country, threw himself at the emperor's feet, and begged so irresistibly, that all hearts were affected, and the soldiers themselves took part in supplicating mercy for Helvetia.* Thus his country was preserved by one man; but instead of being, as hitherto, entitled the ally of Rome, was degraded into union with the province of Gaul.

It, however, remains doubtful whether, even at this period, when the whole land was nominally subject to the Romans, a certain measure of freedom, in its wooded and rocky recesses at least, might not still have continued to exist, compatibly with a nominal allegiance, perhaps even with the payment of a tribute. The remains of Roman settlements, extending from the Albis to the Bernese Oberland, lead to the inference that a connected line of garrisons was kept up for security towards the interior of the country. Roman coins, &c., which have been found in the interior, and even in the higher parts of the mountains, may have come there through the natives themselves. This may be conjectural; but a matter of more certainty is, that Roman habiliments, manners, and usages, became diffused throughout the country, along with their attendant effeminacy, luxury, and moral corruption. The Latin language gradually encroached upon, and in some measure superseded, that of the country. Even in things of common use, and in agriculture, many Latin names, which have not been adopted into the formed and matured dialects of Germany, are to be met with at the present day in

* Tacit. ibid. c. 7. *et seq.*

Switzerland.* All genuine nationality was extinguished, and the very name of Helvetia disappeared. The inhabitants became mere subjects.

The government of Nerva, Trajan, Adrian, and the two Antonines, in almost its whole duration, may be reckoned among such blessings as Providence but sparingly vouchsafes to mankind. Under such rulers, bad administrators are rare, or, at all events, they are kept in check by wholesome apprehensions. Human industry penetrated the fastnesses of the mountains. The Alpine cows became an article of commerce; for though the breed was small and poor in flesh, it was capable of enduring labour, and afforded abundance of milk: the Alpine cheeses gained at that early period the renown which they retain to this day. Experiments were undertaken in agriculture — and the Falernian hills were rivalled by the vineyards of Rhætia. The Helvetians paid peculiar veneration to the god of wine; and preserved his gifts, not as yet in wine cellars, but in wine casks. They worshipped also the sun, by the name of *Belin*, the invincible god; and his sister *Isis*, the moon; the sylphs, their guardian angels; and the shadowy powers, the *dii manes*. But the period must soon terminate in which individual qualities softened the workings of pure despotism and military dominion. The inseparable consequences of boundless prodigality, and consequent rapacity, on the part of the rulers, had made government a mere unpunished system of plunder. Admission to the rights of Roman citizenship, which, under Caracalla, became easier than ever, had the effect of introducing Roman citizens into all situations hitherto filled by natives. Thus the latter came at length to be governed by functionaries, who acted upon wholly distinct interests from theirs; a grievance which rose to its highest pitch in the reign of Diocletian, who conferred upon the higher class of officers powers of proceeding summarily, without calling assessors.

* The following are examples, — Aren (for pflügen, to plough), Bolle (bulla, a bud), Furkel (furca, a pitchfork), &c.

"Woe to the land," exclaims an eloquent Swiss writer *, "on whose judgment seats the stranger sits — at whose gates the stranger watches! Woe to the land divided against itself, and relying on foreigners! Woe to the people which gathers gold, but knows the use of steel no longer!"

Christianity, during this period, spread by degrees throughout Helvetia. Men who were abandoned as a prey to every variety of misery and oppression, must have found a system welcome and encouraging, which taught resignation and patience under suffering, while it held out brighter hopes for the future; which had its menaces for the haughty and tyrannical, and its comforts for the lowly and wretched, and singled out the indigent and despised classes as the most especial objects of divine grace and mercy. The original announcement of the new faith has been ascribed by the legends to a certain Beatus, so early as the first century; in the third century, to Lucius, a Rhætian; at the close of the fourth, to the members of the so-called Theban legion. In like manner, the signatures of bishops or presbyters of churches, in the Valais, at Geneva, Coire, Aventicum, and elsewhere, are handed down to us, bearing date from the fourth century. These, however, are of extremely doubtful genuineness. What is better made out is, that a church existed at the close of that century in the Valais. During the fifth, others were established in the rest of the above-mentioned places.

Meanwhile the Roman power sunk lower and lower. Not the misused people only, but many men of rank and power, encouraged foreign, in order to get rid of domestic, enemies. Under the perpetual minority of the imbecile Arcadius and Honorius, the empire, already more than once dissevered, became permanently parted into Eastern and Western. Precisely at this epoch of exhaustion, more numerous swarms of semi-barbarous nomad nations set themselves in motion than

* H. Zschokke.

at any former period; the roughest and remotest of
which drove the others forwards on the now defenceless
frontiers of the empire. While from the east the Goths
fell upon Italy, while the Vandals and the Suevi attacked
Spain, the Burgundians (also a race of Vandal origin)
marched on the Upper Rhine, from the Oder and Vistula.
(A. D. 409.) Imperial Rome, too feeble to repel them,
granted them, according to former examples, the possession of the larger part of the lands which they had
devastated; thus purchasing their alliance against enemies
yet more formidable.

The Burgundians fixed their residence on both sides
of the Jura, on the lake of Geneva, in the Valais, on the
banks of the Rhone and the Saône. They had adopted
Christianity on their reception as Roman allies—a
title which, by this time, had completely changed
its import; and, instead of future subjugation, augured future mastery. They combined with large
and vigorous outward proportions a character less rude
than that of some other northern nations. In the
quality of peaceable guests and new allies of the empire,
they spared the still remaining towns and other Roman
monuments, and permitted the former owners to retain
their established laws and customs; appropriating, however, to themselves, a third of the slaves, two thirds
of the cultivated lands, and one half of the forests,
gardens, and farm buildings.

Much obscurity, during this period, rests on the history of those regions which are now German Switzerland.
It is not exactly known how far the first Burgundian
empire extended itself over the plain of the Aar. East-
ward of that stream, and over great part of Germany,
the land was over-run by the Alemanni, whose inroads
on the empire may be dated somewhat later than those
of the Burgundians. (A. D. 450.) These new-comers,
embittered towards whatever bore the name of Roman,
destroyed the still remaining fragments of fortresses
and cities, which, in common with all German tribes,
they utterly detested. They did not treat the inhabitants

with cruelty, but reduced them to a state of complete servitude. All Roman landed property they seized without exception, and only allowed the tenants to remain there in the situation of bondmen, and on the condition of paying them dues. This new barbarian torrent overwhelmed the public monuments and symbols of Christianity. Whatever yet remained of the old culture disappeared, or, at all events, concealed itself.

Towards the close of the fifth century, another German race, or rather confederacy of tribes, obtained ascendency. These were the Franks, a sturdy stem of heathens, whose power was established in Gaul by their leader Chlodewig (Clovis — Louis). This chief engaged in hostilities against the Alemanni. In the plain of Tolbiac (Zulpich, near Cologne, on the Rhine) the hostile nations met in deadly conflict. Victory remained long undecided; the fortune of the day seemed even to lean towards the Alemanni. In this emergency, Clovis swore aloud that he would turn, with all his Franks, to Christianity, if he won the field. This, as he doubtless intended, being heard by his Christian Gallic troops, they resolved to show their faith in Christ, in its whole triumphant efficacy. The Alemanni could not stand against the onset of enthusiasts, who felt that they were fighting for the glory of God. The fall of their prince decided them to surrender, and transfer their allegiance to the victorious king of the Franks, and Clovis marched along with them into their territories. Here, however, hostility towards the Franks and their new gods induced many to refuse him obedience. It was not until nine years after his victory that the body of the tribe was brought to submission. Clovis resolved to extirpate a population so unmanageable.

While Clovis raged thus furiously against the Alemanni, his brother-in-law Theodoric, king of the Ostrogoths, wrote to remind him that mercy and moderation better became a monarch than vengeance. As Clovis turned a deaf ear to this wise and benevolent counsel, many of the conquered Alemanni finally threw themselves into

the arms of their intercessor. Thus Rhætia became
added to the dominions of the Ostrogoths; and at length,
in the year 500 of our æra, south-western or Roman
Switzerland belonged to the Burgundians; northern or
German Switzerland was shared between the Franks,
the Alemanni, and the wilderness: Rhætia was possessed by the Ostrogoths. These partitions, however,
were destined to have no long duration. The first
Burgundian empire owed its final dissolution (A. D. 534),
in a great degree, to the family feuds and vices of its
princes. The empire of the Ostrogoths verged to its
fall about the same period. Five successive kings incurred successive losses in war and land. Dietbert, king
of the Franks, took advantage of their weakness to recover
the possession of Rhætia. Thenceforward the Franks
held exclusive rule over the whole extent of Rhætia
and Helvetia.

From this period is derivable, in a general way, without aiming at impossible exactness, the distinction of
the French and German languages in Switzerland. So
far as the dominions of the Alemanni, and since their
subjection those of the German Franks, extended, the
present Swiss dialect of German took its rise from the
original roots of that language. In the lands about the
lakes of Geneva and Neufchâtel, where the power of the
Burgundians was established, the Gallo-Roman popular
dialect kept its ground, from which were formed the
several Romance dialects: from these, again, the Pro-
vençal; and at last the modern French.

More obscure in their origin, however obvious in their
existence, are some characteristic varieties in the divisions of the race itself; for notwithstanding all the
mixtures which have hitherto taken place, and all
local exceptions, a marked dissimilarity exists between
them. The more rounded contours of the western inhabitants are distinguishable at once from the strong
features of the eastern. The latter may conjecturally be
traced to the Alemanni; while the former are more
probably inherited from a Frankish stem.

CHAP. II.

HELVETIA UNDER THE GERMAN EMPIRE.

500—936.

EARLY INSTITUTIONS OF THE GERMAN TRIBES. — LAWS. — RULES
OF EVIDENCE. — TRIAL BY ORDEAL. — TRIAL BY BATTLE. —
HELVETIA UNDER THE FRANK KINGS OF THE FAMILY OF
MEROVEUS. — IMPROVED CULTIVATION. — INFLUENCE OF THE
CLERGY. — DECLINE OF THE MEROVINGIAN RACE. — ITS FALL. —
PEPIN. — CHARLEMAGNE — VISITS HELVETIA — ENCOURAGES
EDUCATION AND AGRICULTURE. — JUDICIAL AND ECCLESIASTI-
CAL POLITY. — PARTITION OF THE EMPIRE OF CHARLEMAGNE.
— INCURSIONS OF THE MAGYARS, OR HUNGARIANS. — MEA-
SURES OF HENRY THE FOWLER. — GROWTH OF TOWNS.

THE Frank kings of the family of Meroveus were the
third exclusive rulers of Helvetia. As no fixed laws of
succession existed, the country belonged, under their
government, now to one head of the whole Frank dominions, now to several princes, amongst whom those
dominions were divided, and who were no less divided
by disputes among themselves. Omitting the intermin-
able feuds of these princes, the perpetual alternation of
conquests and losses, and other incidents equally little
momentous, we shall rather attempt a rough draught of
the social and judicial institutions of the German populations at that period, in order to trace the gradual
revival of Helvetia from a state of deep and utter desolation.

The population, in those central parts of Europe
which had been occupied by branches of the great German family, was a mixed race, compounded of the
conquerors, the aboriginal inhabitants of the country,
and the later ingrafted colonies of Rome. The first
claimed the exclusive right to be lords, while the two
latter were looked upon as slaves of the soil; or, at the

utmost, as an inferior and ignoble race of men, neither
in rights nor in honours on an equality with freemen ;
treated with little or no regard in matters of legislation ;
and, above all, excluded from the privilege of bearing
arms,—the proudest badge of freedom, and its only
security.　Military service was the first of public duties.
The assembly of the people, in which every freeman
had a voice, pronounced on all public affairs of importance ; and the monarch could not arbitrarily set
aside its decisions.　In peace, indeed, the king was only
first of his peers, but in war-time his command was
almost absolute ; and, as wars were almost incessant
since the period when the German tribes had extended
their incursions over the south of Europe, the people
became more and more inured to obedience.　The
people might be said to consist exclusively of the
conquering army.　Individual warriors settled themselves on scattered landed possessions.　About a hundred
farms or manors constituted a hundred (cent).　Over
this a centenary, or constable, was appointed, who held
a court analogous to the old hundred court in England,
which took cognizance of all cases concerning freemen
or conquered nations.　The public place for the administration of justice was called *mallus*.　Over larger
circles or districts counts were appointed ; over whom
dukes presided, who were commonly the leaders in
war.　Besides the original and ordinary allotments
after victory, to all freemen, of the spoils and conquered territory, which thus became their independent
property (*allodium*), the kings made separate grants to
those who had done them special services, under the
Roman denomination of *beneficium* ; in later ages.
feudum, or fief.　The grantee was thereby placed in the
condition of a vassal, and under special obligation to
arm in defence of his feudal lord.　Fiefs at first were
not hereditary, nor even given for life ; but, in the course
of time, the vassals found means to render them inherit-
able, and almost independent of the monarch.　Such
was the rise of hereditary nobility ; which, while on the

c

one hand it set limits to the royal power, and reduced it in some countries nearly to nothing, on the other hand depressed the common freemen to the condition of serfs.

The laws partook of the rudeness of the period, and were few in number: these, however, were tolerably intelligible, and consisted less in commands than in prohibitions. Their main object was protection of property; for in those ages theft was viewed with more abhorrence than murder, since even a coward can make himself master of things unarmed and inanimate. This abhorrence of the cowardly crime of theft went so far, that, according to the Saxon laws, a horse-stealer was punished with death; while a money fine would expiate even the murder of a nobleman. The judge who let a robber escape was proceeded against as guilty of a capital crime. Whoever accepted a secret composition for theft was punishable equally with the thief. Whoever was charged by five impartial witnesses with theft must die. Hardly any other crime besides theft was punished with death, but treason and breach of trust. Most crimes had their money price; by which a double advantage was given to the rich over the poor, as the penalty was proportioned to the rank of the person against whom acts of violence (then the most frequent crimes) were committed, and was calculated thus in an inverse ratio to the pecuniary abilities of the payer; while non-payment entailed the loss of personal freedom, and degradation to the state of feudal bondage. The rudiments of trial by jury existed at this period. Apprehension of the abuse of evidence, or rather ignorance of its use, introduced appeals to the judgment of God through the medium of the ordeal. The accused was made to plunge his hand into boiling water, take hold of a red-hot iron, or set foot on a red-hot ploughshare. The limb which had been thus tried was put in a sealed bag; and the appearance which it presented on the third day was decisive of the party's guilt or innocence. Several other trials of this description came into use; and their application lay almost entirely in the hands of the clergy. Deceptions, which were only too easy, threw doubts at length on the aptitude of this instrument of justice; but, when once the path of reason has been swerved from, men only glide from one absurd aberration into another. Single combat now superseded the ordeal, as a method of proof less easily eluded; a method of which the vogue is not surprising at a period when irregular vindications of right by *voies de fait* were so frequent. Women, and others unable to bear arms, were, in general, permitted to procure capable substitutes. These and similar modes of trial were, at least, not worse than the torture, and those other inhumanities which in later times were introduced in the nations of German origin from the laws of other lands, and through the spiritual tribunals.

In the year 613, Clothair II. succeeded in uniting the whole empire of the Franks, after long internal wars and scenes of violence had taken place. Two years later, in 615, Clothair called his peers, secular and spiritual, together, to restore order in the land, and to remove existing grievances. In this assembly were settled the rights of the several ranks and races; and a basis was laid for the future constitution of the empire. The people learned, by slow degrees, the value of peace and tranquillity. Prosperity was gradually restored to the wasted lands of Gaul and of Helvetia. On the demise of Clothair, in 628, his son Dagobert ascended the throne. What the father had begun the son successfully continued, and administered his realm with vigour, wisdom, and justice.

In these times Helvetia, which in earlier days had counted twelve towns, 400 villages, and above 350,000 inhabitants, and where now nearly 2,000,000 human beings are collected in several thousand towns and villages, lay in great part waste and desolate, covered over with morasses and forests. Here and there a cluster of rude tenements might be met with, around a farm, a fortress, or a monastery. The revival of a country is difficult after long disasters; especially when its natural site and qualities are unfavourable to the rapid growth and bloom of civilisation. The recovery of Helvetia, therefore, could only advance slowly. It commenced, however, under Clothair and Dagobert. Villages and towns arose in many places; and their rise was often favoured by religious foundations. Those of St. Gall, Disentis, Zurich, Lucerne, and Romainmotiers, may be traced to the times of which we have been treating. The bishops, — who, like their clergy, very generally lived in wedlock, — were elected by the latter and by the people, and afterwards confirmed by the king.

While the clergy, as in most rude nations, was exclusively in possession of such knowledge as existed, a few individuals only among the laity could at that time read, and still fewer could write. This brought into the hands of the clergy, besides their spiritual power over the conscience, considerable political influence; and enabled them, in a manner, to monopolise the functions of ministers, envoys, and agents in all the most important affairs of monarchs and great men. Into their hands fell the education of the upper classes, and the composition of history, — including, of course, the formidable instruments of praise and blame. Their influence was enormous in the diets of the empire; and, when Clothair demanded contributions from them, they complained, not of tyranny, but of sacrilege. Yet kings, who knew how to vindicate the dignity of their office, maintained a wholesome ascendency over the synods of the clergy; and these again opposed themselves, not unfrequently, to clerical, social, and moral abuses.

Soon after the time of king Dagobert, the Merovingian dynasty began to verge towards ruin. The effeminacy, tyranny, and vices of these princes brought them, finally, into contempt with their subjects. They gave over the government altogether into the hands of their prime functionary, the mayor of the palace (*major domûs*); who was also commander-in-chief of the army. The elevation of Pepin of Heristal to that dignity, through the support of the nobles, in the year 687, is enough to

show that the royal power had dwindled away to a
shadow. Under the vigorous administration of his son,
Charles Martel, the royal person ceased to appear at
all, except in the annual popular assembly of the
Franks on May-day. The Frank monarchy seems
indeed, at this time, to have nearly reached the ideal
of constitutional aristocracy. The king was a mere
puppet in the hands of the men of influence; and the
mayor of the palace played the part of responsible
minister, in executing the mandates of this virtual representative body. Six monarchs of the Merovingian
dynasty were cut off, within the space of forty years,
by sword or poison. Of few of these can history make
any honourable mention. At length, when in addition
to unworthiness came impoverishment, (for the Mero-
vingians, in order to maintain themselves on the throne,
were forced to alienate their hereditary domains in favour of their proud and rapacious nobles,) these princes
lost entirely the regards of the people. In the year 751,
two centuries and a half since the erection of the Merovingian dynasty by Clovis, Childeric III. was deposed
from the throne by the assembly of the people at Soissons,
thrust aside into a convent, and succeeded on the throne
by the mayor of his palace, Pepin the Little, who founded
the new Carlovingian dynasty. The whole proceeding
was sanctioned by the blessing of pope Stephen III.

The Carlovingian dynasty, founded by Pepin, received its name from his son Charles; who not only
excelled his father in greatness, but exalted himself
high above the mass of his contemporaries. His
reign, contrasted with that of his son Louis, who succeeded him, exhibits an instructive example how, with
resources nearly similar, by means of skilful administration, a vigorous prince can elevate himself along with
his people, and even efface the memory of important
errors and blemishes; while, on the other hand, an incapable ruler, without bad dispositions, may not only
make himself individually contemptible, but cripple and
confine the national energies.

Pepin, with consent of his nobles, had, in 768, divided his kingdom between his sons, Charles and Carlomann; and the early death of the latter did not leave the former free from the suspicion of having hastened it by poison. Charles, shortly after his accession, put an end to the Lombard kingdom in Upper Italy. The Saxons, in the regions of the Lower Elbe and Weser,—who, notwithstanding many defeats, persisted in the most courageous resistance,—were brought into subjection, after thirty years' warfare, and compelled to embrace the Christian religion. The Arabs, who possessed Spain, were driven back as far as the Ebro. In the east, he forced Bavaria to acknowledge his supremacy, and extended his power as far as the Raab in Hungary. Yet he was not a mere insatiable conqueror: he directed his unremitting attention to internal administration. Through his capitularies, he aimed at improving the mode of administering justice; and the earlier institution of circuits, made by royal commissioners, was called into new life under his reign.

He was crowned at Rome as emperor, by the pope, in the year 800,—a solemnity which enhanced the outward dignity of his throne, but placed his feeble successors in a dangerous state of dependence on the spiritual authority, and fortified the prejudice which, for ages afterwards, shook the independence of thrones no less than the internal repose of nations. Similar in its tendency was the law enacted by Charlemagne,—that bishops should be nominated, not by the royal authority, but by the clergy and people in every diocese, without any other recommendation than merit.

Helvetia had her share of the provisions made by Charlemagne, with a wisdom far beyond his age, for the popular instruction. Among the schools which he established or reformed was that of Zurich, where the grateful recollection of his bounty was preserved by an annual celebration. He also introduced vine-cultivation into Helvetia; and peopled several districts by transporting thither the conquered Saxons. He occasionally made

some stay at Zurich; and enriched the cathedral church
with his donations. We read, moreover, that men from
the Thurgau served in his campaigns, whose strength
and spirit attracted general notice.

After the death of Charlemagne, Helvetia, notwithstanding the frequent partitions of the empire, and the
internal disorder occasioned by them, enjoyed peace for a
century. The land flourished greatly during this period,
under what was called the *Second* or *Little* Burgundian
kingdom, which was founded by count Boso of Vienne,
and which maintained itself for more than an age independent of the sinking Carlovingian dynasty. Many
common-lands were divided, and converted into arable.
In the Valais, and even in the neighbourhood of Zurich,
vines were cultivated. The inhabitants, formerly scattered, now collected themselves into farms and villages, in
which commonly stood a baronial tower or mansion.
Every village had a special jurisdiction, under its *vogt*,
or bailiff. The whole district assisted in the trial of important cases. The general assembly, which was held
in the open air, was joined by every one who possessed
seven feet of land before and behind him. The elders
took the first place; the count stated the case; and every
man gave judgment on it as God had given him understanding. After the case had been thus debated, the
judges, properly so called, stepped into the circle,—that
is to say, into the middle of a ring formed by the rest
of the meeting,—and that which they declared was received for doom. The monastery of St. Gall, already
wealthy and powerful, distinguished itself for science
and for discipline. It was not, indeed, an age of native
learning; nor had St. Gall much to boast of in the shape
of intellectual productions of its inmates or tenantry.
Here, however, the books of the fathers and ancient
historians were read and copied; and many a now extensively diffused Latin work might have been lost to
the modern world but for the toils of these obscure
monks, inhabiting a corner of the Thurgau. The use of
religious foundations, in the infancy of national culture,

may be likened to that of firs planted to screen the growth of young trees. Oak and beech may long survive their dark and withered nurses; but it was these whose formal and sombre lines could alone have served effectually to fence the tender saplings from the bleak gales of the north.

The partition of the empire of Charlemagne between the two branches of his family, which established themselves on the thrones of France and Germany, at which the separate histories of those countries may be considered to commence, and the extinction, not long afterwards, of the Little Burgundian line, threw Helvetia under the power and protection (such as it was) of the German empire, restored by Otho the Great from amidst the ruins, which were all that remained of the lofty pile of Charlemagne. The decline of the Carlovingian race was made to subserve their own aggrandisement by the counts and by the rest of the nobility. Pepin and Charlemagne, by frequent changes, and by strong control of their functionaries, had imposed checks on the increase of the power of the counts. But now the lords, great and small, spiritual or secular, turned to good account the weakness of the government. Many of them aimed with success at absolute independence. The great nobles exercised oppression over the less powerful members of their own order; and exacted from them oaths of allegiance, as though they were their masters and monarchs. In effecting their designs, the counts made frequent appeals to arms, without asking the consent of their princes; and rendered the empire, which they ought to have protected, a theatre of ravage and desolation. Even the servants of the church began to stretch their holy hands, in all directions, after the treasures of this world. Enriched by perpetual pious bequests, they at length found themselves strong enough to push their pretensions, if need were, at the point of the sword. This struggle for aggrandisement gave occasion for continual strife betwixt the clergy and nobles, whose plans were perpetually crossing each other.

The lords and counts, who ruled during this period in Switzerland, domineered over the land uncontrolled; and only feared or flattered the German emperors when they hoped to increase their power by their assistance. Union among themselves they never knew, or knew at times only of instant and universal peril.

Such peril hung over all in the days of Henry I., surnamed the Fowler. A fearful scourge, — the irruption of hordes of absolute barbarians, — from which the land had been exempted during more than four centuries, broke out afresh, shortly after the opening of the tenth century. The Magyars, or Hungarians, like the Huns, their savage predecessors in former ages, extended their multitudinous and mischievous incursions into the very heart of Germany, into Switzerland, and even into Italy and France. They wasted the whole face of the open country, and exercised savage cruelties on the unarmed inhabitants. On the other hand, their ignorance could effect little or nothing against fortified and well-provisioned places.

The principal mode of defence adopted by Henry was at once the most effectual, as against so rude an enemy, and the most permanently useful to the country, long after the immediate emergency had passed away. He built walls around a number of defensible places, as a refuge for the property and persons of the country people. The fortifications of Zurich, of Soleure, and other Swiss towns, are generally referred to this epoch. To this epoch also belongs the first foundation of the class of burghers, whereby Henry the Fowler has merited to be viewed as in no small degree the founder of all modern civilisation. It is true that he could not contemplate all the effects of his own measure; of part, indeed, he could not have the slightest conception. This does not detract from the wisdom and benevolence of his purpose, in contending with the reluctance of the German tribes of his kingdom, who, accustomed as they were to vagabond licence, unwillingly sat down in walled towns, and looked upon these sanctuaries of popular rights as prisons. To counterweigh these prejudices, Henry con-

ferred on the towns a number of important favours
and privileges; which, in many points, placed the
burghers on an equality with the nobles. The lesser
nobles themselves, who, as we have seen, were elsewhere
exposed to oppression by the powerful men of their own
order, received, along with ordinary freemen, a due
share in the management of civic concerns. All the
other settlers, moreover, were looked upon as freemen,
with the exception of those who were bondsmen of convents or cloisters already existing within the walls of the
town. Thus, at the sides of the nobles and the clergy
arose a new class — that of the burghers; which, in the
sequel, came to take part in the municipal administration, and assert a higher degree of independence.

It is probable that Henry saw, in his new municipal-
ities, the cradle of a third estate in his kingdom: it is
certain, at least, that the birth of a rival and formidable
interest was viewed with jealousy by the higher nobles
and clergy. These tyrants had extended their powers
arbitrarily, not only over their vassals, but over those
who might at any time have voluntarily courted their
protection. They demanded of them new contributions
and services. Freeholders, or freemen, were descendants, for the most part, from the race of the Frank conquerors. Some of them, indeed, were descendants of the
conquered; to whom freedom had, at different times,
been conceded. Almost every where, however, they
lived mixed and confused with bondsmen, and did not
always keep a jealous watch for the maintenance of their
freedom. Thus, amidst the pressure of warfare, indigence, and ignorance, freemen were confounded with,
and counted for, serfs. Such was the state of things
throughout Switzerland; it was such, indeed, throughout the German empire universally. The free class of
the common people was almost entirely extinguished;
and the German race was nearly reduced to the state of
so many others. From this degradation Henry's institution of towns rescued it. The inhabitants of these
towns, fortified by strong walls and close internal union,

could defend themselves from all assaults of violence,—could harbour the oppressed, as guests or citizens,—and could reinforce their internal strength by alliances. In effect, the burghers could soon bid defiance to the nobles, and even balance the political weight of the clergy. It was not long before the towns committed themselves in strong and successful rivalship with these formidable influences. While the nobles were impoverished by disastrous feuds, by senseless extravagance, by changes in the value of commodities, &c.; the towns, on the other hand, flourished in the possession of free constitutions, active traffic, wealth, power, and imperial favour,—as they supported the emperor's warlike undertakings with men and money, and on all occasions adhered to him more faithfully than the nobles. Such was the rise of Henry's institution; not, indeed, sudden, as if by the stroke of a magic wand, but vigorous, though gradual in its progress.

CHAP. III.

DYNASTY OF ZÆRINGEN IN HELVETIA.
1090—1240.

POWER OF THE CHURCH. — HENRY IV. — POPE GREGORY VII. — DYNASTY OF ZÆRINGEN IN HELVETIA. — THE CRUSADES — THEIR EFFECTS. — IMPROVED CONDITION OF THE COUNTRY. — BERCHTHOLD IV. — AUGMENTS THE NUMBER OF FORTIFIED TOWNS—ENCOURAGES THE BURGHERS BY IMMUNITIES.—BERCHTHOLD V. — LAYS THE FOUNDATION OF BERNE. — ERECTS IT INTO A FREE TOWN OF THE EMPIRE. — REFUSES THE IMPERIAL CROWN. — LAST OF THE LINE OF ZÆRINGEN. — FREE MEN OF SCHWYTZ AFFORD THE FIRST DEMONSTRATION OF THEIR EXISTENCE.

IT was reserved for the eleventh century to see the growth of a power which, under the banners of a sacred institution, and through the union of invisible weapons with others of more earthly temper, extended itself equally over sovereigns and their subjects. Invariably fixed on one purpose; apparently quiet, as long as no

occasion offered for acting; pliant and flexible under
the pressure of fear for its own safety, and ever prompt
and dexterous in the use of opportunities; it had formed
and matured a regular offensive system, with formidable
resources and auxiliaries; and only required a daring
leader, a suitable field, and careless opponents, to show
itself in its whole extent and under its true colours.

Helvetia hoped in vain to enjoy repose beneath the
wide-extended wing of the German empire. The obstinate, protracted, and destructive strife which raged
between the emperor and the pope, engendered the
most violent disorders even in its mountain recesses.
During a century and a half, the German empire had
been governed by a vigorous line of princes, who raised
the imperial power to such a pitch, that the revival of a
dominion such as Charlemagne had planned did not
appear beyond the bounds of possibility. The rise of
such an enormous power was prevented by the papacy.
Hitherto the popes had been under the sovereignty of
the emperors; the influence of the latter had decided
their elections, and superintended all their proceedings.
The popes had long wished to be freed from this burdensome supervision. Many members of the clergy
likewise, tired of a state of tutelage under their archbishops and bishops, hoped to gain a freer field of action,
by magnifying the more distant authority of the papacy.
The popes, besides, well knew how to take advantage of
the weakness and dissensions of the secular powers;
their disputes with the princes or bishops; the love of
freedom in the towns; the love of power in the nobles;
but especially of those cases in which the emperors
sought papal mediation and arbitrement. Even in the
reign of Henry II., whose attachment to the priesthood
may probably have gone farther towards procuring the
honour of saintship for him than even the strict piety of
his life, the imperial confirmation of the papal election
was no longer treated as necessary. The emperor Conrad, busied with other matters, did not attend to Rome.
But, in 1039, the imperial throne was ascended by his

son, under the title of Henry III. Since Charlemagne,
no prince had stood at the head of the German people,
who with such energy preserved the imperial dignity
inviolate, and ruled with so much vigour every part of
his extended empire. After many great undertakings,
he had leisure to turn his eyes towards Rome, which was
at that time distracted by the contending claims of three
popes. Henry deposed all three, and re-established the
ordinance that no papal election was valid without the
imperial confirmation. So long as he lived, German
prelates occupied exclusively the papal chair; but his successors in vain sought to maintain a similar influence.

On the demise of Henry III., in 1056, the imperial
crown descended on the head of his son, Henry IV.;
who, at the time of his father's death, was a child of
less than six years old. He gave evidence, at an early
age, of great qualities, of a fiery spirit, and chivalrous
disposition. He was spoiled, however, to such a
degree by the injudicious treatment of his guardians,
that his noble natural faculties were defaced,—without,
however, being utterly extinguished,—by wanton levity,
pride, passion, vindictiveness, and boundless ambition.
Under his reign, the discord between emperors and popes
broke out into open warfare, which raged through nearly
half a century, and at a later period blazed out anew.

Contemporary with Henry IV. was Hildebrand, better
known by the name of pope Gregory VII. Few characters in history have been eulogised or censured with
more vehemence than that of this prelate. Some have
represented him as a monster in human shape, —
nay, with a laughable distortion of his name, as a
hell-brand. Others paint him in angel hues, as an
honour to human nature. Neither side pays any regard
to truth. Born at Siena or Saone, an Italian town,
the son of a blacksmith, Hildebrand entered early into
the spiritual profession. He showed talents of a high
order; was invited to the papal court; and here, by that
ascendency which belongs to great over common minds,
he soon became the soul of all undertakings. He had

set it before him as the aim of his life, to exalt the successor of St. Peter, the delegate of God upon earth, over all kings and princes, and to annihilate the influence of the emperor, as of every other secular ruler, in ecclesiastical matters. This plan was followed by Gregory throughout his whole life with such skill, perseverance, strength, and singleness of purpose, as to rank him amongst the most 'extraordinary characters in history. In his times the grossest disorders and abuses had crept in amongst the higher and lower clergy. Extravagance, immorality, vice of every kind, had ceased to be a rarity amongst them ; and, as the dignities of the church were bought and sold, the most unworthy were often found in the highest places. Inspired with the most ardent zeal for the freedom of the church, and for the morality of the spiritual order, Hildebrand resolved to lay the axe to the root of these evils. Even while only papal chancellor, he toiled towards his end by multiplied ordinances ; and when he deemed every thing ripe for his grand object, he ascended at length the papal throne, as Gregory VII., A. D. 1073. Having contrived to obtain the emperor's assent to his nomination, though the election had already taken place without his concurrence, Gregory at once set to work in the accomplishment of his schemes against the secular power ; and struck the first blow in the year 1075. A triple and solemn prohibition went forth to the clergy on the several points of celibacy, simony, and investiture.

The blow was now struck—the measures of Gregory fell like lightning from heaven; and the conflagration threatened to involve all Germany. The spiritual and secular powers stepped into the lists, and struggled for superiority ;—the one with the aid of abused faith and the most audacious assumptions ; the other, backed by the sword, and based on titles hallowed by centuries.

It was not surprising that Henry should oppose with his whole power the papal ordinances, which endangered to such a degree the imperial dignity. But the pope also put forth his utmost strength, and found numerous adherents among the discontented nobles. A schism took place throughout the whole empire. Provinces, archbishoprics, towns, monasteries, — nay, many private families,—were the prey of internal divisions. Sincerity and confidence, the corner-stones of human society, seemed to disappear from the earth. Subjects revolted against their princes ; children took arms against their parents. All the bonds of family affection were loosed ; and what mankind had regarded hitherto as holy and inviolable, was trodden under foot with contempt. When the papal anathema finally went forth against the emperor, while, on the other hand, the ban of the empire fell on his opponents, confusion reached its highest pitch ; and, besides the grand struggle which was soon to begin, a thousand petty feuds broke out through the whole extent of the empire ; which were fought for and against pope and emperor, often indeed merely under cover of their names, for the gratification of private rapacity, passion, or some long-cherished hatred.

Helvetia, at this period, offered no agreeable aspect. Its first and most powerful prince, duke Rudolf of Swabia, along with Berchthold of Zæringen, duke of Carinthia, and many other princes, had revolted from the emperor. The country was divided betwixt the parties : Rudolph was ascendant in Swabia ; the emperor, in Burgundian Helvetia.

Through the excommunication launched against Henry, Gregory freed from their oaths of allegiance all the imperial vassals and subjects, and solemnly declared that even emperors, kings, and princes, with all their powers, were subject to him, the pope ; who, as divine plenipotentiary, was warranted to give and take away thrones. Gregory was resolved to try the first application of this principle on the emperor himself, the first of secular princes, — an enterprise in which success was possible ; the rather that Henry, in the heart of his empire, had powerful enemies, who would willingly see him humbled, even partly at their own expense. Henry, in whom Gregory's measure excited rage rather than fear, as the

invisible power of the papal anathema was not yet known
by experience, retorted by a scornful deposition of the
pope.   Thereupon the latter lanched a new excommunication, and pronounced the deposition of the emperor himself.   An impression most unfavourable to
Henry was produced by this extraordinary measure. His
enemies exulted ; for their cause had now become that
of the church, and their customary war-cry from thenceforward was " St. Peter."   Henry's friends became discouraged ; and events took such a turn, that the princes
at length threatened to give effect to the papal sentence,
if Henry did not clear himself from it within the term
of a year.   Had the latter been a man of blameless character, the power of a mere word could not have struck
him down thus ; for the word itself acquired its irre-
sistible effect entirely through the public opinion.   But
his errors and presumption had made him enemies innumerable, who now were glad to veil their revenge with
the pretext of religion.   In this situation, the emperor
had no resource left but to creep with his wife and
children into Italy, in the depth of winter, amidst un-
heard-of difficulties and dangers, without money, without
escort, through the mountain passes occupied by Rudolf
and the rest of his enemies.   On his arrival, he was
hailed with loud acclamations by his Lombard vassals ;
and nothing but that want of true spirit, which depresses
the presumptuous in the day of ill fortune, could have
prevented him from marching on the pope at the head
of an army, and induced him to prefer imploring
remission of the sentence at the price of the hardest conditions and the deepest humiliations.   With rage and
revenge in his heart, he returned to Germany.   Here
he found duke Rudolf of Swabia enthroned as anti-
Cæsar.   But he found, too, a strong party of adherents,
in the free towns, in the clergy, who were mostly averse
to Gregory's innovations ; and amongst all who felt indignation for the dishonour done to the German name,
and sympathy for their deeply humbled emperor.   Now
began a war of extermination, by which even a large

portion of Helvetia was depopulated. Gregory, who at first regarded the scene of confusion quietly, now fulminated new excommunications, but in vain. In vain he sent his favourite Rudolf a consecrated crown, with the arrogant inscription, " *Petra dedit Petro, Petrus diadema Rodolfo.*" The fortune of war declared itself in favour of Henry. In a decisive battle at Merseburg, in 1080, Rudolf was mortally wounded, and his hand, which had been cut off in the combat, being shown him, he is said to have to have repentantly exclaimed, " That is the hand which I pledged in swearing fealty to the emperor !" His fall was regarded as a judgment of God, and Henry's adherents gained the ascendency. The archbishop Gilbert of Ravenna was elected anti-pope, as Clement III. Gregory, banished from Rome, died in exile at Salerno, A. D. 1085. Henry's subsequent fortunes, the rebellion of his sons, and his death in the year 1106, do not concern the history of Switzerland so much as the foregoing occurrences. The main dispute was smoothed by a tardy compromise, in 1122, between Henry V. and Pope Calixtus II. The pope retained investiture by ring and staff, as a symbol of his spiritual jurisdiction. Enfeoffment of secular possessions, with the sceptre, was recognised as belonging to the emperor. But the conflict between spiritual and secular supremacy was not to be stilled for any lengthened period.

After the fall of Rudolf of Swabia, the anti-Cæsar, at Merseburg, his vacant dukedom was bestowed by the victorious Henry IV. on his son-in-law Frederick of Hohenstaufen. Rudolf's son, count Berchthold of Rheinfelden, contested, in a long war, the possession of his father's domain, with its new owner. Berchthold died in the year 1090, by which event the rights of the count of Rheinfelden were transmitted to his brother-in-law Berchthold II. of Zæringen. The nobles in Ulm recognised the new duke immediately, and tendered him the oath of allegiance. Frederick of Hohenstaufen prepared for a renewal of the war with fresh vigour ; but Berchthold well knew that the land was tired out by protracted vexations, and he himself preferred a moderate fortune to the doubtful issue of warfare. He, therefore, appeared in the presence of the emperor at the diet of Mentz, in 1097, and there surrendered the ducal office and dignity into Frederick's hands, terminating by this submission the four and twenty years' hostility, maintained by his house against Henry IV. As a recompense for this renunciation, Henry shared the sometime duchy of Swabia or Alemannia between the two candidates, so that Swabia properly so called was allotted to Frederick, while Helvetia was conferred upon Berchthold, almost in its present extent. This arrangement finally separated Swabia from Helvetia, and extinguished the very name of Alemannia. Thus the land was tranquillised; and thus the beneficent powers of the princes of Zæringen was established in Helvetia. They found the land in a far from happy condition. Long and furious warfare had engendered insecurity, immorality, distress, and disorder. On the other hand, foundations pious and useful for the times, increased in number, and promoted culture physical and moral. The towns, too, acquired more and more importance; on the whole, the accession of the dynasty of Zæringen seemed to announce an era of more general well-being.

While such were the mutual relations between Germany and Helvetia, a series of events, of which the first scene lay in Asia, produced effects in the whole of of Christian Europe, which for their magnitude may well claim attention.

The more difficult it is to infuse new ideas into mankind, the more strongly such ideas work when once they have found entrance. As several of the nations of antiquity were accustomed to visit sites supposed holy, where oracles were uttered or any other wonders worked, as the Jews performed certain religious exercises only in the temple of Jerusalem, even so an opinion spread in the course of ages amongst Christians, that pilgrimages or travels to remote places, to which especial

sacredness was attributed,— prayers and penance offered
up in such places, — must have efficacy far superior to
that of acts of simple piety confined within the circle of
home. Pilgrimage to the holy sepulchre became more
and more frequent; and so long as the Arabian power
extended over Palestine, the Christian pilgrims met with
mild treatment. But when the Arabs were forced to
yield to the Seldschuk Turks, the pilgrims were often
treated with harshness and cruelty by the latter. The
conviction at length arose, that it was a duty to reclaim
the holy place from such hands. Peter of Amiens, a
hermit of doubtful character, brought the long collected
elements of wrath to an explosion. The pope, who
might be well assured of gaining a great influence in
the guidance of the popular force, and even over the
princes, promised absolution of sins and a crown of
eternal glory to all who should join the holy expedition.
In the year 1096, the first crusading army set out,
composed of numerous volunteers, in great part from
France. In 1099, they made themselves masters of
Jerusalem and the neighbouring country.

At different times, after shorter or longer intervals,
during the course of the two following centuries, emperors, kings, princes, bishops, dukes, counts, with a
multitude of priests and monks, whole bands of burghers
and peasantry, nay, troops of women, and even of children, marched against the infidels. The first electric
impulse was renewed in the sequel, partly by similar
means of excitement, and partly to preserve from ruin the
newly established empire in the East. Rome neglected
no means of fuelling the zeal which had been spread
through all classes of society. In exact proportion as
the monarchs of Europe fixed their views on the East,
while they weakened their dominion at home, the papal
power was inevitably aggrandised; and as these wars
were regarded as religious concerns, the spiritual authority was more than once successful in uniting the whole
forces of the West in its own hands. Incalculable
profits besides resulted to the clergy from the accom-

plishment of pious vows and donations, and to this general movement many monasteries owe their origin. These were founded by some count or baron, either in fulfilment of a vow in time of need and peril; or, in order to testify gratitude for his fortunate return; or, finally, to close his life in practices of devotion.

As almost every great convulsion of nature or humanity, notwithstanding all the mischief it may occasion, directly or indirectly produces salutary consequences, so from these expeditions, although their principal end was attained in only a transient manner, and several successive generations suffered severely from them, there still resulted many beneficial effects, and these were extended widely over Helvetia.

Many noble lords had found their death in the crusades; many families were impoverished and forced to alienate their properties. In this way the large landed estates were brought into numerous hands, whereby not only freemen but bondsmen improved their situation, and were enabled to acquire property. The latter class were treated with more humanity by their masters, lest they should march off in a body with the crusaders; and received tracts of land from the owners for cultivation, on the payment of ground rents and other dues. Thus the vassals were encouraged to exertion and economy; many of them succeeded in still farther bettering their condition, and in buying off their old or recent burdens and obligations. Similar acquisitions were also made by the towns; admission into which from this period became easier for the vassals of the nobles.

Thus a gradually altered aspect was taken by Helvetia, in common with the other lands on this side the Alps, partly through the growth of the towns, partly through the effects of the crusades. Improvements were effected in agriculture. Not only many better modes of laying out the land were introduced from the examples of other countries, but new species of vines, fruit trees, vegetables, and grains were imported. The dukes of Zæringen, besides that they possessed over

Helvetia the delegated prerogatives of the empire, owed likewise to the free election of Zurich, and of other towns, the office of their *kast-vogt*, or *schirm-vogt*, which in English may be rendered *warden*, or *patron*. The ecclesiastical establishments, not being in general sufficiently armed against external violence, found it expedient to have secular protectors, on whom they could rely for safety and defence. They, of course, chose some powerful lord; and these in their turn, as the office conveyed much power and influence, were ever solicitous to obtain it: many even succeeded in making it hereditary. In German the officer is called *kast-vogt*, or *schirm-vogt*, which in some Latin muniments is sometimes rendered *castaldus*, but more commonly *advocatus*. The cities and free states in their infancy accepted likewise of such protectors, who afterwards often became oppressors.*

In the year 1152, Berchthold IV. stood at the head of the house of Zæringen. He had numerous dependants, but even more numerous enemies, who envied his preponderant power. In order to keep these within bounds, and to strengthen himself against the nobles of Burgundy, Berchthold walled in many existing hamlets, or built new towns, and gave them extraordinary privileges. In these the love of freedom, of tranquillity, or of profit, collected together a multitude of persons, who naturally adhered with steady fidelity to the duke, by whom their new position had been given, and was secured to them. On the other hand, the duke intruded no one as a citizen, nor prevented any from changing their places of residence at pleasure; so that free and bondsmen vied with each other in pressing into the towns. The latter became free when their masters did not claim them within the term of one year, and prove their vassalage by the oath of seven witnesses. The burghers imposed taxes on themselves. They were obliged to march no farther in the wars of the duke than so that they might still sleep at home the same

* Planta, vol. i. p. 112.

night. Every burgher must possess a house, as pledge
of his allegiance. In good or evil fortune they stood
each for all, and all for each. Thus simple were the laws
and customs observed by the rising class of burghers.
These laws and regulations, indeed, were calculated, not
for the general good of a state, but for a single town,
and for those who belonged to it. This apparent selfishness may be pardoned, if we recollect the necessities and
circumstances of the period. At the time when towns
were founded, nothing like patriotism, far less zeal for
the general rights of humanity, could exist. The burgher
who was heartily attached to his town, and the knight
who cherished love for his prince, and cultivated the
virtues of his order, was regarded as fulfilling his whole
duties. For in those times the burgher viewed his town
in the light of his father-land, and the citizen knew no
state but the court of his prince. A closer bond between
the individual parts of a commonwealth, the sacrifice of
private to public interests, respect for the rights of
others, in a word, a general love of country, was the
product of a more advanced age. Besides, the nobles
and clergy strove with their whole strength to keep down
the growing power of the citizens. This imposed on
them the most vigilant regard to their own interests, and
the most complete union among themselves, so that the
well-being of others could not be taken into account.

Berchthold V. followed the example of his father in
laying the foundations of towns; for the dukes of Zæringen governed on a plan grounded upon, or rather
prescribed by, the circumstances of the times. They
found their power menaced by the nobility, and were
therefore obliged to seek its humiliation. All the nobles
of Burgundy revolted from the government of Berchthold V., so that he was forced to live in a state of open
warfare with his subjects. The duke twice defeated the
insurgents.

About this time he formed the hamlets of Burgdorf
and Moudon into little towns; yet he still sought a more
advantageous site, which should be nearer the possessions

of his enemies, and such that the foundation of a town upon it should cause no apprehensions to his adherents. A little hamlet, called Berne, lay near the fortress of Nydeck, on a peninsula which is washed by the Aar. The banks of the rapidly flowing stream are on all sides high and steep. On the site of the present town lay a considerable pasture ground, and behind it a thick wood. On every side were visible only a few farm-houses and villages. The strong-holds of the nobles frowned from every height in the neighbourhood.

About a month after Berchthold had defeated them, he commissioned Cuno of Bubenberg to surround Berne with walls. Cuno exceeded the prescribed extent of ground, and soon afterwards it was thought fit to extend still further the limits which he had set to the town. For a long time the duration of the new town seemed doubtful. The climate was raw, the region unattractive, the enemy's vicinity dangerous. To counterbalance these disadvantages, however, Berchthold placed it as a free town of the empire, under the emperor's immediate protection, and thus rendered it independent of his own house for the future. Allured by this extraordinary boon, many of the inferior nobles, who valued freedom, which they could not enjoy in a state of isolation, gathered themselves together into the town, to secure by brotherly union this most precious of all possessions. Such were, for example, the Erlachs, Bubenbergs, and Mühlerers. Numerous artificers were attracted by hopes of profit. Even in its increased extent the town could not contain the increasing multitudes; and as the land-owners preferred besides to live upon their property, Berne acquired many out-burghers, who added much to her strength.

Soon after this epoch, Berchthold fell into a feud with the imperial house. The emperor Henry VI. died before it was well finished. Many German princes now wished to place the crown upon the head of duke Berchthold, partly moved by hatred to the house of Hohenstaufen, which at that time sat upon the throne, and partly by respect to that of Zæringen. A succession of five admirable princes had inspired a good opinion of this noble stem, which seemed exactly suited, by its wealth and power, to maintain the imperial rank in a dignified manner. Although, however, Berchthold loved, at other times, to aggrandise his power by any means, sometimes, indeed, more dexterously than honourably, yet he declined, with prudent modesty, this perilous elevation; and renounced a claim which, even with arms in his hands, he could not have well supported; as he had reason to fear the worst from the disaffection of his Burgundian subjects, and had learned, by striking examples, that their fidelity was not much to be depended upon in warfare. But, in any event, Berchthold could be but a powerless emperor, and accordingly preferred to be a powerful duke. For the renunciation of the throne, he received compensation from Philip the brother of the late emperor, and lived in peace thenceforwards with the imperial house of Hohenstaufen. Twenty years longer he administered his domains with uninterrupted prosperity and glory. He surpassed all the princes of the empire in wealth, in power, and in reputation; and reigned a true father of his people, as well as a firm sovereign of his nobles. His arms were, in general, victorious; although, through the unfaithfulness of his armies, he experienced the mutability of fortune. He was the last of his race, his sons having died before him, and he followed them on the 14th of February, 1218.

It was probably not so much from love of freedom that the princes of the Zæringen line took part with the towns and the people, as because they wished to triumph by the aid of the towns and the people over the powerful disaffected nobility. This object being nearly accomplished, the line became extinct, without having stained its reputation by completing its dominion over Helvetia through the subjection of the burghers and the peasantry.

Under the dynasty of Zæringen, in the midst of so
many bishops, counts, and burgher-corporations, the
name of the free men of Schwytz was, for the first time,
heard in a dispute about their boundaries with Einsiedlen.   These people had long lived in the enjoyment of
tranquil happiness, subject to no one but to God and
to the empire.   They had hitherto attracted so little
notice, that the monks of Einsiedlen were able to conceal their very existence from the emperor.   Henry II
had made a grant to these monks of the waste lands in
their neighbourhood.   The abbot claimed as much as
he chose as waste and unenclosed land ; and accordingly
included in his claim the pastures, hills, and plains, bequeathed to the men of Schwytz by their forefathers.
The country people, however, neither yielded to the
claims of the abbot, nor to the sentence of the emperor, and maintained their rights so strenuously under
Conrad III. of Hohenstaufen, that every effort employed
against them was fruitless, and even outlawry and ban
effected nothing.   They maintained themselves by vigour and resolution in their possessions, which were
finally secured to them by Frederick II., a better disposed or better informed emperor.

CHAP. IV.

TIMES OF RUDOLPH AND ALBERT OF HAPSBURG.

1218—1308.

BIRTH OF RUDOLPH OF HAPSBURG. — HIS EARLY CONDUCT AND
CHARACTER.—INTERREGNUM IN THE EMPIRE.— FIRST LEAGUE
OF URI, SCHWYTZ, AND UNTERWALDEN WITH ZURICH.—RUDOLPH
SUPPORTS THE TOWNS, AND EMPLOYS THEIR ARMS AGAINST
THE NOBLES. — ACCEPTS THE VOGT-SHIP OF THE FOREST LANDS,
AND THE MILITARY COMMAND OF ZURICH. — CONCILIATES THE
ABBOT OF ST. GALL, IN ORDER TO ATTACK THE BISHOP OF
BASLE. — ELECTED EMPEROR. — PARTIAL CHANGE IN HIS
CHARACTER. — HIS FEUD WITH SAVOY. — HIS FEUD WITH
BERNE. — HIS DEATH. — STATE OF THE EMPIRE.

THE same year which witnessed the extinction of the
race of Zœringen saw, in the birth of count Rudolph
of Hapsburg, the rise of a more illustrious dynasty.
The family from which he sprung was ancient and
powerful ; though Rudolph himself inherited from his
father, Albert IV., who died in a crusade in 1240, only
a moderate portion of lands and subjects. Most part of
the hereditary property of his house was in the hands
of his maternal uncle. As landgrave of Alsace, and
count of the Aargau, the power which Rudolph possessed was, by the ancient love of freedom subsisting
in the subject population, confined almost to the empty
name of lord of the land. Rudolph took possession of
this far from brilliant heritage with a temper of mind
impatient of its trammels ; and was impelled to seek,
by means of martial enterprise, a position more commensurate with his wishes. At this epoch he was a
fiery youth of two and twenty, qualified, by the prepossessing friendliness of his manners and address, to
awaken confidence in the hearts of all around him. In
every situation, oppressed with the greatest cares and

anxieties, Rudolph remained tranquil and cheerful. His manners had the unconstrained simplicity and openness which characterise a truly great man.

At first, indeed, fired with impatience for higher fortunes, Rudolph despised the paths of timid prudence; and started, like a thoughtless, hot-headed youth in his career. This excessive eagerness rather impeded than aided his purposes. Before he had attained his fortieth year, he had drawn on himself the hatred of his father's relations, was disinherited by his uncle on the mother's side, and excommunicated more than once by the church. Afterwards, however, when such checks had taught him prudence, and he had learned to subdue his passions, his affairs took a better aspect. A memorable evidence, observes Müller, that fiery youths should not allow the vigour which resides in them to be relaxed by disgust at the past errors of their youth, but should manfully struggle onwards in unshaken hope of better times.

About this period (1254) the extinction of the imperial house of Hohenstaufen took place; and disorder reached a higher pitch in Germany than ever, as the empire remained long without a head. In these times, which were called the Interregnum, injustice and violence gained the upper hand in a frightful manner. The corporal right of the strongest, called *faustrecht*, was the only one which was held in any respect, and discord rent asunder the bonds of order and morality. The greater princes broke loose from their ties towards the empire, waged wars amongst themselves, and were in no haste to elect an emperor. The castles of the nobles, which still frown on every eminence, were just so many nests of birds of prey. Highway robbery was regarded as a knightly sport, an honourable source of gain, or an innocent amusement. Armed gangs lurked in every corner, ready to pounce upon travellers, to levy contributions on them, or rather to seize their whole property: — happy were those allowed to escape with bare life and freedom.

No German prince was willing to start as a candidate for the crown, which an Englishman, duke Richard of Cornwall, had shortly before actually *bought* of the archbishops of Cologne and Mentz and the rest of the electoral princes for a much larger amount of solid gold than it was worth. So low had the opinion of the imperial dignity fallen, that it had now become an object of distrust or contempt. Every one chose rather to take advantage of the prevailing anarchy, in order, by oppression of the feeble, to promote his own personal aggrandisement, than to join in any effort for the general welfare. In circumstances like these, disorder necessarily increased daily; acts of violence became more and more frequent, so that the greater and lesser princes and counts, prelates, knights, and towns, lived in perpetual and destructive feuds with each other; the stronger fell on the weaker; and the well-disposed and peaceable sighed with their whole soul for an emperor to protect and defend them.

Shortly before this miserable epoch, in which Helvetia with the rest of the German empire was delivered over to every species of violence and injustice, the three districts of Uri, Schwytz, and Unterwalden, closed their first league for mutual aid and defence with Zurich.

It would have been easy for count Rudolph to cooperate with the other nobility for the oppression of the towns and rural districts of Helvetia. But he possessed the rare faculty of extracting the best uses from all circumstances amongst which he lived, and preferred to protect the citizens and country people against the violence of the great, and of the wild robber chivalry. As military commandant of the town and country districts, by using the arms and treasures of the burghers, he undermined in succession each of his noble rivals, of whom many in birth and power were his equals, many his superiors. The imperial towns and free lands in Helvetia which would have found, but for Rudolph, no protection against injuries, threw themselves unconditionally into his arms. The burghers, whose civic

rights and regulations had accustomed them more to
order and obedience than the nobles, chained conquest,
as it were, to the banners of Rudolph, through their discipline, the main requisite to military success. Their
industry and traffic furnished him with the means of
protracting, without damage to himself, feuds which
impoverished the nobility, and of winning superiority
by delay ; and as he constantly displayed affability
even towards the lowest, with all the other qualities
which most adorn princes, the good fortune by which
he never was forsaken won him the confidence and love
of the whole people, while similar good fortune in others
would only have awakened alarm and envy.

Rudolph's grandfather, in 1210, had obtained for his
house the vogt-ship, or office of imperial bailiff, over the
three lands of Uri, Schwytz, and Unterwalden. This
vogt-ship was at that time felt as a burden by a free
people; and it was only with reluctance that they yielded
to necessity. Finally, in 1240, they were enabled to
shake it off. In the Italian wars of Frederick II. a
select band from the forest cantons served him with extraordinary courage and fidelity. Even excommunication,
which terrified so many, could effect no alteration in their
fearless adherence. In return, and as a token of his
favour, Frederick relieved them from the vogt-ship of
Hapsburg, and gave to each district a charter of enfran-
chisement, importing that the men of Schwytz had of
their own accord chosen the immediate protection of the
emperor. But when this headless empire, in the years of
the interregnum, was turned into a theatre of discord,
and on every side was delivered up as a spoil to rapine
and violence, these districts voluntarily renewed the
abolished office in 1257, in order to acquire in Rudolph of Hapsburg a powerful ally—a generally beloved and brave leader. Shortly afterwards Zurich
also conferred on him the office of her military protector, which had already been refused by the arrogant
baron Luthold of Regensberg, who, according to his own
expression, regarded the town as caught in a net, sur-

rounded as it was by his castles. From 1266 to 1268 these
fortresses of his were taken one by one by those burghers
whose alliance he had repelled, led by the holder of that
office which he had scornfully rejected. Utzenberg, a
fortress of Luthold's ally, the count of Toggenburg, had
the same fate, and the trade of Zurich flourished in
greater security.

Thus Rudolph supported the towns and rural districts, and employed their co-operation, in return, to
break the force of his own personal antagonists. While
his feud continued yet undecided with Regensberg and
Toggenburg, and in order to meet with less divided
forces the bishop of Basle, against whom he was also
engaged in hostilities, he disarmed, by friendly surprise
and cordial advances, abbot Berchthold of St. Gall, who
was already preparing to take the field against him. The
abbot now supported instead of opposing him : the town
of Basle soon came to terms : the bishop also, after his
lands had been laid waste, purchased peace. This was,
however, not of long continuance : hostilities were renewed upon the first pretence which offered ; and Rudolph
again laid siege to the town in 1273, when the intelligence arrived that the electors assembled at Frankfort
had chosen him for emperor, on the ground that he was
one of the most upright in times of prevalent injustice.
His election had been principally owing to the influence
of Werner, archbishop of Mentz, who, on a journey
several years before into Italy, had been treated in an
uncommonly friendly manner by the pious count Rudolph of Hapsburg ; and had said to him on taking leave
that he only hoped to live long enough in some degree
to repay his kindness. Now when, on the death of
Richard of Cornwall, those princes who assumed to themselves the right of election to the vacant throne were
assembled for that purpose at Frankfort, he proposed to
them the pious count of Hapsburg, as the worthiest
possible object for their choice. The burggrave Frederick of Nuremberg, a near relation of Rudolph, echoed
his praises ; and as most of the electors chanced to be

unmarried men, he hinted to them that Rudolph had six daughters at their disposal in marriage. Upon this hint, the affair was arranged with marvellous celerity, and the election to the empire wore the air of a family compact. Basle opened her gates to the new emperor ; while the bishop, almost beside himself with rage and consternation, cried, *Lord God! set thyself fast upon thy throne, else surely will this Rudolph pluck thee down from it.*

Rudolph, however, was not to be dazzled by the brilliance of his new elevation, as little souls are apt to be on less accessions of dignity. He preserved his affability, forgot not his old friends; and it was long before " commodity, the bias of the world," made him deviate from the wise moderation displayed in the first years of his government. He not only continued the chartered franchises of the imperial towns and territories in Switzerland, but also those of Lucerne, Soleure, Schaffhausen, Mulhausen, and others. He raised the abbot of Einsiedlen and the bishop of Lausanne to the dignity of princes of the empire. On the other hand, in recompense for his benefits, he enjoyed the firm adherence of the mass of the population. Auxiliaries from Switzerland distinguished themselves fighting at his side against the powerful king of Bohemia. The men of Zurich formed part of his body guard, and the treasures of the town supplied him with loans.

But with the increase of the emperor's fortune some alteration took place, during the latter years of his government, in the uprightness of his character. Like most princes, whose throne is not hereditary, he sought to aggrandise his house by every means during his lifetime. Already, with the consent of the German princes, he had raised his sons, Rudolph and Albert, to the dukedoms of Swabia and of Austria. He next turned his views upon Helvetia, and commenced hostile measures against Berne and Savoy. Rudolph had conceived the idea of restoring the old kingdom of Burgundy, for the benefit of his favourite son Hartmann: this involved him in warfare with the house of Savoy, whose possessions

were put in jeopardy by his project. The emperor made
two successful campaigns against this house; but the
object of his whole undertaking was frustrated by the
early death of Hartmann, who was drowned in the
Rhine.

Not more fortunate in its issue was the feud of Rudolph with Berne, which he besieged with 15,000 men
in 1288. He was soon, however, obliged to draw off
his forces, as the military skill of those times could effect
nothing against a town surrounded on three sides by a
rapid stream, protected by steep banks and walls, and
defended by stout burghers. An attempt to take the
town by surprise in the following year was frustrated by
the resolute self-devotion of the citizens, and the timely
aid of Wale of Gruyeres. From this time forth the
emperor ceased to meddle much with Helvetia; and,
three years afterwards, death put an end to his far-pro-
spective purposes. Eighteen years after his accession to
the throne, or, to use the expression ascribed to himself,
" after he had been raised from the hut of his father to
the palace of the emperor," in the seventy-fourth year
of his age, he fell ill on a journey to Spires, and died at
the town of Germersheim, which he himself had founded.
Except when the ambition to enlarge his domains misled
him into abuse of his good fortune, his dealings had
been mostly upright and equitable; and so highly had
his administration in civil affairs been popular, that his
memory was long held in honour; and " *He has not
Rudolph's plain dealing!*" was a common saying in Germany.

Although the restoration of peace in the empire procured safety and protection for the upper ranks, yet the
lower were still subjected to multiplied oppressions. Innumerable castles of barons, counts, and other nobles,
were spread over the whole face of the country. With
the increased taste for splendour, excited by attendance
upon courts and tournaments, and with the discovery of
new modes of luxury, new wants were created in proportion. These were supplied, in many cases, by rich

revenues, water and land tolls, imposts and dues of different kinds, which were paid by serfs and vassals, ground and quit rents, hens, eggs, &c. Others were not contented with hereditary possessions. The emperor Albert himself doubled the taxes in his domains; and many powerful men did the same. Similar sources of revenue were enjoyed by the spiritual dignitaries and cloisters: all of these, the mendicant orders only excepted, possessed sovereign power over their vassals.

From this time forward many monasteries succeeded, through papal or episcopal favour, in appropriating to themselves the tithes of churches and parishes: this was called *incorporating;* and the only charge which lay upon the new tithe impropriators was the acquittal of certain very limited payments to the priests, with the additional obligation, in some cases, of repairing the church buildings, and relieving the poor. Many nobles sought and found improvement of their fortunes in the holding of offices under lords spiritual or secular; and there were others who, from this period till far into the following century, drove a regular trade of robbery in the neighbourhood of their strong-holds. They imposed contributions on their neighbours, waylaid passing tradesmen and travellers, sometimes took them prisoners, and compelled them to pay ransoms.

Here and there bondsmen had succeeded in buying themselves free of their obligations, or in holding their lands as hereditary fiefs, in consideration of certain fixed annual payments. Freedmen of this kind, indeed, as yet were rare; but out of them a new class of peasantry gradually formed itself; and those who had bought themselves wholly free came at length to be ranked in the same line with the previously existing class of freemen.

Heavy oppression, however, weighed on the great body of bondsmen. They were bound to an infinite number of services; chained to the glebe which they cultivated; were not even allowed to marry without leave from their lords; and the children belonged to whatever master the parents had belonged to. On the death of a serf, a portion more

E

or less of his effects, such as his best head of cattle, his best clothes or arms, were regularly claimed by the lord. Nevertheless the rights of the liege lord, as well as their practical exercise, exhibited considerable varieties.

In the towns which exempted themselves by purchase from their dues and obligations towards their spiritual and temporal lords, or acquired extended franchises as a reward for services done to the latter, knowledge, and the arts of life diffused themselves. Since the close of the twelfth century, the language of the country was more and more employed in public transactions, and now began distinctly to assume that character from which the modern German has developed itself. Those who possessed superior knowledge were treated with respect; poetry became a favourite occupation among the cultivated part of the nobility, which formed in those times a larger proportion than in the subsequent centuries; and men of talent in the class of burghers united in the same study. These poets, who received the name of Minnesingers, selected the subjects of their verse from the more tender passions, and the pleasures or vicissitudes of life, and taught lessons of practical wisdom through the medium of examples and apologues. In the towns also, exclusively of the cloisters, schools were established, which, notwithstanding their deficiencies, could not fail to produce good effects.

Through the unlimited power of the hierarchy, and notwithstanding the energetic resistance of several bishops and abbots, the opinion had been almost universally diffused, that whatever the church, that is to say, the pope, erected as a rule of faith, must be received with implicit credence; and that out of the pale of that church was no salvation. The conservation of what was called the true faith was entrusted to the order of Dominicans. Imprisonment, torture, death at the stake, were the destiny of heretics. But as the human mind struggles with most vehemence under external pressure, independent opinions became too rife to be crushed by persecution: the effect of these was aided by the abandoned lives of the clergy, of whom a large number were hated by the people. The monaster of Rutiy near Rappersweil was pulled down, while yet unfinished, by the neighbouring peasantry; and while, on the one hand, these foundations were enriched and multiplied, on the other they remained a constant mark for the rapacity of the more powerful nobles. The authority of the papal court itself often found in cloisters and monasteries the most determined resistance; and the earliest energetic re-action against it was brought on by the unparalleled assumptions of Boniface VIII., the contemporary of Albert of Hapsburg. This prelate had explicitly advanced the doctrine, that all secular power was only held by princes in trust from the pope, and remained at his discretion and disposal. It was precisely this excess of oppression which, as commonly is the case, brought the world by degrees to its senses. The papal bulls were powerless against Philip the Fair of France, although his character was by no means free from blame. The pope's inflexibility in this instance was of evil consequence only to himself; and the power of princes, at least in temporal matters, became gradually placed on a firmer footing.

CHAP. V.

ÆRA OF HELVETIC EMANCIPATION.
1308—1334.

ALBERT OF HAPSBURG. — AIMS AT ERECTING A DUKEDOM IN
HELVETIA. — TYRANNY OF GESSLER AND BERENGER. — OATH
OF RUTLI. — WILLIAM TELL. — DEATH OF GESSLER. — CAP-
TURE OF ROTZBERG AND SARNEN. — LEAGUE OF THE THREE
FOREST CANTONS. — DEATH OF ALBERT OF HAPSBURG. —
CRUEL REVENGE FOR HIS MURDER. — RECOGNITION OF SWISS
FREEDOM. — INVASION OF SWITZERLAND BY DUKE LEOPOLD.
— BATTLE OF MORGARTEN. — PERPETUAL CONFEDERACY OF
THE FOREST CANTONS. — SIX YEARS' TRUCE WITH AUSTRIA.
— SIEGE OF SOLEURE. — MAGNANIMITY OF THE BESIEGED
BURGHERS. — RENEWAL OF THE TRUCE WITH AUSTRIA. —
RECEPTION OF LUCERNE IN THE CONFEDERACY. — STATE OF
INDUSTRY — COMMERCE — AND RELIGION.

ALBERT, the eldest and sole surviving son of Rudolph
of Hapsburg, the founder of the imperial house of
Austria, united with undoubted bravery other respectable
qualities. But he was hard, unfeeling, rapacious and
unscrupulous in his views of aggrandisement. That
cheerful adhesion and confidence which had attended
his father's administration, and even the first years of
his own, were soon succeeded by opposite feelings. He
was feared by all, hated by many, loved by none, and
the father's truest friends were speedily alienated by the
son. No sooner had the men of Schwytz heard of his
accession, than they hastened to renew their league of
reciprocal protection. Albert was resolved to succeed to
all the honours of Rudolph, during whose lifetime attempts had been made to secure the imperial crown for
him. At that time the princes had the prudence to defer
the nomination of an emperor. But on Rudolph's death
Albert made so sure of the succession, that he seized on
the imperial insignia without waiting for the decision of
a diet. He now received the first proof of the disesteem
in which he was held, by his claims being entirely overlooked in the election, which fell upon count Adolphus
of Nassau. But the new emperor possessing neither

power nor popularity, and having besides contrived to disoblige the archbishop of Mentz, whose influence had a principal share in raising him to the throne, he was very soon deposed from it, through the agency of that prelate, at a diet of the electors held in Mentz; and Albert, who in the interim had conciliated their suffrages, was raised to the imperial throne in his stead. This illegal act was shortly after ratified by the fortune of war; and in a final throw for empire, poor Adolphus lost his crown and his life.

Albert aimed at erecting a new dukedom in Helvetia, and at uniting all the scattered domains of his family by the acquisition of whatever lands of others lay between them. He proposed to the free and contented inhabitants of Uri, Schwytz, and Unterwalden, whose districts inconveniently separated his rich possessions, to exchange their direct dependence on the empire for the more powerful and permanent protection of the house of Austria. But the foresters viewed with fixed distrust the advances of their emperor; they were perfectly well acquainted with the value of their own freedom, and were the less likely to barter it for Austrian protection, as they had long regarded with anxious apprehension the increasing power acquired by the house of Hapsburg. They accordingly made answer, that their only wish and prayer was, to be left in the condition of their forefathers. They begged that they might not be taken from under the guardianship of the empire, and subjected to that of any one prince in particular. Moreover, they demanded the appointment of imperial commissaries (landvogts or bailiffs), in order to be relieved from the administration of Albert's officers, whom he had set over them, contrary to established rights and usages. Albert complied with this demand; but, in order to disunite and harass them, he sent, instead of one vogt, two. These were, Hermann Gessler of Brauneck, and Berenger of Landenberg; men of rude and imperious temper, who, as if their master's instructions were not arbitrary and large enough, interpreted them in the most extended sense,

and indulged their personal pride by a haughty deportment towards the people, who were wholly unaccustomed
to such treatment. Remonstrances and complaints to
the emperor only redoubled the wrongs complained of;
and these were barbed by insults more provoking than
the wrongs themselves. Excessive tolls and duties, and
unprecedented imposts for the maintenance of garrisons,
formed an item in the list of grievances. Gessler built
a fortress at the foot of the St. Gothard, which he inso-
lently named Uri's Restraint. Landenberg went on with
equal violence in Unterwalden, where Henry of Halden,
an aged and zealous friend of freedom, lived in the
Melchthal. Landenberg imposed the fine of a yoke
of oxen on this man, for some slight, or pretended
offence of his son, Arnold of the Melchthal. On his
hesitating to give them up, Landenberg's messenger
sneeringly said, that if the boors wished to have bread
to eat, they might draw the plough themselves. On
hearing this, the young man Arnold, yielding to a fit
of passion, broke one of the servant's fingers, and fled
from the bailiff's vengeance. Landenberg had the father
of the fugitive arrested, and demanded to know his son's
place of concealment. It was vain for the old man to
protest ignorance — not only were his oxen seized, and
a heavy fine imposed upon him, but his eyes were put out
to expiate the venial act of his son. That puncture, says
an old historian, went so deep into many a heart, that
many resolved to die rather than leave it unrequited.

Every act of Albert's vogts seemed purposely adapted
either to crush all independence of feeling, or to provoke
the people to some precipitate act of overt resistance.
Those whom the vogts thought fit to regard as dangerous, were, in spite of the ancient popular franchises,
sent to foreign prisons. At Altorf, Gessler caused a hat
to be set upon a pole, as a symbol of the sovereign
power of Austria, and ordered that all who passed by
should uncover their heads, and bow before it. He
taunted Werner Stauffacher, a freeman entitled to bear
arms, at Steinen, in the district of Schwytz, " that he, a

vile peasant, should have built himself a new house, without asking permission of his liege lords." This man, who had the fortune to possess a wife of good understanding, communicated by her advice with other men of like dispositions, who felt with pain equal to his own the daily aggravated oppressions borne by their countrymen, as well as the affronts offered personally to themselves. He selected for his first confidants, Walter Fürst of Uri, and the deeply aggrieved Arnold of the Melchthal. They bound themselves by oath to endure no longer the degrading wrongs inflicted on their countrymen, to restore their ancient freedom, and to league themselves for that purpose with other men deserving of their confidence; above all, to expel the domineering vogts, but without throwing off their allegiance to the emperor and the empire.

When one and the same resentment of injustice is extended over whole tracts of country, the communications of resolute men are sure to be met speedily by individual confidence and adhesion. Each of the sworn confederates chose confidants. They were wont to assemble, at first accompanied only by few, in the dead of night, at Rutli, a meadow slope under the Seelisberg by the lake of Uri, to consult for the salvation of their country, and to give and receive intelligence of the progress of their efforts, and the friends who had been won to their cause. At length on Martinmas-eve (11th November), 1307, Walter Fürst, Werner Stauffacher, and Arnold of the Melchthal, each brought to the accustomed place of rendezvous ten trusty companions, to whom they had confided their enterprise. These three-and thirty clasped each other's hands, and took a solemn engagement that no one would ever desert the rest, and that all would devote their united strength to restore their invaded franchises, without, however, despoiling others of their goods, their rights, or their lives. At the moment when the beams of morning struck the neighbouring Alps, and seemed as signal-fires to light them on their enterprise, the three leaders raised their hands with their comrades, and swore a league by that God who fashioned all men for equal freedom. The men of Schwytz and Uri wished to proceed to the immediate execution of their project; but those of Unterwalden, who did not feel assured that they could take easy possession of the fortresses, advised delay, and their reasons found acquiescence.

Soon after occurred the famous episode of William Tell *, momentous to the main plot in its issue. This man, who was one of the sworn at Rutli, and noted for his high and daring spirit, exposed himself to arrest by Gessler's myrmidons, for passing the hat without making obeisance. Whispers of conspiracy had already reached the vogt, and he expected to extract some farther evidence from Tell on the subject. Offended by the man's obstinate silence, he gave loose to his tyrannical humour, and knowing that Tell was a good archer, commanded him to shoot from a great distance at an apple on the head of his child. God, says an old chronicler, was with him; and the vogt, who had not expected such a specimen of skill and fortune, now cast about for new ways to entrap the object of his malice; and, seeing a second arrow in his quiver, asked him what that was for? Tell replied, evasively, that such was the usual practice of archers. Not content with this reply, the vogt pressed on him farther, and assured him of his life, whatever the arrow might have been meant for. " Vogt," said Tell, " had I shot my child, the second shaft was for THEE; and be sure I should not have missed my mark a second time!" Transported with rage not unmixed with terror, Gessler exclaimed, " Tell! I have promised thee life, but thou shalt pass it in a dungeon." Accordingly, he took boat with his captive, intending to transport him across the lake to Kussnacht in Schwytz, in defiance of the common right of the district, which provided that its natives should not be kept in confinement beyond its borders. A sudden storm on the lake overtook the party; and Gess-

* See the Appendix.

ler was obliged to give orders to loose Tell from his fetters, and commit the helm to his hands, as he was known for a skilful steersman. Tell guided the vessel to the foot of the great Axenberg, where a ledge of rock, distinguished to the present day as Tell's platform, presented itself as the only possible landing-place for leagues around. Here he seized his cross-bow, and escaped by a daring leap, leaving the skiff to wrestle its way in the billows. The vogt also escaped the storm, but only to meet a fate more signal from Tell's bow in the narrow pass near Kussnacht. The tidings of his death enhanced the courage of the people, but also alarmed the vigilance of their rulers, and greatly increased the dangers of the conspirators, who kept quiet. These occurrences marked the close of 1307.

On new year's eve, 1308, the conspirators obtained possession of the castle of Rotzberg in Nidwalden. A girl had drawn one of them, who was her lover, up at midnight, by a rope, into the castle; by his assistance twenty more were introduced in the same manner, and the garrison, thus surprised, was overpowered without difficulty. With morning-dawn, twenty men of Oberwalden went with new year's presents to the castle at Sarnen. Berenger, who was coming out to church, let them enter the gates without hinderance, seeing them unarmed. Whereupon they fixed on their staves the pike-heads which they had carried concealed, and blew the agreed signal-note on their horns to thirty others, who lay in ambush and armed in the neighbouring alders. These hastened up, and this formidable stronghold was thus captured almost without resistance. The garrison was dismissed free, on taking a solemn engagement not to revenge the past, and not to overstep their assigned limits. The triumphant people now demolished several other fortresses, amongst the rest, the unhappy Gessler's yet unfinished *Restraint of Uri*. The nobles gladly joined the league of freemen and vassals, as they preferred sharing their freedom, to becoming slaves along with them; and on the following Sunday the

three lands engaged themselves reciprocally through
their envoys in the terms of the same oath which had
been taken at Rutli.   But, as generally happens to the
founders of great changes, they were far from forming
an adequate idea of what they had done.

Albert, whose unquiet and grasping policy was continually provoking fresh ˙ enemies, had just seen his
project of annexing Bohemia to his family domains
frustrated, and in Thuringia his Swabian troops had
suffered a severe defeat.   He heard with great indignation the revolt of the forest cantons ; but he wished
first to finish another feud which he had begun, with
slight pretence of right, against Otho of Granson, bishop
of Basle, and accordingly laid siege to his castle of
Furstenstein.   At the same time, he forbade the inhabitants of Lucerne, Zug, and the rest of his subjects on
the frontiers, all intercourse with the forest cantons, and
excluded the latter from entrance into the markets of
the former.

Duke John, son of the late duke Rudolph, who had
already reached his twentieth year, and saw the sons of
the emperor enjoying high consideration and dignities,
had often begged the emperor, his uncle, to make over
to him his father's domains, or a part of them.   But
the emperor put him off, and on the renewal of his
entreaties, is said to have reached him a coronet which
he had made of a broken twig, with the words, that this
would become him better than ruling lands and people.
The insulted youth knew that this refusal of the emperor was displeasing to both spiritual and temporal
lords ; he knew the hatred felt for Albert by the nobility
of the Thurgau and the Aargau (districts upon which
he himself had claims), and he also knew their favourable dispositions towards his own person.   He seized
the opportunity of the emperor's return, on the 1st of
May, 1308, to Rheinfelden from his castle at Baden,
where he had held a consultation with his intimate
advisers on his enterprise against the three cantons ; and
just as Albert had crossed the Reuss at Windisch, and

was separated from the rest of his suite for a moment,
duke John, baron Walter of Eschenbach, and Rudolph
of Balm fell upon him and murdered him in the face
of open day, and left him to die in the lap of a poor
woman on the spot. Terror and astonishment filled the
whole land. The inhabitants of Zurich shook the dust
from their gates, which had not been closed for thirty
years previously. It was dreaded by the emperor's
adherents that an extensive league had been formed
against his house. On the other hand, the blinded
assassins, after the deed was perpetrated, found out for
the first time their want of support from any quarter,
and now only endeavoured to save their lives by a
rapid flight. Elizabeth, the widow of the emperor,
came to a compromise with the bishop of Basle, and
issued warnings to the towns and villages not to give
harbour or concealment to the murderers. Hostile
preparations were not only suspended with regard to
the three cantons, but intercourse and transport of
goods were thrown open again between them and the
territories of Austria, and advances made to a friendly
understanding. They who only sought to maintain
their old rights, and their immediate connection with
the empire, behaved themselves throughout with moderation and equity.

For some time after Albert's death, the house of
Austria directed its whole efforts to secure the imperial
crown for his eldest son Frederick. It was not until
this scheme had failed of success with the German
princes, who hated the whole family for Albert's sake,
that the Austrians turned their thoughts to the execution
of that revenge which they had resolved upon against
that prince's murderers. The ban of the empire was
pronounced upon them by the new emperor, Henry VII.;
and as the murderers themselves were not to be
found, their innocent relatives, friends, servants, and
subjects were, with inhuman cruelty, hunted down and
extirpated by the family of Albert. The principal
promoter of these horrors was Agnes, queen of Hun-

gary, the late emperor's daughter, a woman unacquainted
with the milder feelings of piety, but addicted to a certain sort of devotional habits and practices, by no means
inconsistent with implacable vindictiveness. In gratifying this passion she forgot all female dignity; and
is even said to have waded in the blood of three and
sixty innocent sufferers, with the exulting exclamation,
" This day we bathe in May-dew !" Not till numerous
castles had been dismantled, the whole resources of
multitudes annihilated, and more than a thousand innocent persons, men, women, and children, had perished
by the hand of the executioner, was an end put to this
series of horrors, by which indeed the wealth of the
house of Austria was increased, but by which at the
same time it had provoked so many enemies, that the
consequences of these events contributed not a little to
frustrate its designs against the freedom of Helvetia.

The emperor, Henry VII., who had testified his
favour to the Austrians by the outlawry of the regicides,
gave evidence, on the other hand, of his gracious
dispositions towards the forest cantons, by recognising
their freedom and independence on any power but that
of the empire. The Austrian princes were highly displeased by this step; but being occupied with their
bloody revenge for the murder of their late chief, they
were obliged to suppress their anger for a season. The
emperor imagined he had tranquillised Helvetia; but
he had no sooner set out on an Italian expedition, than
open hostilities broke out between the forest cantons
and the subjects of Austria. These disturbances might
probably have proved of no great consequence, if the
emperor had not met his death in Italy. For the moment, indeed, another direction was given by that event
to the ambition of the Austrian family, which now exerted every means in its power, for the second time, to
secure the crown for Frederick, but in vain. A majority of the electoral princes, still averse to that house,
declared themselves for duke Louis of Bavaria. The
latter candidate likewise enjoyed the adherence of the

forest cantons, who had excellent reasons for wishing
to see the imperial power in any hands rather than in
those of a duke of Austria. This election contest proved
the occasion of a furious war in Germany and Helvetia.
In the latter country the old dispute about boundaries
was revived between Einsiedlen and Schwytz, and was
carried on by both sides with excessive heat and violence.
Frederick, whose house had been invested with the pro-
tectoral rights of kast-vogt* over Einsiedlen, used this dispute as a pretext to attack the forest cantons; and though
Schwytz alone had offended in the matter, lanched
the imperial ban against all three. Louis again absolved
them from the sentence. On the other hand, duke
Leopold prepared his whole powers at once to wreak
the hereditary hatred of his family, — to protect the
(alleged) rights of so renowned a religious foundation,
and to revenge upon the forest cantons the slighted
claims of his brother. He threatened to tread the boors
under his feet, and carried with him waggons full of
cordage wherewith to bind or hang up their ringleaders.
He marched in person to Baden, where he held a council
of war. A triple attack on the same day was resolved
upon. The main body, 15,000 or 20,000 strong, was
to advance from Zug under Leopold himself; count
Otho of Strasburg, with 4000 men, were to march
over the Brünig; 1000 Lucerners to cross the lake
and fall in with the other forces at Stanzstadt in Unterwalden. The main army arrived at Zug in two divisions. Heavy-armed cavalry, then the pride and
strength of armies, led the van in large troops, without
sufficient discrimination of the mode of warfare demanded by the nature of the country. The flower of
the nobility of Hapsburg was in this army, amongst
others the ex-vogt Berenger of Landenberg, and Gessler's relations. Fifty burghers of Zurich also, all in
uniform clothing, marched along with it, according to
treaty. The duke himself, a tall majestic figure, pre-
senting the very ideal of chivalrous heroism, rode in

---

* For an explanation of this title, turn to the foregoing chapter.

the front of his warriors, confident of victory; and
dreamed not of the wonders which a people urged to
extremities can achieve in the defence of its freedom.

The Schwytzers, whom the main attack threatened,
were so far from being intimidated by it, that they scornfully rejected a dishonourable peace.   On receiving reinforcements of 400 men from Uri, and 300 more from
Unterwalden, they offered up their prayers to God, their
only Lord and Master, according to ancient usage in
the forest cantons, and stationed themselves, 1300 in
number, on the ridge of the Sattel.   An old man, Rudolph Reding of Bibereck, infirm in body, but listened
to respectfully by the people for his military talents and
experience, had given them the wise advice to take this
position.   If the narratives of several historians are to
be trusted, Reding's advice was grounded on a specific
warning received from Henry of Hünenburg, an Austrian noble, who had shot into the Swiss outposts an
arrow with a label bearing the inscription, "Beware of
Morgarten!" and had thus given them previous information of Leopold's plans, whether moved by love of
freedom, or by natural compassion for the imminent destruction of so many brave men.   On the eve of the battle
fifty men appeared before the lines of the Schwytzers.
These had been banished their country during the former
times of disturbance; but as soon as they were acquainted with its danger, they resolved, by joining the
combatants for freedom, to become once more worthy of
the land they had lost.   The forest cantons, however,
would not admit them within their frontiers, nor receive
them in the ranks of their combatants.   Nevertheless
they remained true to their purpose.   They stationed
themselves just beyond the frontiers on an eminence
above Morgarten, and prepared to act their part in the
reception of the enemy.

On the 15th November, 1315, with the first dawn of
day, the Austrian troops made their appearance.   The
helmets and cuirasses of the knights gleamed in the sun-

shine.   As far as the eye could reach glittered the spears
of the first army which had ever been drawn out against
the forest cantons; and the Swiss may be supposed to
have contemplated so novel a phenomenon with emotion.
The narrow way between the ridge of Morgarten and
the lake was soon crowded with the close column of
horsemen. This was the instant chosen by the fifty Swiss
exiles, who had collected fragments of rocks and trunks of
trees during the night, and now hurled them on the enemy
from their height, crushing horse and man.   A mode of
attack so startling produced terrible disorder.   The
horses became restive, reared, threw their riders, broke
the ranks, and many of them plunged into the lake.
The Swiss troops on the Sattel took advantage of this
moment of panic.   They rushed down hill in tolerable
order, fell on the enemy's flank, struck down the heavy-
armed knights by the vigorous use of their clubs and
halberts, and completed the confusion of the Austrians,
whom the slippery state of the half-frozen road rendered
yet more helpless, and unfit for making any defence.
The knights attempted to fall back on the infantry, and
to gain room; but the latter had not space to open their
files.   Many of them consequently were trodden down
by the cavalry—many cut to pieces by the confederates
—no prisoners made—no quarter given.   The Austrians
lost the flower of their nobility; and amongst them fell
two Gesslers, with the ex-tyrant Landenberg.   The
infantry suffered even more severely, as the narrowness
of the defile afforded no room for their evolutions.
After a slight resistance, the whole mass was dispersed
in disorderly flight.   The fifty men of Zurich alone,
with those of Zug, had fought bravely; and were slain
man by man upon the spot where they had stood.   The
whole affair was terminated by nine o'clock A. M.; and
thus the Schwytzers won a complete victory in the
space of an hour and a half, through the courage and
dexterity with which they took advantage of the nature
of the ground, and of the injudicious confidence of their
enemy.   Leopold's adherents had with difficulty succeeded

in saving the duke's person from the horrors of the fight.

On the following morning count Otho of Strasburg marched, with several thousand troops, over the Brünig on Obwalden, in concert with 1300 men of Lucerne, who landed at Bürgenstadt. These were met by the victorious men of Unterwalden, reinforced by 100 fresh volunteers, and were forced back on their ships with great loss. Strasburg's troops also, struck with panic, took to flight on all sides, leaving their baggage behind them.

It was easy to foresee that no permanent tranquillity would be procured to the three cantons by their victory; they were therefore obliged to study means of rallying their forces for the farther prosecution of the conflict; and the most effectual seemed to be a permanent confederacy. On the 13th of December, 1315, the envoys of the forest cantons held a meeting at Brunen, to conclude a perpetual league of self-defence against all internal and external enemies—a league, to use the words of the great annalist of Switzerland*, distinguished from most political arrangements and alliances, by extreme simplicity and innocence;—by seeking, not the attainment of interested or ambitious ends, but the welfare of the public alone, and the preservation of freedom, justice, and peace; and, finally, by calling a federal state into existence, which resisted the assaults of time during so long a period, only because it was not grounded, like other federal unions of that century, merely on commercial connections, but on the maintenance of the holiest rights of humanity—a noble end, extorting respect even from the most rapacious neighbours, until at length the hour arrived (that of the French revolution), destined to establish a new order in the world, to separate the durable from the decayed and obsolete social elements, to bring about the destruction of much evil, the continuance, or at least the regeneration, of much good. This league was long the only bond and law of the confederacy; but

* J. von Müller.

before the close of the sixteenth century, a Frenchman found occasion to write—" *Laxata sunt invicti illius fœderis vincula negligentiâ reipublicæ.* It was about this time that the name of *Swiss* came first into use with their neighbours, as a general designation for the members of the confederacy, which may be accounted for by the chief part having been acted by the Schwytzers, in the feud with Einsiedlen, and the battle of Morgarten.

On the 19th of June, 1318, a peace, or rather truce for a year, on equitable terms, was concluded between Austria and the confederates, which was afterwards prolonged to six years. By the terms of this armistice the freedom of the confederates received fresh confirmation : on the other hand, they bound themselves to enforce within their territories the payment of all revenues belonging to the duchy of Austria. In the mean time, notwithstanding the external show of repose, frequent occasions of offence kept up the old grudge on both sides.

The dukes, after the ill success of their arms against the confederates, turned them next against the other adherents of Louis. Duke Leopold laid siege, with a strong body of men, for ten weeks, to the town of Soleure, which espoused the Bavarian interest. With the aid of the Bernese, however, the town was so well defended, that he sought in vain to force it to capitulate, and equally in vain endeavoured to terrify its commandant, count Hugo of Bucheck, by threatening him, unless he would surrender the town, with the death of his eldest son, who was a prisoner. Father and son alike despised the menace. Another proof of no less magnanimity, the more deserving remark, as it occurred in an age when all extremities were looked upon as allowable against an enemy, was given to duke Leopold in the course of this siege. He had caused a bridge to be thrown across the Aar, above Soleure, in order to cut off supplies from the town, as well as to keep up communication between the divisions of his army upon both sides of the river. This structure was, however, soon

in danger from the force of the stream, which heavy
rains had swelled to an unusual height.   In this
emergency, Leopold had it loaded with stones, and
posted a body of troops upon it; but the bridge, unable
to bear the double weight, gave way, and Leopold's soldiers were plunged into the rapid stream below.   At
such a moment the men of Soleure regarded them not
as enemies, but as fellow-men, in need of assistance.
They threw themselves into the river, at great risk to
themselves, and not cnly rescued their foes from death,
but cherished and restored them in the town, and sent
them back to the camp without exacting ransom.   This
trait of generosity touched the prince, who was far from
being destitute of that quality.   Moreover, he had small
remaining hope of success, and was no longer disposed
to contend in arms where he had already been overcome
in magnanimity.   He requested entrance into the town,
with a train of thirty knights only; made a present to
the burghers of a banner; and concluded with them an
honourable peace.

The treaty betwixt Austria and the confederates had
lasted about six years, when Louis summoned the
Schwytzers, in 1323, to aid in the war of the empire
against Austria.   In this, as in its former contests, the
latter power was unsuccessful; and duke Leopold's life
is supposed to have been shortened by disappointment.
In 1326, the armistice with Switzerland was renewed
by his brother and successor, duke Albert.   In the
same year the forest cantons, which adhered with remarkable loyalty to the emperor, followed him in an
expedition to Italy.   Excommunicated on that account in 1328, they knew, as they had known before,
how to reduce to nothing the force of that so much
dreaded sentence, by setting the alternative before their
priests, of doing their duty, or of leaving the country.
Against such determined resolution, pope John XXI.
felt himself powerless, and said of the clergy who chose
to remain in the country, that their conduct was unrighteous, but prudent.   In fact, the pope had never

any power against the people, but only against princes whom he robbed of the people's fidelity. The cantons were in such high esteem with the emperor, on account of their unvarying attachment, that in 1316, an imperial decree annihilated all the rights of Austria in their territory.

In 1332 the forest cantons admitted a fourth member to partake in their perpetual union. We have already seen that the town of Lucerne, in the reign of the emperor Rudolph, had come, by an iniquitous purchase, under the power of Austria. It was only the most flattering promises which induced the town to subject itself to the new domination; but no long time had elapsed before these promises were forgotten, and the Austrians began to encroach beyond their just rights. However discontentedly this was seen by the burghers, they nevertheless bore it with patience, nay, exerted themselves actively in the cause of the house of Austria, and in the wars against the forest cantons suffered extensive losses. By way of showing gratitude for these services, the dukes withheld the subsidies which had been promised to the town, and forced upon it depreciated coins, and augmented imposts. An opinion had, however, gained ascendency, that even the power of princes had its limits, and that the chartered rights of freemen must not be sacrificed entirely to these earthly divinities. The burghers therefore assembled, and concluded a twenty years' peace with the confederates. The nobles opposed a violent resistance to the measure, of which the only result was, that a second popular meeting closed an everlasting league with the forest cantons.

The men of Lucerne, however, like their confederates, were forced to pay the price of freedom in blood. A treacherous attempt of the Argovian nobility, whose property lay within the Austrian territory, and who first had recourse to open war, but in vain, was fortunately frustrated by the steadiness of the burghers; and an armistice at length took place, by the emperor's mediation, between Austria and the forest cantons, by the

terms of which Lucerne preserved its league with the
three others, with reservation of the rights and dues of
Austria.

Notwithstanding all the feuds and disturbances, which
crowded upon each other during so short a time, prosperity made progress in the land.   Towns and convents
vied with each other in diffusing cultivation even
throughout the wildest mountainous regions.   Considerable commercial intercourse also was maintained with
Italy, Germany, France, and Flanders.   Zurich and St.
Gall possessed linen and silk manufactures ; the pasture
lands produced hides, wool, cheese, and butter ; in Berne
and Freyburg, cloth-making and dyeing establishments
flourished ; the western districts traded in iron, horses,
hawks, and horned cattle ; Geneva in southern fruits and
spices.   The trade in gold was prohibited, and that of
silver restricted.

Religion still appeared in all its primitive simplicity.
Wealthy knights still knew no better method of per-
petuating their memory in the land than through the
medium of bequests for the foundation of cloisters.
The respect in which the monks were held, however,
already began to decline, by reason of their flagrant
violations of the rules of their order, in spite of frequent
attempts at reformation of their discipline.   Accordingly,
no fault was found with the conduct of the forest cantons,
who, when under excommunication, as we have seen, in
1328 left their priests free to perform divine service or
quit the country.   No fault was found with the clergy for
accepting the former alternative.   Again, it was heard
without disapprobation that the men of Basle had
seized on a distinguished papal legate, who had dared
to affix to the walls of their church the bull of excommunication against the emperor Louis, and had drowned
him in the Rhine.   Such violent acts were perfectly in
the spirit of the times.   The Zurichers cared so little
for the bulls of the pope, that in 1331 they drove the
clergy out of their town for obeying them ; and for
eighteen years there was no divine service in Zurich,

except such as was rendered by the bare-footed friars. The whole population often resisted ecclesiastical ordinances, when they ran against their old traditional usages, and detected with instinctive sagacity whatever was indifferent or useless in them. Such was in those times the state of Switzerland, which contained sufficient elements of those great changes which we shall presently see effected in its polity.

CHAP. VI.

FROM THE REVOLUTION OF ZURICH TO THE LEAGUE WITH APPENZELL.

1335—1412.

SITUATION OF ZURICH. — CHARACTER OF THE BURGHERS. — FORM OF GOVERNMENT. — RUDOLPH BRUN. — EXCITES A REVOLUTIONARY MOVEMENT. — ELECTED BURGOMASTER FOR LIFE. — DEFEATS A CONSPIRACY OF THE NOBLES. — APPLIES FOR AID TO THE FOREST CANTONS AGAINST DUKE ALBERT OF AUSTRIA. — THE LATTER BESIEGES ZURICH. — IS COMPELLED TO RAISE THE SIEGE. — LEAGUE OF THE EIGHT ORIGINAL TOWNS AND LANDS OF THE CONFEDERACY. — PEACE OF THORBERG. — CHARACTER OF RUDOLPH BRUN. — HIS TREACHEROUS COMPACT WITH AUSTRIA. — BERNE. — DISTINGUISHED FOR A SPIRIT OF ENTERPRISE. — OBNOXIOUS TO THE BORDERING NOBILITY. — ATTACKED BY THE COMBINED FORCE OF THE NOBLES AND THE EMPEROR. — BATTLE OF LAUPEN. — BERNE'S PLANS OF AGGRANDISEMENT. — ROGER MANESSE'S WISE ADMINISTRATION OF ZURICH. — DECLINE OF THE NOBILITY AND CLERGY. — BERNE AND SOLEURE DEFEAT THE COUNT OF KYBURG. — DUKE LEOPOLD OF AUSTRIA ENTERS SWITZERLAND. — BATTLE OF SEMPACH. — ARNOLD OF WINKELRIED. — THE BAD PEACE. — UNEXPECTED INROAD OF THE AUSTRIANS. — BATTLE OF NAEFELS. — DESCRIPTION OF RHÆTIA. — THE MEN OF APPENZELL REVOLT FROM THE ABBOT OF ST. GALL. — ARE REINFORCED BY THE SCHWYTZERS. — ENGAGE AN AUSTRIAN ARMY AT THE STOSS. — AGAIN AT THE WOLFSHALD. — DEFEATED AT BREGENZ. — RECEIVED AS ALLIES OF THE CONFEDERACY. — RENEWAL OF THE TWENTY YEARS' TRUCE WITH AUSTRIA.

ON the pleasant site of the old Helvetian Thuricum stood the town of Zurich, long renowned for industry, intelligence, wealth not too unequally distributed, and genuine civic spirit in its burghers. A general and constant love of the laws had, for ages, been the chief support of their government. The cordial and familiar usages handed down from their forefathers did not easily admit of innovation, and these usages, as in free states they ought to be, were uniform and simple for all. The citizens retained their family names, even after they had acquired lands and lordships, and never became ashamed of their original vocations. The confluence of foreigners, and the general easy condition of the inhabitants, contributed to the flourishing appearance of the town. Nor were science and art strangers in Zurich. The renowned songsters of those times, the Minnesingers, found hospitable welcome with the principal burghers. Nowhere more effect was produced than at Zurich by the doctrines (enlightened for those times) of Arnold of Brescia, a scholar of Abelard, and one of the most acute and enquiring spirits of his age. He gained there many adherents to those principles of resistance against clerical and papal usurpation, the expression of which he expiated afterwards at the stake. We have already seen, that even papal interdicts neither frightened nor subdued the men of Zurich. They often enacted laws which seemed oppressive to the clergy, who were placed by them on a footing of equality with other classes, and forced to bear their share of contributions to the public burdens. They resented with indomitable spirit the aggressions and affronts of the nobles, and repaid them by the capture and destruction of their strong-holds. Thus, Zurich enforced respect for herself from the proudest of her neighbours, and formed alliance with every free town from the Main to the St. Gothard. Yet, with a population exceeding 12,000, and consisting, for the most part, of free burghers, the town possessed hitherto no domain without its walls, except the forest on the banks of the Sihl.

The supreme powers of the state were vested, practically, in the council, a body consisting of twelve knights

and twenty-four burghers, who exercised those powers
by rotation, a third part of them holding office during
four months, wielding, independently of the remaining
two thirds of its members, the whole executive functions
of the commonwealth : powers rendered in some measure dictatorial and discretionary by the provision that,
in unforeseen cases, they should act for the public interest, according to their best judgment.   Thus the
whole affairs of the state came by degrees under the
management of a few influential families, principally
attached to the pursuits of war and chivalry. The body
of the citizens, the bold and intelligent traders and
handicraftsmen, became tired, at length, of subordination
to these dignitaries, especially as many practical grievances were complained of in their administration.   It
was said they took no care but for themselves, and those
who belonged to them ; gave no reckoning of the moneys
of the town, received the inferior burghers with intolerable haughtiness ; proceeded, in short, in all respects in
an arbitrary manner.   Discontent, for a while, exhaled
in murmurs, till a member of the obnoxious body itself
came forward, and made common cause with the disaffected burghers.   This was Rudolph Brun, a man of
noble birth and large fortune, a knight, and a member
of council, who possessed precisely the qualities indispensable for a popular leader.   His condescending
familiarity made him a favourite of the common people,
and he had skill to take advantage of every circumstance
which offered, and to veil revenge or ambition under the
aspect of true patriotism.   That the cause which Brun
espoused was good, is manifested by the warm participation of such men as Roger Manesse — that his heart
was bad, has been probably inferred from the tenour of
his public life.   Revolutions would too often find but
little favour in history, if their justification depended on
the characters of their leaders.

Independence of feeling had planted itself amongst
·the burghers of Zurich, with the increase of their wealth

and their knowledge, and prompted them to express more
and more loudly their desire to be united in political
guilds or companies. They listened, therefore, with
open ears to Brun's representations that their rulers
disregarded their duty, and were reducing the town,
originally free, beneath the yoke of an intolerable
tyranny ; that he himself was hated by the council, because love to his fellow-citizens ever prompted him to
lift his voice against these abuses ; that the burghers
could only free themselves by exerting their own strength,
and that for his part he was ready to sacrifice life and
estate in their service. His adherents increased daily in
number. Many good and honourable men joined his
party, who perceived the pressing need of a reformation
in the state ; many who might have been ill used by a
member of the council, or condemned by a judicial sentence, which was alleged of Brun himself ; there were
many in whose cases legal judgments had been given
unfavourably, and, therefore, as to them, it would seem
unjustly ; many whom the subversion of the existing
order might flatter with the hope of personal benefit, the
re-establishment of a ruined, or the foundation of a new
fortune ; many, in fine, whom levity, a bold and lively
temper, or a reckless and licentious disposition, prompted
to take part in any daring design, which afforded hopes
of disorder, and destruction of all legal and moral
restraint.

On the 1st of May, 1335, the first section of the
council was on the point of quitting office, while the
second only waited for the sanction of the people, in
order to succeed to its functions. Now, however, this
necessary sanction was withheld until an account of the
public money should be given ; and this demand was supported in the council by Rudolph Brun, Roger Manesse,
and by several other members. The rest, however, treated
it as a popular ebullition, which in a short time would
subside of itself, and exhausted their whole stock of
petty artifices to draw the affair into length, and gain

time. This course had been adopted on a much better acquaintance with the temper of the council than with that of the people. After six weeks of inaction, Brun industriously promulgated that the lords of the council only meant to mock and delude the commonalty. This intelligence brought a multitude round the doors of the hall of council, who terrified its members with their concourse and clamour. Some declared for the burghers, others, in fear for their personal safety, precipitately fled from the city. A popular assembly was held in the church of the Franciscans, in which it was resolved to bring to account all the members of the late government, to reform the constiution, and to place provisional sovereignty in the hands of Rudolph Brun and his friends. By the new constitution, framed under their auspices, all handicraftsmen were classed under thirteen guilds, the foreman of each of which should sit in council. One moiety of this body was henceforth to be composed of burghers, the other of nobles, and the whole was to be subject to renewal every half year. Brun caused himself to be elected burgomaster for life, and contrived to retain considerable power in his hands; while a prudent reservation of the rights of the empire, and the sanction of the emperor, prevented the accession of a formidable enemy to the infant democracy.

It had already natural enemies enough. Rarely do those whom a social revolution has degraded from distinguished eminence find themselves without friends at home—without allies abroad;—and still more rarely are .they capable of renouncing their hereditary pretensions with a good grace. The ancient lords of council and their adherents could not forget their former functions and dignities. They entered into a secret league with the count of Rappersweil, the barons of Bonstetten, Mazingen, and others; and the night of the 24th of February, 1350, was fixed for a general massacre of the democratic party. Some of the conspirators had re-entered the town secretly; others had acquired and abused the public confidence in their peaceable intentions, and numerous auxiliaries approached the town by land and by water. A baker's boy is said to have discovered the conspiracy at the moment of its meditated explosion; and the town was saved by Brun's skill and decision, supported by the bravery of the citizens. The loss of the conspirators was enormous; and, besides those who perished in the conflict, or by drowning in the river, thirty-seven died on the wheel or by the sword of the executioner. The Zurichers, with the aid of Schaff-hausen, soon made themselves masters of Rappersweil; and, a few days before Christmas, Rudolph Brun, in contempt of his own promise, burned the town, abandoning the helpless inhabitants to the rigours of the season and to famine. But when, in the following year, duke Albert of Austria threatened severe retaliation for these outrages, the burgomaster addressed himself to the league of the forest cantons for reinforcements and reception into their permanent confederacy. Uri, Schwytz, Unterwalden, and Lucerne, which had long regarded Zurich as their principal mart and bulwark, accepted her proposals with alacrity; and, on the Walpurgis night of the year 1351, closed with her a perpetual league of reciprocal aid against all enemies, reserving only the rights of earlier allies of the emperor and the holy Roman empire.

Albert now began to press the Zurichers more closely, and demanded satisfaction for the burning of Rappers-weil,—a town which had belonged to his relative,—as well as for all other injuries done to the dependants and adherents of Austria. He advanced at the head of 16,000 men, and, moreover, called the people of Glarus to arms as his auxiliaries. On their refusal, as they alleged that they were under the immediate protection of the empire, and acknowledged no obligation to aid in the private feuds of Austria, the duke resolved to send troops into Glarus, where he himself was protector of the monastery of Seckingen, and from whence he

might overawe Schwytz and Uri, and deter their population from assisting the Zurichers. This design was,
however, frustrated by the confederates from the forest
cantons, who achieved the occupation of Glarus by an unexpected inroad in mid-winter. The people of Glarus
pledged their faith to the Schwytzers; sent 200 men to reinforce the garrison of Zurich; defeated Walter of Stadion,
as he marched upon their territory, at the head of Austrian forces from Rappersweil, and captured and destroyed the castle of Naefels. Admission into the league
of the confederates rewarded these achievements of their
new allies.

On the side of Zug the confederates were still exposed to attack, and the connection of their forces was
interrupted. Two thousand six hundred men from Zurich
and the forest cantons approached the town, and received oaths of fidelity from the neighbouring districts,
reserving only the rights of the duke of Austria. The
town itself, which was held by a strong garrison, at first
made a vigorous defence, till the burghers, becoming discouraged by the assaults of the besiegers, solicited a
three days' truce. Delegates were despatched by them
to duke Albert, who described to him the straitened
situation of the town; but the duke, instead of attending
to them, turned to question his falconer whether his
birds had been fed; and when asked whether his subjects
did not concern him more than his birds, replied, " Go!
if you are conquered, we shall very soon reconquer you."
Resentment of such wanton disregard did not fail to
produce a new disposition in those who had been its
objects; and Zug immediately joined the league of the
forest cantons and Zurich, on nearly the same conditions
as the latter town,—Glarus having already, on the 4th
of the same month, acceded to the same eternal confederacy.

Duke Albert, instead of wasting his resources in
petty hostilities against Zug and Glarus, prepared to
crush the force of the confederates at one blow, by the
capture and subjection of Zurich. In this enterprise he

tasked the whole strength of his hereditary domains and
allies.   The elector of Brandenburg, with many other
secular princes, five bishops, six and twenty counts, the
towns of Berne, Soleure, Basle, Strasburg, and Schaffhausen swelled the ranks of his auxiliaries.   He exhausted his domains by extraordinary imposts.   The
stout defence of the Zurichers, however, soon made it
evident that, against a people so steadfast, united, and
dauntless as the Swiss, no glory could be gained by contending; while, moreover, the dearth of provisions in
the camp of duke Albert became such as threatened
absolute famine.   In this emergency, the elector of
Brandenburg offered his mediation, and despatched confidential messengers to treat with the Swiss.   Scarcely
had an answer been received from the town, when its
inhabitants saw the enemy draw off from their walls;
the Bernese alone retained their position.   The terms of
peace were arranged through the elector's intervention;
and in these, as in all previous ones, the privileges and
leagues of the confederates were maintained inviolate.
Berne was now received among their number: her recent
alliance with Austria, which was known to have been
merely in compliance with existing engagements, had
not destroyed the sense of common interests with her
neighbours.

Such was the alliance of the eight towns and districts,
which, for more than a century afterwards, received no
new member into the body of their original confederacy.
In this league, the three forest cantons alone, Uri,
Schwytz, and Unterwalden, properly speaking, formed
the old and genuine Switzerland.   They alone, who had
admitted all the others into their everlasting league,
were in alliance with all of them;—with Lucerne, whom
they had aided to emancipate herself from Austria; with
Berne, whom they had voluntarily assisted in emergency;
with Zurich, whose cause, when forsaken by all others,
they had adopted; with Zug and Glarus, whom they
had conquered only to confer on their inhabitants friendship and freedom.   On the other hand, no particular

bond of union existed between Glarus and Lucerne; no immediate league had been formed between Zurich, Berne, and Lucerne; the Bernese were under no obligations with regard to Zug and Glarus. The forest cantons remained the pivot—the keystone—of the whole confederacy,—the remaining five being leagued with them, and only through *them* with each other. Their energy preserved that union, of which the only object was the maintenance of the spirit of freedom, while, in other respects, every canton retained its independence and the liberty of constituting at pleasure its own internal administration, laws, and institutions. It was only in the course of time that reciprocal engagements betwixt the other cantons were agreed to, which, in like manner, reserved to each contracting party unlimited powers in their own internal arrangements. This league continued to flourish only so long as its organisation continued correspondent with the wants of the time—until its animating soul, the spirit of freedom and self-sacrifice, had departed from the frame of the confederacy —until many desired to retain freedom only for themselves, along with absolute domination over their subjects; while others could not resolve to raise their arm for the defence of their confederates in extremity, so long as they entertained the delusive hope of remaining undisturbed amidst the ruin of their brethren.

After this pacification, the duke of Austria endeavoured to compel the people of Zug to renounce their connection with the Swiss league. But they answered, that the treaty of peace had maintained that league inviolate; and that they would yield to no other claims than such as the duke could rightfully make. Albert on this laid the whole affair before the emperor, their common liege lord; and a diet at Worms condemned the Swiss league, on the alleged ground that members of the empire could not bind themselves together without the concurrence of their head. Weapons more effectual than sophistry were marshalled to support this decision. Summonses were sent to all the feudatories of Austria

as well as those of the empire; and all the imperial
towns were called to aid with their militia. Charles IV.
himself advanced in person with a force of 4000 knights,
and at least 40,000 foot and horse; and laid siege to Zurich. These mighty preparations, though directed against
a garrison of barely 4000 men, were equally ineffectual
as those of the duke of Austria had been in the preceding
year. The Zurichers besides contrived artfully to indicate that their quarrel with Austria did not affect their
allegiance to the emperor, by displaying, on a lofty
tower, the ensign of the holy Roman empire—a black
eagle on a golden field. They followed up this demonstration with a petition from a number of their barons,
burghers, and magistrates; and these overtures, combined with the impression made by the spectacle of their
steadiness and union, induced the emperor, after a siege
of only twenty days, to disband his army, and to leave
the Swiss confederacy in quiet.

It being found that the confederates were not to be
coerced with arms, an attempt was made to break their
force by producing disunion amongst them. Brun,
whose conduct was arbitrary on all occasions, subscribed,
with a few other members of council, a separate treaty of
peace in the name of his town; and, moreover, an alliance
with Austria, which might well displease the confederates, as its provisions were more binding and extensive
than those of their league; nay, in certain cases went
to supersede it. The interest of their trade, which was
ever uppermost with the Zurichers, may have moved
them to close so sinister a compact, the evil effects of
which were, however, averted by the steadiness and fore-
sight of Schwytz. As duke Albert would not yield up
his pretensions, and the emperor persisted in declaring,
" that the Swiss should not, on pain of the imperial displeasure, regard Schwytz and Glarus as their allies,"
the confederates held a diet at Lucerne. Zurich did not
appear, and remained neutral. Schwytz, however, declared that the decree should be resisted, and the event
reposed in God's hands and their own. The Austrians

demanded the submission of Zug and Glarus, which was refused until the duke should give his sanction to their league with the confederates. The Austrians threatened; on which the men of Schwytz raised their banner, and espoused the cause of Zug and Glarus in the name of all the confederates. Duke Albert, however, did not find it advisable to renew the war. He was old and infirm; pain and impatience had lamed his spirit for action; he no longer cherished hopes of conquest; and he therefore acquiesced in the arrangement of existing points of dispute, through the mediation of Peter, baron of Thorberg, by whom a treaty was accordingly concluded with the confederates, which was commonly known by the name of the peace of Thorberg.

Rudolph Brun, to whom the foregoing transactions owed their original impulse, was versed in all the wiles of a party leader. He knew how to attract the crowd by every art of persuasion, and while his power was small, and the issue of his plans remained doubtful, to avoid the least appearance of violence. Intrepid, when the victory depended on words — inflexible, as long as he had nothing to be afraid of — he could sometimes be courageous through the mere dread of death, and his natural timidity made him habitually vigilant. His abilities were better adapted for civic transactions than great affairs, — yet, perhaps, the only quality which he wanted as a magistrate, was the strength of mind to act with uprightness. Notwithstanding all his failings, he possessed the attachment of many, to whom the revolution which he led brought economical or social advantages. His renown was at its highest pitch in the fourteenth year of his government, through the flourishing state of affairs, which was ascribed to his administration. But on examining his character, as it developed itself from year to year in the elevated position where he fixed himself for life, it exhibits a less favourable aspect; at the point of time especially, when, after having procured for his native town the protection of the confederacy, he

ruined his own patriotic work by an unseasonable compact with Austria, not without suspicion of sordid
motives in the transaction. Yet it cannot be denied
that Brun's undertakings gave a firmer seat to internal
freedom in Switzerland, as we shall presently see external perils combated by the energies of Reding and of
Erlach.

While the burghers of Zurich employed themselves
in overthrowing aristocratical sovereignty within their
walls, at Berne the nobles joined their strength with
that of the commons in repelling aristocratical aggression
from without. The rapid growth of the town in wealth
and importance, and its numerous territorial acquisitions
and purchases, aroused the jealous pride of the counts
and barons in its neighbourhood. Berne had long been
distinguished by an active and ambitious spirit, impatient of control or restraint, and which nothing but the
altered state of Europe could have prevented from advancing as resistlessly to greatness as had been done
under more favourable circumstances by the most renowned republics of antiquity. Constantly intent on
leaving no debt unpaid, whether of hostility or friendship, they pursued progressive aggrandisement on the
ruin of their enemies, or by reconciling and receiving
them into the privileges of citizenship. This system
created a numerous body of out-burghers, the protection
of whom involved the town in everlasting feuds, which
might sometimes be considered unavoidable, but were
often waged from eager love of glory, or as offering an
occasion of aggrandisement. Agriculture and arms
engrossed the nobility; trade and the mechanical arts
were exercised by the people. Public affairs came by
degrees, under the direction of a certain number of families; and though the burghers were, by law, to be
consulted in all state-occasions, yet the authorities dispensed with that formality on pressing emergencies;
emergencies which could not fail frequently to recur
amidst the enterprises of Austria, and the barons in the
neighbourhood, and which, by calling off the popular

attention to external attacks, were apt to favour domestic usurpation.

In the hundred and twenty-seventh year after the building of Berne, the higher and inferior nobility of Aargau and Burgundy combined their whole force for its destruction with the barons and counts in the Uecht-land. The dukes of Austria joined this combination; and the emperor Louis sanctioned its proceedings through his envoys. A beginning was made by petty provocations and affronts; but more serious measures were taken after a general assembly of the nobles in the town of Freyburg. At this meeting all the injuries were enumerated, alleged to have been suffered from Berne, whose burghers, it was said, aimed at the ruin of the nobility. Hostilities were determined, and commenced against the obnoxious town; all commerce and intercourse with it closed. Berne sought no protector, and her citizens neither exhibited trepidation nor blind ardour. The council, under the avoyer, John of Bubenberg, resolved, that satisfaction should be given to all equitable demands, but that force should be repelled with force; and as all negotiation with the nobles was fruitless, an appeal to arms remained the only alternative. Laupen, a small town in the Bernese territory, was already threatened by the combined force of the emperor and the nobles, consisting of 15,000 foot and 3000 horse, led by 1200 knights, in complete armour *, and 700 barons, with crowned helmets. The victory or overthrow of Berne was now to decide the freedom or servitude of the whole of western Switzerland. The peasantry who fled into the town for refuge brought frightful accounts of the near approach, the overwhelming forces, and the merciless dispositions of the enemy. They were minded to leave not a human creature alive in Berne, but to put whatever had life in it to the sword without pity. Each of the hostile leaders had already selected a mansion in the town, of which, after their assured success, they meant to take possession. Mean-

* Ferreis muris armati.

G

while the nobles gave themselves up to an arrogant security; while the burghers, on the other hand, put forth
their whole defensive strength, and determined rather to
bury themselves in the ruins of their town than to ask
or accept mercy from the insolent invaders. As the
first aim of the enemy was directed against Laupen,
where only a small garrison was posted, under the
knight of Blankenburg, they swore by God and all the
saints to sacrifice life and goods in the defence of the
place, and issued a decree, that " if any father had two
sons, or if in any house there were two brothers, one of
each should march to the relief of Laupen." Six hundred men marched accordingly under the younger Bubenberg.

The Bernese, having thus provided for the first instant
emergency, proceeded at more leisure to levy the force
of their out-burghers, elect a general, and solicit the
support of the confederates. Though the term of their
original league with the forest cantons had expired,
these brave allies were foremost in advancing to their
succour. Nine hundred able warriors marched across
the Brünig to Berne; and the whole force of the town
advanced upon Laupen on the 20th of June, 1339, under
the command of Rudolph of Erlach. Erlach drew up his
troops in good order, assigning to the allies, and first of
all to the forest cantons, the post of honour against the
enemy's cavalry. He himself, at the head of the troops
of Berne, prepared to attack their infantry, and gave
the signal for the engagement, by exclaiming, " Where
be now those gallant youths who were wont to bid defiance to the enemy in their revels at Berne, adorned
with flowers and feathers ? The honour of your town
is now in your hands. — Follow her banner ! Follow
Erlach!" On this the youths of Berne rushed round the
banner ; the slingers advanced ; and having discharged
three volleys with considerable execution, fell back into
their former position. This retrograde movement was
taken for a flight in the rear of the army, which was
occupied by young inexperienced combatants, who

wheeled about, and fled into the neighbouring wood.
Their flight occasioned wavering and disorder in the
main body. At this critical moment Erlach showed the
soul of a great leader, whose presence of mind is not to
be shaken by the most untoward accidents. He cried
to the troops with an air of cheerful confidence, " My
friends, we shall now conquer, for the chaff is threshed
from the corn !" Then, waving his sword, he gave the
command for a charge. The nature of the ground had
not allowed the enemy's infantry to extend its lines
sufficiently; and the want of subordination and of union
which prevailed amongst an army under so many rival
chiefs, rendered it utterly unable to maintain its ground
against the compact mass of the confederates. After a
short and feeble resistance, the infantry threw away their
arms, and took to flight in utter disorder. The forest
cantons, the men of Soleure, of Hasli, and of Sieben-
thal, were still engaged in doubtful strife with the cavalry. Already they were on the verge of utter defeat,
and had only maintained their ground through the obstinate stand made by the forest cantons ; when the men
of Berne attacked the enemy at once in flank and in
rear, and the victory was now complete on all points.
The field was strewed with the bodies, arms, and horses
of the nobility. So total was their overthrow, that the
baron of Blumenberg no sooner heard the numbers and
the names of the fallen, than exclaiming, " God forbid
I should survive such men !" he spurred his horse upon
the ranks of the forest cantons and found what he sought,
an honourable death. Seven-and-twenty banners of the
imperial towns and nobles fell into the hands of the
victors, who, after a short pursuit of the fugitives, re-
assembled on the field of battle, fell down on their
knees, and returned thanks to Him who had given them
the victory over their enemies. The garrison at Laupen
heartily sympathised with the joy of their victorious
brethren ; and Erlach paid his tribute of acknowledg-
ment to the valour and the discipline of his army. He
then gave orders to remain on the field during the night,

according to the usage, partly to prove on whose side
was the victory, and partly to take care of the wounded.
Early on the following morning, the conquerors marched
homewards.   A priest, with the holy sacrament, led the
procession ; next in order went the conquered banners,
arms, and accoutrements ; and the procession was closed
by the march of the conquering army.   In this manner
they reached Berne, and entered the city amidst exulting
shouts of welcome from the people.   Erlach, having
saved his country, laid down the authority with which
in the hour of need he had been invested.   Berne re-
,.ewed her league with the forest cantons, and gave them
practical tokens of her gratitude.   The celebration of a
solemn divine service was ordained on every future an-
niversary of the day of Laupen, that pious remembrance
and ardent emulation of its glories might be preserved
through all succeeding generations.

The triumphs of Swiss valour were soon saddened by
the breaking out of that great plague, which visited with
its ravages the greater part of Europe and Asia, and of
which the most vivid delineation ever written (except
that of a similar pest by Thucydides) has been preserved in the Decameron of Boccaccio. Whole towns were
depopulated. Estates were left without claimants or
occupiers. Priests, physicians, grave-diggers, could not
be found in adequate numbers; and the consecrated
earth of the churchyards no longer sufficed for the
reception of its destined tenants. In the order of
Franciscans alone 120,430 monks are said to have
perished. This plague had been preceded by tremendous earthquakes, which laid in ruins towns, castles,
and villages. Dearth and famine, clouds of locusts, and
even an innocent comet had been long before regarded
as forerunners of the pestilence ; and when it came it
was viewed as an unequivocal sign of the wrath of God.
At the outset, the Jews became, as usual, objects of
umbrage, as having occasioned this calamity by poison-
ing the wells. A persecution was commenced against
them, and numberless innocent persons were consigned,

by heated fanaticism, to a dreadful death by fire, and their children were baptized over the corpses of their parents, according to the religion of their murderers. These atrocities were in all probability perpetrated by many, in order to possess themselves of the wealth acquired by the Jews in traffic, to take revenge for their usurious extortions, or, finally, to pay their debts in the most expeditious and easy manner. When it was found that the plague was nowise diminished by massacring the Jews, but, on the contrary, seemed to acquire additional virulence, it was inferred that God, in his righteous wrath, intended nothing less than to extirpate the whole sinful race of man. Many now endeavoured by self-chastisement to avert the divine vengeance from themselves. Fraternities of hundreds and thousands collected under the name of Flagellants, strolled through the land in strange garbs, scourged themselves in the public streets, in penance for the sins of the world, and read a letter which was said to have fallen from heaven, admonishing all to repentance and amendment. They were joined, of course, by a crowd of idle vagabonds, who, under the mask of extraordinary sanctity and humble penitence, indulged in every species of disorder and debauchery. At last the affair assumed so grave an aspect, that the pope and many secular princes declared themselves against the Flagellants, and speedily put an end to their extravagances. Various ways were still, however, resorted to by various tempers to snatch the full enjoyment of that life which they were so soon to lose, at the expense of every possible violation of the laws of morality. Only a few lived on in a quiet and orderly manner, in reliance on the saving help of God, without running into any excess of anxiety or indulgence. After this desolating scourge had raged during four years, its violence seemed at length to be exhausted.

Rudolph of Erlach, the hero of Laupen, had on the close of the war withdrawn himself from the stage of

public life, and lived to an advanced age on his property
near Berne. There he remained in his castle, honoured
by all, in modest retirement: his children were at a
distance from him; and while men and maids were
busied in husbandry, the old man often was left under
the sole protection of his hounds. The sword which
he had worn in his country's battles hung on the wall.
In this solitude he was visited one day by his son-in-
law, Jost von Rudenz, who had on many occasions
excited Erlach's displeasure. A bitter altercation is
supposed to have taken place between them; and Rudenz, in an excess of rage, snatched the sword from the
wall, struck down the old hero, and escaped. When
intelligence of the murder reached Berne, the whole
population, horse and foot, sallied forth to seize the
murderer; who, however, was not taken, and is supposed to have shortly afterwards met his death in some
unknown manner. Thus fell Erlach.

Even in peace Berne pursued with great success her
plans of aggrandisement by feuds, or by acquiring cas-
tellan jurisdictions, and also made many purchases of
territory at this time, by which the town became so
much involved in debt, that nothing but the spirited
exertions of the burghers could have cleared away its numerous embarrassments. While such was the external
progress of Berne, the internal tranquillity of the town
became disturbed by the strife between the higher ranks
of nobility and the lesser nobles, as well as the respectable
burghers. These dissensions were, however, composed
with much discretion, moderation, and equity; a few suspicious characters were removed from the council, and
future encroachments on the part of the authorities were
provided against by judicious regulations.

Zurich, under the wise and moderate government of
Roger Manesse, who, on the death Brun, succeeded to
the dignity of burgomaster, sought a remedy in dili-
gence and industry for the serious wounds which severe
and protracted warfare had inflicted on the morals and
the wealth of its population; whose numbers had, more-

over, been diminished by one eighth. The first aim of the government of Zurich was to ameliorate its impoverished condition ; the second, to set limits, by strong sumptuary laws, to the decay of moral discipline, and to new modes of extravagance; the third, to secure the freedom of the burghers by wise amendments in a defective constitution, which had bestowed upon the burgomaster more extensive powers than should be given in a free state to any one. Thus, in four and twenty years of almost uninterrupted peace, Zurich gradually rose to even more than her former prosperity. Berne could certainly boast of greater power than Zurich, of more illustrious rulers, of a more high-minded and warlike people. Zurich, on the other hand, pursued with greater energy the arts and undertakings of peace; and while Berne advanced with rapid strides to the rank of a powerful commonwealth, bore away the palm of civilisation and improvement.

Lucerne, torn by perpetual party contests, and externally exposed to the power of Austria, remained far behind Berne and Zurich.

Zug and Glarus were quiet and contented, as it was no longer in the power of Austria to invade their rights and liberties.

The forest cantons felt but little concern about the outward world, and followed the still tenour of their pastoral life ; but they were not the less endowed with a free spirit, and prepared at any moment to fight for their freedom, friends, and country. While the confederacy thus enjoyed its liberties, the towns of St. Gall, Schaffhausen, Basle, Soleure, Sion, and Lausanne, struggled eagerly to attain the like advantages.

The forest cantons, along with Zurich, Lucerne, and Zug, adopted, in 1370, a set of regulations very remarkable for those times, which were known under the title of the Pfaffenbrief, the object of which was to hinder the abuse of clerical influence, to abolish the impunity enjoyed by ecclesiastics, even in cases of enormous criminality, to narrow the operation of their intrigues and their vindictiveness, and to render them amenable to the native laws and tribunals. The pecuniary wants of princes and nobles prompted bolder and bolder measures against the clergy; the towns taxed them; the peasantry refused to pay any longer many services of vassalage imposed by their authority; and the church vassals themselves, especially in the district of Appenzell, hardly maintained the semblance of obedience to their mandates.

The power of the nobility declined with that of the clergy, as the great barons set themselves to vie with the magnificence of the princes of Austria, Savoy, and Milan: thus preparing their own ruin by the abandonment of their primitive manners, as well as by the consumption of their patrimonial wealth. The noble houses of Montfort, Neufchâtel, Kyburg, and a few others, maintained themselves with difficulty between the rising Swiss republic and the growing powers of Austria and Savoy.

During the peace with Austria, the confederacy had to repel two other assaults of hostile power. No prince or town was at that time sufficiently rich to support standing armies; or if there were any whose wealth might have enabled them to do so, they would hardly have dared to combat the repugnance of their people, who justly regarded standing troops as an instrument for their subjection. In case of war, the nobles with their squires followed for a certain time their prince's banner on horseback, while the common people served on foot; belligerent towns, on the other hand, called out their burghers and out-burghers. This mode of conducting war had obvious disadvantages. As the vassals of princes were only obliged to a limited term of service, a large army not unfrequently disbanded just at the moment when the best success might have been expected; and as the nobles and people felt the constant recurrence of warfare more and more burdensome, it often happened that military service was refused. Other disadvantages, more-

over, were inseparable from these imperfect military arrangements, which often crippled the conduct of the best
planned undertakings. And if the towns had not exactly
the same impediments to struggle with, as were often
opposed to princes by the turbulence of their vassals,
they had others perhaps equally embarrassing. The
wealth acquired in trade introduced effeminacy, decay of
martial spirit, and dread of death; and gave rise to the
wish to free themselves by any means from a personal
share in warlike expeditions. To liberate towns and
princes from these difficulties, bold and enterprising men
soon offered their services: these men, who, for the most
part, were poor nobles, or burghers and peasants anxious
to distinguish themselves by deeds of valour, levied on
their own account large troops of rapacious rabble, often
to the number of many thousands. Thus escorted, they
roamed about, maintaining themselves and their armies
at the cost of the unfortunate lands which lay in their
line of march; and offering their mercenary services, for
one or more campaigns, to towns and princes. When
dismissed by one employer, if they did not immediately
find another they betook themselves to predatory excursions on their own score. Not a few of these leaders
were murdered by their own band; many met a disgraceful death on the scaffold; but, on the other hand,
some won for themselves domains and principalities.
Their formation was the first trace and original germ
of standing armies; and has considerable resemblance
to the manner in which partisan corps are formed
in modern warfare. As the invention of this mode
of making war belonged to Italy, the leaders of these
troops received the Italian name of *condottieri*. One
of these mercenary captains, Arnold of Cervola, a man
of acknowledged courage but indifferent reputation, had
fought in the pay of France against England: after the
close of that war, he marched through several districts
at the head of twenty, thirty, or even forty thousand
men; and, spreading devastation around him, advanced

upon the town of Basle. On other occasions he avoided attacking fortified towns with his ill-disciplined troops, who were totally devoid of all preparation, practice, and appetite for services which required patience and order: but Basle had only just been rebuilt after a wasting earthquake: its trenches were in many places still choked with rubbish, which gave unusual facilities for storming. At this moment of terror Basle begged for aid from the confederates ; and in a few days Berne and Soleure, which were leagued with that town, sent 1500 men to its assistance. As soon as they were received in the suburbs, the leader of Berne addressed them :—" Having been sent to venture all for you, faithful and true friends and colleagues, post us where the danger will be greatest." A day later, 3000 picked troops arrived from the other cantons to defend Basle, as a bulwark of the confederacy, although they had then no direct league with it. Cervola, who had heard of Swiss valour and Swiss poverty, found it advisable to turn his march northwards without an attempt on Basle: in the following year (1366) he was despatched by his own followers, in Provence.

Ten years after the menaced inroad of Cervola, Ingram or Ingelram de Coucy, count of Soissons and earl of Bedford (titles both conferred on him by Edward III. of England, whose daughter Isabella he had received in marriage), proclaimed a feud against Austria, that power having refused to pay the marriage portion of his mother Catharina, daughter of the late duke Leopold, slain at Morgarten, on pretence that the towns and lands assigned for its payment had fallen for the most part into the hands of the confederates. In Coucy's army were many English in splendid armour, with gilt helmets, or high-crowned iron caps (Germanicè, *gugel*-hats, or capuches,) whom the cessation of the war between France and England had reduced to an unwelcome state of inaction, and who willingly joined the standard raised by a son-in-law of their monarch. Besides these excellent warriors, from whom the bands of Coucy were sometimes

called the *Englanders,* and sometimes, on account of
their strangely fashioned hats, the *Guglers,* Coucy picked
up numerous recruits in France and the Netherlands,
and was also reinforced by the remains of Cervola's army.
With these bands, which carried terror before them,
spread devastation around, and left misery behind them,
he began his expedition against Austria. Leopold now
applied for the assistance of the confederates, which was
afforded with alacrity on the part of Berne and Zurich,
as the open country of these cantons was equally exposed to attack. But the forest cantons declared that
they would not sacrifice their people in order to protect
the lands of a hostile power from invasion ; they would,
therefore, view the course of the war merely as spectators ; and if the enemy should reach their borders,
they hoped, by God's assistance, and by the vigour of
their own right arms, to be able to defend themselves.
They adhered to this determination, although they would
have done better to take up arms in defence of the
Aargau, not on the duke's account, but because it was
an avant-mure of Zurich and Berne. On the approach
of Coucy's force, an unaccountable panic seems to have
taken possession of the Austrians and their Swiss allies :
the invaders plundered and laid under contribution the
whole country from the Jura to the gates of Berne and
frontiers of Zurich. As the produce of these tracts hardly
sufficed to feed their own inhabitants, such dearth and
desolation ensued, that many not insignificant towns
could with difficulty defend themselves from the wolves.
Coucy's army itself suffered dreadfully ; and the oppressions which it was forced, for self-preservation, to heap
on the land, brought the people at last to despair and to
resistance. Three thousand English warriors were defeated near Buttisholz, by a few hundred inhabitants of
Entlibuch (a district among the mountains that decline
from the higher Alps towards the Aargau), assisted,
however, by straggling bands from Lucerne and Unterwalden. As the conquering men of Entlibuch were
riding home on English horses, exultingly displaying the

arms and ornaments of the vanquished, the baron Peter of Dorrenberg, as they passed his castle, cried out,— " O noble blood, alas! that peasants should wear your decorations."—" That hath come to pass," replied an Entlibucher, "because we have this day mingled noble blood with blood of horses." A mound, called the English barrow, near the wood of Buttisholz, still remains as a monument of the action.

Count Rudolph of Kyburg, one of the few remaining powerful nobles, expiated a treacherous attempt to surprise the town of Soleure, over which he claimed some jurisdiction, by the loss of a great part of his hereditary domains; as the citizens of the town in question took their revenge, with the aid of Berne, by inroads on his lands and those of his friends. Berne, with her accustomed policy, took the opportunity of appropriating Thun as well as the bailliage of Griessenberg.

Though the recent peace still remained unbroken, many secret causes of discord were in active operation, which could not fail to produce a new and sanguinary contest. The support which the count of Kyburg had received from the Austrian territories had awakened the distrust of the confederates, while the ruin of that ancient house, and the growth of the power of Berne, had exasperated the ill-will of the nobles towards the confederacy. Duke Leopold III. of Austria, who resembled in pride as well as in courage that Leopold who had fought with the confederates at Morgarten, brought bitter complaints against the confederates for receiving into their league, in defiance of treaties, Entlibuch, Sempach, Meyenberg, Reichensee, and other places, on which he had claims, as either subject or mortgaged to him: he charged Lucerne with breaking into his castle of Rothenburg in time of peace, and Zurich (whether with or without foundation we are only enabled by history to conjecture) with having planned a similar inroad upon Rappersweil. On the other hand, besides the share which Leopold had, contrary to his solemn engagements, taken in the count of Kyburg's quarrel with the confederates, he had violated several points in the late pacification, and had done injury to the trade of the confederates, by the erection of a bridge at Rappersweil, as well as by the exaction of new tolls and dues at that place and at Rothenburg. And if Leopold had hitherto taken no further steps against the confederates, his forbearance was not so much attributed to love of peace, or regard to the faith of treaties, as to the obstacles which were laid in his way by circumstances. As soon as these were overcome, he marched into the Aargau, and swore a solemn oath, by God's assistance, to dissever "that insulting league of the Swiss, the source of so much unrighteous warfare."

The hatred of the nobles now broke forth against the free-burghers, so that messages of defiance reached the confederacy from 167 lords temporal and spiritual, which, in order to enhance their stunning effect, were delivered in twenty messages successively. At this crisis Berne declined taking the part in the common danger which seemed enjoined by gratitude for the aid of her confederates at Laupen, on pretence of an eleven years' truce with Leopold; of which, however, the term was to expire in a few months. The other cantons reinforced the Zurichers, against whom the first attack was apprehended, with 1600 men, and ravaged in conjunction with them the neighbouring lands of Austria; but on the news of a threatened inroad on Lucerne, the force destined to garrison that town was detached thither, while the Zurichers protected their own walls against the division of the ducal force by which they were menaced. Meanwhile the duke marched rapidly towards the interior of the country, at the head of a body of picked troops; and on the 9th of July, 1386, met the Swiss advancing from Zurich in the neighbourhood of Sempach.

Arrogance and scornful menace heralded the march of an enemy confident of a sure and easy victory. Cords, as on a former occasion, were prepared to hang the expected captives. A certain baron of Hasenburg, who

suggested prudent caution, received the punning nickname, *heart of hare* (Hasenherz) ; and, in order to owe
the honour of victory solely to themselves, the heavy-
armed nobility dismounted from their horses, cut the
long peaks then in fashion from their shoes, and formed
an extended line of battle, seemingly impenetrable,
through the formidable length and close array of the
presented spears. The Swiss had nothing but boards
attached to their left arms by way of bucklers, but
charged manfully notwithstanding their rude accoutrements, in reliance on their God, and in the cause of their
country. Their leaders fought in front of the battle,
and many of them soon fell before the levelled spears of
the enemy. It was then that Arnold of Winkelried, a
knight of Unterwalden (for the chivalry was not all on
one side), resolved by his heroic death to render an im-
perishable service to his father-land. Exclaiming, "I will
make way for you, confederates — provide for my wife
and children — honour my race!" — he rushed upon the
spears, and grasping several with his arms, he bore them
to the ground with the weight of his body, over which
the confederates forced their way through the broken
ranks of the enemy, who were unable to manœuvre from
the closeness of their array, and half smothered under
the sultry summer's sun in their ponderous armour.
The high-souled Leopold fell beside the sinking banner
of Austria, resolved to share the fate of those true followers who had sacrificed themselves in his cause. More
than 600 of the higher and lower nobility were left on
the field, with about 2000 of their less distinguished
adherents. The slaughter would have been greater had
not the Swiss yielded too eagerly to the appetite for
plunder. Fifteen banners fell into the hands of the
victors, who lost about 200 men ; but amongst these
some of their bravest. The avoyer Gundoldingen, a
man in high esteem among his countrymen, and deeply
imbued with the spirit of a republican government, died
repeating the words, " Tell the men of Lucerne to retain
no avoyer longer than a single year in office."

Leopold IV., surnamed the Proud, continued during several months longer the war commenced by his father against the confederates. He enjoyed the aid of a numerous and powerful body of nobles, eager to revenge their friends and relatives slain at Sempach, or to vindicate the honour of their order. Yet this feud, in which Berne, Zurich, and Lucerne took principal parts, resembled a mere predatory excursion more than any thing else. Berne seized the opportunity to aggrandise herself, and gained a firm footing in the Oberland. Lucerne destroyed several strong fortresses. Zurich did the same, and distinguished herself by valiant deeds of arms in the Wehnthal. But the conquest of the Austrian town of Wesen, in the Gaster, by the seven old cantons, alone deserves notice here, not so much on account of the importance of the acquisition as of its consequences. Since neither fame nor profit accrued from these events to the house of Austria, and the confederates themselves were tired of this desultory warfare, a year and a half's truce was easily mediated by several imperial towns. This was called the *Bad Peace*, on account of the numerous acts of ill faith which were exercised on both sides while it continued, and because its whole duration was employed not in pacific transactions, but in warlike preparations. At that time the minds of the confederates were penetrated with such hatred against Austria, that they could not hear the name of that house without exasperation. Whoever spoke well of Austria was regarded as an enemy —whoever should have adorned his hat with peacock's feathers, the ducal ensign, would have lost his life by the fury of the people. It is recorded that no peacock was permitted in all Switzerland; and *Peacock's Tail* became the most offensive of all nicknames. The national antipathy rose to such a height at this time, that many writers, not without ground, refer to this epoch the definitive separation of the Swiss confederation from the German empire.

Towards the close of the truce, the Swiss garrison in the conquered town of Wesen were surprised by a

treacherous junction of the burghers with the Austrians;
and the vogt, with all who could not escape over the
walls, were murdered. The confederates advanced from
the lake of Zurich, but did not attempt to penetrate
through the strong body of Austrian troops collected in
the neighbourhood; and the men of Glarus were left to
themselves for the space of nearly two months, while
the mountain-passes were blocked up with snow. Nevertheless, they rejected the conditions proposed by the
enemy, which amounted, indeed, to nearly entire subjection. Unexpectedly, on the 9th of April, 1388, a hostile
army, several thousand strong, made its appearance from
the neighbouring lands of the Aargau, Thurgau, and the
remote Swabian territories, and attacked the fortress of
Naefels. A handful of 200 men, commanded by Matthew of Bühlen, though reinforced by 300 others who
came up from the neighbourhood, were not strong enough
to maintain an unfinished line of fortifications extending
across a valley from one hill to another. Their entrenchments were forced, after a stout resistance. While the
enemy, confiding in their far superior numbers, and des-
pising the insignificant bands of Glarus, dispersed in
every direction in quest of plunder, Bühlen collected his
handful of men on the mountain ridges near Ruti. Even
in an open country resolute men are capable of great
things; and little bands of warriors cut their way from
all quarters to their country's banner floating from the
height. The men of Glarus, reinforced by a few Schwytzers
and other chance auxiliaries from the valleys in their
rear, by a succession of spirited charges, brought the
enemy first to wavering and confusion, and at last to a
disorderly flight. The bridge at Wesen gave way beneath
the pressure of the fugitives. Above 3000 common men
and 183 knights fell on the field, or found their death
in the lake and in the river. The entreaties and magnificent offers made by the sorrowing relatives for leave
to build a convent on the field of battle were rejected by
the community of Glarus, who justly feared that such a
foundation might, in course of time, find means to ap-

propriate the best lands, acquire a dangerous influence, and encourage that of foreigners. The same community ordained that, on each succeeding April, the principal able-bodied member of each family in the district should go in procession to Naefels, passing every spot and stile which had witnessed the achievements of their forefathers. Then and there should be read before the assembled people the history of the day of Sempach, the events in the Gaster, and, finally, of the victory of Naefels. After the celebration of mass for the souls of their brave ancestors, and due commemoration of their constancy in the cause of freedom, the people were allowed to relax in moderate festivity.

After incessant hostilities waged for more than thirteen months, some imperial towns succeeeded in effecting a truce, or peace, as it was called, for seven years, in which the Bernese acquiesced with reluctance. In this peace the confederates retained their actual conquests. Zurich, Uri, and Unterwalden, however, acquired nothing. The event of the war, and the terms of peace, shook to their foundations the financial resources of Austria, as well as its power and influence on the popular mind in Switzerland. The attempt was therefore renewed to sow disunion among the confederates, and subdue those spirits by fraud which had only been roused by open violence. Duke Leopold gained over to his interests the burgomaster Rudolf Schön, and the majority of the council at Zurich. Without the knowledge of the great council, and in spite of the remonstrances of the rest of the confederates, who watched their proceedings with attention, they closed with Austria a still more binding alliance than that of Brun had been. Zurich therein exempted herself from guaranteeing the recent conquests of the confederates, &c. The envoys of the latter had recourse to measures justifiable only by the peculiar relations and danger of the confederacy. They employed their personal influence in the streets and public places on the members of the great council and congregated burghers. The ascendency of the government rapidly fell, as it had

H

only been based upon arts of intrigue and coercion. Its
members were displaced, and, in part, banished; the
Austrian league dissolved, and changes made in the constitution, in consequence of which, the former rulers were
superseded by firm friends of the confederacy.

Convinced of the necessity of adopting regulations
conducive to internal strength and harmony, the confederates concluded as a body that state compact which
received the name of the Sempach declaration, which
was intended to prevent the recurrence of the disorders
which had marked the late war, and which prohibited
self-revenge among the confederates, provided for the
safety of commerce and intercourse, the maintenance of
discipline, and the prevention of unnecessary violence
and plunder among the soldiery. The seven years'
peace with Austria was prolonged, in 1394, for twenty,
and in 1412, for fifty years. While the influence of
that power sunk in Switzerland; while one ancient, proud,
and powerful house was extinguished after another, two
new confederations became organised in the east. Rhætia
was the one, — the other was Appenzell.

Enclosed by rugged chains of the higher Alps, and
possessing a climate rapid in its vicissitudes, from eternal
ice to almost Spanish sultriness, Rhætia presented, in
the times of which we are treating, a strange mixture
of free communities with the bondsmen of the church
and the nobles. Already had a century elapsed since
the confederates had achieved their freedom, when the
Rhætians, for the first time, manned themselves to
struggle for that glorious object. They formed alliances, partly amongst themselves, and partly with the
neighbouring confederates; but their struggles were as
yet too undecided, their internal relations too confused
and unregulated, to deserve farther notice for the present.

With more decision, and therefore with more effect,
the district of Appenzell entered on the struggle for independence. It consisted of some half-dozen nameless
hamlets, at the northern end of the ancient Rhætian
territory, where an insulated group of mountains, like a

sort of natural fortress, rises high above the circumjacent country. The snow-crowned head of the Sentis seems to tower supreme over wide tracts, from the Tyrol, over the distant Swabian plains, as far as Wirtemberg. Arrogance, combined with oppression and tyranny, first aroused in the inhabitants of this obscure region a force which had been hitherto unknown to themselves, but which extended its workings over a wide circle, until arrogance and imprudence on their own part again limited its results within a narrower field. Cuno, of Staufen, was invested, in 1379, with the dignity of abbot in the monastery of St. Gall, which for a considerable time back had appropriated the imperial and all other dues throughout the four districts around it. Cuno held the wisdom of a ruler to be best shown by extension of his rule; his servants also delighted in surpassing their lord's excesses, and in barbing his oppressions with insult. Cuno refused to confirm the prescriptive franchises of the peasantry, or to gratify their wish to have their officers selected from the natives of their own district; augmented the dues and imposts to which they were liable, and exercised his feudal rights with the most tyrannical rigour. At length, the four districts under his government combined for common resistance; but the ferment was for once appeased through the good offices of impartial towns and nobles in the neighbourhood. These conciliatory labours were however rendered useless by attempts on the part of the abbot and his officers to avenge themselves on the abettors of the recent discontents. Rigours made still farther rigours necessary; and in January, 1401, the four districts leagued themselves with the town of St. Gall, which had been irritated already by the abbot. They expelled that prince's officers, and threw up their allegiance. Constance, and five other imperial towns, which had shortly before allied themselves with the prince-abbot, as well as with the town of St. Gall, again succeeded in dissolving the league of the citizens with the mountaineers. When the commons of Appenzell found that force was about to

be employed against them, they unanimously swore to a
firm union. They now sought an alliance with the Swiss
confederacy; but Schwytz alone answered their advances. The abbot now allied himself more closely with the
Swabian towns, and, through their mediation with St. Gall,
where the princely name and influence still worked
powerfully on the leading men, and attempted to coerce
the combined mountaineers by force of arms.

But the latter had received reinforcements from the
ever-ready Schwytzers, and had moreover been joined by
volunteers from Glarus, though that canton was precluded, by its league with the confederates, from entering
into open alliance with Appenzell. On the 15th May,
1403, the well-appointed enemy, 5000 strong, while
attempting to penetrate towards Speicher, received, in
the hollow road before Vögeliseck, a signal overthrow
from 1800 ill-armed shepherds of Appenzell, backed by
a handful of men from Schwytz and from Glarus. Few
of the conquerors lost their lives, while 400 of their
enemies perished; and the town of St. Gall atoned for
its courtly subservience by the loss of its leaders and
many of its citizens. Nevertheless, the men of St. Gall
and Appenzell renewed their league in 1404, unrestrained
by any resentment of their losses on the part of the
former. Abbot and monks made their escape to Weil,
while the Appenzellers, ever advancing in boldness, received lands and villages into their league, without regard
to existing rights, and maintained the cause of the vassals
of the nobles against their lords, who regarded them
from thenceforth as their enemies. This rendered it
easy for the abbot to stir up the nobles of the Thurgau
and others to participate in the war against these disturbers of the peace; and he was thus occasioned also to
court the assistance of duke Frederick, although hitherto
the holders of the abbacy had always cherished distrust
against his house. Scarcely had the duke resolved to
aid the prince-abbot, when the deeply outraged count
Rudolph of Werdenberg, whom the rapacity of Austria
had robbed of his paternal estates, presented himself as a

comrade to the Appenzellers. In order to silence any thing like distrust, he submitted himself to voluntary hardships, which an ordinary knight's page of those times would have thought unendurable. He went clothed like themselves, often with bare feet, and fought in their ranks; but his courage, as well as counsel and experience, soon placed him amongst the number of their leaders.

On a rainy day of June, 1405, the main body of duke Frederick's forces advanced to the borders of Appenzell, through the Rheinthal, and began to ascend the Stoss; where the short turf of the meadows, slippery from the rain which had fallen, afforded no sure footing for the heavy-armed troops. Four hundred men of Appenzell, with some from Glarus and Schwytz, rolled fragments of rock and beams of wood down on the enemy, who had hardly advanced midway up the hill, when Rudolf of Werdenberg gave the signal for onset. Then rushed the men of Appenzell with loud shouts on the already broken lines of the Austrians; and the slippery soil favoured their barefooted bands as much as it embarrassed those of the enemy. The rain had, besides, rendered the cross-bows of the latter unserviceable. Notwithstanding these disadvantages, the Austrians fought desperately, till a new array of combatants appeared on the heights in the rear, who seemed designed to cut off their retreat. The sight of a new enemy entirely broke their courage, and they fled down hill precipitately, pursued by the men of Appenzell; whose *wives* and *daughters*, in shepherds' smocks, composed the dreaded reserve, of which a distant apparition had inspired too great a panic to wait for the correction of a nearer view.

Duke Frederick, in the mean time, had advanced from another quarter, and carried his ravages, at the head of his glittering chivalry, up to the very gates of St. Gall. Finding the place too strong for his means of attack, he fell back again upon Arbon, when his disorderly line of march was assailed by the burghers of St. Gall, divided into several small detachments, from which considerable loss was sustained by the ducal force at Hauptlisberg.

The duke was sorely stung by this disgraceful reverse;
but still more so by the news of the disastrous rout at
the Stoss. He had now recourse to artifice for revenge;
and giving out that he designed to retreat from Arbon
to the Tyrol, he drew his forces off towards the Rhine;
but, on arriving at the village of Thal, he wheeled his
troops suddenly round, and led them up the Wolfshald,
towards Appenzell. He hoped to take the pastoral population by surprise; but his intention was already
known at Appenzell. Four hundred men rushed down
on the disorderly troops of Austria, who were toiling
upwards without the least apprehension or precaution.
They had time, however, to take a strong position in a
churchyard, and the battle was fought obstinately on
both sides. At length, the Austrian lines were again
broken, and the ducal army driven down the Wolfshald
with enormous slaughter. The duke was by this time
really sick of the contest, and retreated to the Tyrol in
good earnest.

The hitherto unheard name of Appenzell was now
spread far and wide by renown. Even during the winter
months they besieged the castle of Bregenz, which had
often annoyed the neighbouring inhabitants. But they
were blinded by the self-reliance grounded on good
fortune, so far as to utter open threats against the Swabian
nobles, and thus raise up new allies to their enemy.
A combination was formed against them, called the St.
George's Shield, or League; and their scattered bands,
enfeebled by the rigours of winter, were attacked on the
13th of January, 1408, at break of day, by a body of
above 8000 well-armed warriors. They rallied their
force as well as they were able; but notwithstanding
the determined stand which they made, in which their
captain fell, they were at length compelled to retreat,
with the loss of many prisoners, and of all their preparations for a siege. But so imposing was the memory
of their tried and proved valour, that their most embittered enemies could not stimulate the conquerors,
however superior in number, to molest their retreat.

The Appenzellers themselves were disposed to terms of peace by this disaster, and made a compromise with the nobles and the abbot, by which the latter was finally compelled to acknowledge their independence ; and duke Frederick of Austria having recovered his possessions, the cause of warfare ceased in that quarter. They confined themselves thenceforwards to the defence of their own freedom, which they sought to secure by alliances with powerful lords in their neighbourhood ; but still more by procuring themselves reception from the confederacy : not, indeed, into the rank of a separate canton, but into the number of their citizens and countrymen. The conditions on which this privilege was granted them were directed to secure the confederates from entangle-ment in unnecessary warfare, through the ardour and irritability of the Appenzellers. To this end the latter were obliged to promise never to take up arms without the consent of the confederates ; to give them aid in all future wars with their whole force ; while, in wars undertaken on their own account, they contented them-selves with such aid only as the confederates might choose to afford, and for which Appenzell was besides to pay. Moreover, the confederates reserved the right of adding to, or taking from, the articles of the treaty at their discretion.

The confederates could look without alarm to the approaching close of the Twenty Years' Peace, for their freedom and repose were firmly established, while the former predominance of Austria existed now no longer in Switzerland. Confusion and distress prevailed on all sides,—in Germany, in France, in Spain, in Italy, and, most of all, in the ecclesiastical state. The confe-deracy alone enjoyed order and repose. The wars of princes at that time were carried on with unwieldy heavy cavalry, and their infantry was wretched. But the Swiss understood the art of war better. Compelled to fight on foot by their poverty, as well as by the nature of the country, and opposed for the most part to

superior numbers, they were forced to watch atten-
tively every advantage, to trust to a resolute onset and
immovable steadiness, and to baffle by their quickness
of manœuvre the unwieldy numerical force of their
antagonists.   Thus the confederacy stood prepared for
all events when the peace of twenty years came to a
close. Duke Frederick of Austria wished to prolong it ;
and in order to obtain this end he was obliged, besides
conceding other points to the confederates, to confirm
for fifty years their possession of all the conquests actually held by themselves or their allies of Soleure and
Appenzell. Thus a century after the Austrian pride and
arrogance had commenced the war against the freedom
of Switzerland, the latter had come so triumphantly out
of the conflict, that duke Frederick was glad to conclude
a treaty with them on any terms.

CHAP. VII.

FROM THE COUNCIL OF CONSTANCE TO THE BATTLE OF ARBEDO.

1414—1422.

STATE OF THE CONFEDERATION. — OF THE CHURCH. — GREAT
SCHISM. — COUNCIL OF CONSTANCE. — FLIGHT OF POPE JOHN.
— OUTLAWRY OF FREDERICK DUKE OF AUSTRIA. — CON-
QUESTS OF THE CONFEDERATES. — ERECTION OF FREE BAI-
LIWICKS. — CAPTURE AND DEPOSITION OF POPE JOHN. — DIS-
SOLUTION OF THE COUNCIL OF CONSTANCE. — FRANCESCO
POGGIO. — GIPSIES. — THE MAZZE. — FEUD OF URI AND
UNTERWALDEN WITH PHILIP VISCONTI DUKE OF MILAN. —
MARCH OF THE SWISS ON BELLINZONA. — BATTLE OF ARBEDO.

THE history of the Swiss has been traced in the foregoing pages since the loss of their original savage
freedom : we have seen them in the power of foreign
nations; we have hailed the re-appearance of their
native spirit, the vigour and good fortune which ac-

companied their struggles with their powerful an_
tagonists. But precisely this good fortune induced
gradual deviations from the noble maxim on which
their league was founded, that of making friends in_
stead of acquiring subjects. This deviation had already
become perceptible in the towns which we have seen
acquiring new domains by conquest or purchase; it
has already been remarked in Schwytz and Uri; and
the recital of the following transactions will present
it in a still clearer light, and will also display its
natural effects in the perilous out-breakings of intes_
tine feud and civil discord. The aggrandisement of
particular cantons excited the envy of others, which
was inflamed to the highest degree by the sustained and
sedulous efforts which the former made to preserve and
to increase their acquisitions. As at this time the body
of confederates had no reason to fear attacks from any
of their neighbours, the feeling of reciprocal obligation
died away by degrees among themselves. The previous
bonds of union became relaxed so much the sooner as
the confederates had yet to receive such lessons from
experience as were bestowed in later times on their
descendants: vanity and selfishness usurped the place of
public spirit; and even when the leading men in a
canton were not actuated by personal ambition or rapacity, they took it for a proof of the purest patriotism to
aggrandise their canton at the expense of the rest, and
did not renounce their projects of aggrandisement,
though they endangered the peace, or even the existence,
of the confederacy. We shall presently see Zurich, in
alliance, first with Austria, and afterwards with France,
contending, during fourteen years, with its utmost
strength and energies, against the other confederates
united. A war from which this, if no other lesson may
be extracted, that the same people is capable of the
brightest or the darkest deeds, according as it yields to
the sway of pure or impure impulses.

The affairs of the church about this time arrested the

attention of governments as well as individual enquirers.
The disorders of the ecclesiastical polity, and the evils
thereby engendered, had increased in rapid progression.
Negligence of their functions and encroachments over
their limits on the part of the clergy brought contempt
on their order. The consequences of this contempt
were schisms and ghostly extravagances, in spite of the
exertions made by a few superior spirits, who, so far
as was allowed by prevailing prejudices, endeavoured to
disseminate sounder ideas on religious subjects. It was
now that those Flagellants appeared, who were not to be
satisfied with the penances of the strictest monastic
orders. These were followed by the Beghards and Be-
guines, whose associations originally were framed for
laudable objects, but soon collected crowds of idle vagabonds, and encouraged all the rude exaggerations of
false devotion. The Beghards were first favoured then
suppressed, and their places of meeting, for instance at
Basle, transferred to institutions of charity. Precau-
tions were adopted against them, as well as against their
hordes of sturdy beggars, and *all deviations* in matters
of faith were visited in some places, Berne for example,
with the correction of fire and sword.

Three popes, of whom each had his own phalanx of
adherents, then stood in opposition to each other. The
original constitution of the church had been abandoned
many centuries back, in which the bishops issued orders
in all clerical concerns, as the *overseers* of spiritual communities. On the other hand, the doctrine of *one*
visible head of the church had gradually obtained the
ascendency; and thus from a plurality of popes, each
anathematising the others, arose manifold perplexities.
Nor had the horrible persecutions of the Albigenses,
against whom a crusade had been preached, sufficed to
crush the efforts of those who sought to restore the
church in some measure to its primitive form. These
efforts were revived by the Waldenses. In England,
where from time to time clear views on the subject had

contended with the pretensions of the hierarchy, John Wicliffe, in the latter half of the fourteenth century, strove against a whole host of clerical abuses, combated the frauds of the mendicant friars, and translated the Holy Scriptures into his mother tongue. He, too, was assailed with the accustomed persecutions; but a part of his doctrines strayed to a congenial soil in Bohemia, and found a distinguished apostle in John Huss, whom the council of Constance afterwards condemned to the stake, in contravention of its own safe-conduct.

The necessity of church reform began to be felt in all Europe; and, through the exertions of the emperor, a general assembly of the church was, after many delays, appointed to be held at Constance, towards the close of the year 1414, at which the desired reformation was to be carried into effect by a council of the higher clergy, sitting in the presence of the emperor, and assisted by a numerous body of princes and of delegates from almost every country in Europe. Of the three anti-popes, John XXIII. alone, and with reluctance, had appeared on the summons. But when he found that his own nomination to the popedom was to be brought in question, he betook himself to flight, in breach of his promise, abetted by duke Frederick of Austria. This conduct drew on the latter the ban of the empire, accompanied by the interdict of the council. He was, besides, charged with various other offences, and declared to have forfeited his fief. Many lords, lay as well as clerical, of whom most had been the former friends of Frederick, hastened to declare themselves against the outlaw. The confederates were called to aid against the former enemy, in execution of the ban of the empire; but the proposal that they should violate a treaty which had so recently been sworn for fifty years excited very reasonable scruples. The council, indeed, promised them absolution from that as well as all their other sins; and the emperor guaranteed to them the permanent possession of whatever lands they might conquer from their hereditary enemy: but the forest cantons, as also Zurich, Zug, Lucerne, and Glarus, remained as yet inaccessible to sophistry or temptation.   On the other hand, Berne was anxious to embrace an opportunity so favourable for extending her own territory, and striking a finishing blow to the power of Austria in her neighbourhood.   Accordingly, on the repeated calls of the emperor and the council, to which the other confederates still delayed obedience, Berne armed without waiting for their concurrence.   This aroused the jealousy of Zurich, who would not stay behind and lose her share in the booty.   Finally, the rest of the confederacy gave in to the example of their principal colleagues ; Appenzell and Uri were the only places which still held out.   In order to avoid sharing their expected spoils with their colleagues, the Bernese promptly took the field, before any of the others were in readiness, marched into the Aargau, and besieged Zofingen.   A diet had been held at Sur by the lords and towns of the Aargau, at which it had been proposed to seek an alliance with the confederates, and admission into the rank of a new canton.   This was frustrated by the influence of the nobles, who maintained a firm attachment to Austria.   On this it was resolved by the towns to apply for the protection of the confederacy. Too late ! the Swiss banners were already over the frontiers, and Berne, as usual, foremost of all.   In eight days, with very trifling losses, the Aargau, as far as the Reuss, was in their hands.

At Freyburg in Brisgau, where Frederick and the pope had taken refuge, one messenger of misfortune followed another.   The revolt of large numbers of his vassals, the loss of the Thurgau, of the Aargau, of Alsace, the popular discontent in the dominions yet remaining to him, were announced to the unfortunate duke in quick and stunning succession.   Such a series of reverses at length broke his resolution; and preventing the escape of the pope who still continued obstinate, he repaired to Constance to tender his submissions at the feet of the emperor, who vouchsafed his gracious pardon on condition of the pope being delivered up, and the duke's whole domains being surrendered into his (the emperor's) keeping, until he should graciously please to give them back to his repentant vassal. After many months of humiliation, and a few abortive sallies of impatience, the powerful mediation of duke Ernest, Frederick's brother, procured the restoration of the bulk of his lands, and the removal of the ban and sentence of outlawry.

While Frederick was making his submissions at Constance, the confederates were besieging his castle of Baden, which they had captured, before any notice arrived of the suspension of hostilities. The imperial heralds of peace were within a league's distance of Baden, when the strong and splendid fortress, from which Albert had menaced the forest cantons, where the expeditions to Morgarten and Sempach had been planned, and where the Austrian princes often held their courts, was already in flames. The emperor expressed great indignation, and demanded that the confederates should give their conquests up to the empire. They replied by an appeal to the imperial guarantee by which the permanent possession of their conquests had been assured to them; and when the emperor persisted in his demands, he was given to understand that those who had made the conquests in question would not so easily be persuaded to abandon them. This hint induced the emperor to content himself with a sum of money, in consideration of which he allowed the confederates to retain their acquisitions in perpetual mortgage. The delegates of Uri renounced all participation in the newly conquered lands of the confederacy, and excited the derision of their less magnanimous colleagues by proposing to relinquish them to the emperor, in order not to violate the truce with Austria. The six other cantons came to an agreement on the subject of their common acquisitions, that each in turn should appoint a bailiff over them for two years, and that an annual account of their administration should be given.

If in the establishment of these common, or, so called, free bailiwicks, the confederates swerved from the more enlarged policy of their fathers (who had received Glarus and Zug into the rank of their confederates), and showed that they wished rather to possess indifferent subjects than friends and fellow-combatants in the cause of common freedom, yet the system of rotation in the government of the conquered lands might probably excite less aversion in their inhabitants than would have been caused by a partition of districts which had previously composed one jurisdiction. Gross administrative abuses were at that time out of the question. Sovereignty was exercised in a spirit of great mildness and indulgence to the independent feelings of its subjects. Nevertheless the subsequent abuses in the government of these common bailiwicks, the political insignificance to which their population was consigned, and the moral evils thereby engendered, remain a warning example of the consequences produced by all deviations from the path of correct principle.

After Frederick's submission, the elector of Brandenburg was employed to secure, by fair or forcible means, the pope's person. John was brought a prisoner to Constance; the council made enquiries into his course of life from youth upwards; found it to have been highly vicious and scandalous; declared him to be more deserving of death at the stake than the papal chair, and pronounced a formal sentence of deposition. John lived several years in easy custody; was afterwards released, and went to Florence, where he was favourably received by his successor, and died cardinal bishop of Frascati. The choice of a new pope (Martin V.), which, by an improvident or insidious vote of the council, was made to precede the farther agitation of the points of which the discussion had formed their original object in meeting, restored, indeed, the unity of the papal power, but not the order or discipline of the church, whose new head thought nothing of such urgent importance as to bring about the speedy dissolution of an assembly, the very existence of which he viewed as a menace to the hierarchy.

Cardinal Poggio, one of the first men of what was then the first nation of Europe, present at this council, has left us a description of the gaieties attending it, which exhibits Swiss manners in amusing contrast with those of Italy. In Switzerland, and the neighbouring regions of Germany, the mode of life in all classes was homely and domestic, but by no means sombre or morose. They loved the song and dance; and, in their melodies, pious hymns or martial strains alternated with love-songs. Their games were of an athletic or burlesque kind: gambling was as little in the habits as in the laws of the people. Though the birth of illegitimate children was not a rare occurrence, it appears, according to Poggio, almost incredible how utterly unsuspecting was the confidence of parents and husbands. This may partly be accounted for by the general turn to gaiety, incompatible with dark distrust or deep-laid machinations. Poggio compares the mode of life which he found at the baths of Baden to the ancient Greek descriptions of the games of the goddess of Paphos.

The multitude of masterless servants, forsaken females, and vagabonds of every description, whom curiosity, or the hope of easy winnings, under the pretext of devotion, had collected at Constance, leagued themselves with the bands of sturdy beggars who had long formed a kind of confraternity. About this time, too, swarms of unknown strangers made their appearance, brown in complexion, foreign in aspect, ill supplied with clothing: their leader was named Michael, or, as he styled himself, DUKE MICHAEL OF EGYPT: his followers were known by the name of *Cingari* or *Zingari* (in German, Zigeuner, gipsies). So little was known of oriental languages in those times, that these adventurers could tell what tales they pleased about their origin.[*] They pretended to have come from Lower Egypt, and to belong to the number of those who had not received

* Müller, iii. 115.

Joseph and Mary; that they had now become Christians, and were bound on a seven years' pilgrimage. It has at length been conjectured, from their language, that they were driven out by the great convulsions of India, when the dynasty of the sultan of Ghaur was overthrown by Pir Mohammed Jehan Ghir, the grandson of Timur.

The council of Constance had not yet been closed, and the conquest of the Aargau was but newly completed, when a fresh source of disquietude was opened. Even in remote antiquity, traces of a lively love of freedom had displayed themselves in the Valais. That district had maintained a brave though unsuccessful struggle with Rome; and had always known how to vindicate and extend its freedom against Savoy, and other powerful enemies, whether external or internal. When, in 1411, the confederates surprised and took possession of the valleys of Ossola, the baron Guiscard of Raron, captain-general of the Valais, and co-burgher of Berne, had allowed certain contemptuous expressions to escape him, which had deeply offended the irritable warriors of the forest cantons: accordingly they sent one of their leading men to Berne to deliver their complaints against Raron. Berne replied that it was not in her power to procure satisfaction for them, as Raron's right of citizenship had already expired for some time. The forest cantons now applied to the Valaisans themselves, by whom the power of the family of Raron had long been felt oppressive and dangerous. Guiscard himself lay under the imputation of hating, out of innate pride, all popular sovereignty; and of leaning more to the houses of Milan and Savoy than consisted with his duties as a burgher of the Valais. The popular resentment having now come to a head, it was resolved to crush the baron and his family; but lest the ringleaders of so bold an undertaking should incur danger, an old custom was brought into play to agitate the people.

A young birch was pulled up by the roots, on which was fixed a human countenance rudely carved in wood, and wearing the expression of grief. Below this, in the

stem of the tree, a nail was driven by each of the plotters, which symbolised a solemn engagement to persevere
in their enterprise. In the night this figure, commonly
called a MAZZE, was bound to a tree on a well frequented
thoroughfare. On the following morning, crowds of
passing wayfarers gathered round the tree; the agitators
mixed with them, and thus ascertained the popular temper. As soon as they found it favourable (*i. e.* disposed
for plunder and violence), a bold and well-spoken man
stepped forth as *master of the Mazze,* unbound it from
the tree, and set it up on an open space beside him.
Questions were then addressed to the figure; as, " Mazze,
what is your pleasure?" and its patron was requested
to reply for it. At first he refused with well-assumed
embarrassment; but at last, affecting merely to comply
with the will of the people, he turned to the Mazze;
" Mazze, these good people are willing to help you; —
speak, — name the man whom you are afraid of. Is it
the Sillinen—the Asperling—the Henngarten?" (names
of powerful families in the Valais). The Mazze stood
immovable. " Is it the baron of Raron?" The Mazze
bowed its head, and the master stood beside it in a supplicating attitude. He then addressed the multitude;
" Brave men, you have heard whom the Mazze com-
plains of; whoever will fight for the Mazze, let him hold
up his hand!" A majority instantly showed itself in
favour of the Mazze, and all law and order were suspended. The summons went through the whole land
to the rescue of the Mazze: the obnoxious baron's castles
and estates, as well as those of his relatives, friends, and
dependants, were sacked by a furious multitude; and
nothing but a rapid flight could have saved the lives of
those who were thus solemnly devoted to the vengeance
of the people.

The Swiss had already marched over the Penine Alps
about the commencement of this (the fifteenth) century,
and had permanently occupied the Eschenthal and the
Val Levantina. These conquests drew on them the se-
verest check they had hitherto met with. Philip Maria

I

Visconti, duke of Milan, whose brother had lost the
lands in question, took every means to regain them : he
succeeded, by dint of dexterous negotiation, in obtaining
from the count of Sax Misox, the owner of Bellinzona,
a promise that he would cede the town which commanded the pass into Italy southwards, and into the Val
Levantina northwards. Uri and Unterwalden, however,
obtained by purchase the promised domains ; threw a
garrison into the town ; obtained a confirmation of their
title from the emperor, and took a position which admirably covered their own possessions, while it offered
every facility of attack on the Milanese. Visconti would
have purchased back Bellinzona from the confederates,
but found his proposals rejected, and was reduced to
intrigue in silence : he watched his opportunities for
more than a year and a half, while the confederate garrison gave itself up to a dangerous security. In the
mean time he formed traitorous connections in the town
itself ; and, on the first occasion which offered, his general, Agnolo della Pergola, surprised and took Bellinzona, allowed the Swiss free egress, and took possession
of the Val Levantina as far as the St. Gothard. So soon
as this was known to the men of Uri and of Unterwalden, they made no doubt that the confederates would
instantly take up arms to avenge the affront aimed,
through their sides, at the whole Helvetic body.

But the views of the confederates were exceedingly
divided on the expediency, as well as on the duty, of
maintaining these acquisitions on Italian ground. At
length assistance was promised by Lucerne, Schwytz,
Nidwalden, Zug, and Glarus. The troops of Lucerne,
Uri, Zug, and Unterwalden, 3000 strong, took the field,
without waiting for the rest, and reached Bellinzona
without meeting with any opposition. Here, however,
they were encountered by an army far superior to their
own, commanded by the most distinguished officers in
Italy, and sustained at Arbedo, not indeed an entire
defeat, but severe loss. Disunited and discouraged, the
confederates marched homewards. Success, which had

invariably crowned their arms against the Germans, forsook them now for the first time, when opposed to the troops of Italy.

In the following year, after much negotiation, and many conferences, the confederates concluded a peace with the duke, not on Swiss soil, but amidst Italian influences, of which this treaty bears the stamp in its very phraseology. The cantons are termed *communes*. All their conquests were abandoned—all the title-deeds and the imperial confirmations of them given up.

CHAP. VIII.

WAR OF THE CONFEDERATES WITH ZURICH.

1436—1450.

INHERITANCE OF FREDERICK COUNT OF TOGGENBURG. — DISPUTES OF SCHWYTZ AND GLARUS WITH ZURICH. — FEUD OF SEVERAL CANTONS WITH ZURICH. — PEACE. — LEAGUE OF ZURICH WITH AUSTRIA. — ALL THE CONFEDERATES AGAINST ZURICH. — THE ROTTEN PEACE. — RENEWAL OF THE WAR. — DAUPHIN OF FRANCE ATTACKS BASLE AT THE HEAD OF A BODY OF ARMAGNACS. — BATTLE OF ST. JACOB ON THE BIRS. — LOUIS OFFERS TO MEDIATE PEACE BETWEEN ZURICH AND THE CONFEDERATES. — INTELLECTUAL CULTURE IN THE FIFTEENTH CENTURY. — SCHOOLS. — DECLINE OF POETRY. — FELIX HAMMERLIN OR MALLEOLUS. — INSTANCES OF POPULAR SUPERSTITION.

THE confederates might have already learned from experience how much disunion weakened them, and lessened the respect entertained by foreign powers for their collective force. But their recently made conquests had evoked amongst them the evil spirits of jealousy and ambition. An unreflecting impulse towards aggrandisement had rendered them insensible to the constant truth, that no strength is imparted by constrained and disaffected subjects, and that no acquisitions would com-

pensate the bitterness thus engendered amongst them.
The evil was augmented by the influence of leading men,
who knew how to communicate to the states in which
they presided the contagion of their individual passions,
and took a pride in making their preponderating influence universally perceived and acknowledged. Zurich
not only separated herself from her confederates, but
threw herself completely into the arms of the common
enemy; while even the democratic canton of Schwytz
gave itself up to ambitious projects of aggrandisement.

Count Frederick of Toggenburg had accepted, in the
year 1400, the co-burghership of Zurich, partly moved
by feelings of distrust towards Austria, partly to procure
himself a *point d'appui* in Switzerland itself against the
power of the confederation. The rigours which he exercised on his subjects, while the example of the conquering people of Appenzell encouraged the oppressed to
resistance, rendered alliance very desirable with a place
of leading importance, through which he might make
himself sure of the confederates. He renewed his right
of citizenship in 1405, and, besides, obtained the freedom
of Schwytz.

Rudolf Stussi, burgomaster of Zurich, at that time
stood in high consideration with the count, and with the
rest of the confederates; but, unfortunately, he knew not
how to bear his honours meekly. It happened that his
son, when on a visit to count Frederick, made himself
laughed at for his arrogance by the count's young relations, as well as the other young nobles at his court.
The count endeavoured to pacify Stussi's resentment on
the occasion; but the irritated vanity of a blinded father
rendered the latter forgetful of the dignity of his station
no less than of the good of his country. The confidence of
his countrymen, and his own distinguished position among
them, were by no means enough to satisfy his pretensions, so long as others were not compelled to feel their
whole weight. The count soon afterwards lost a law-
suit at Zurich against the inhabitants of Siegberg, by a
sentence which he considered an unjust one. In conse-

quence, when Zurich desired that Frederick should name his heir, in order to know to whom he meant to transfer his civic rights; the count held out hopes that he meant to name his wife, the countess Elizabeth, who was particularly attached to the Zurichers; but, instead of this, he fixed on other relations, and shortly before his death he agreed with Schwytz upon a permanent jurisdiction over Toggenburg and Uznach, with reserve of the time which the common rights with Zurich had yet to run. He left his wife only the life-rent of his inheritance, and died on the 30th of April, 1436, having, as some thought, purposely aimed in his last testamentary dispositions at throwing matter of discord among the confederates.

The heirs, supported by Schwytz and Berne, of which some of them were burghers, proceeded to enforce their claims. Schwytz exacted oaths of allegiance in Tuggen and the Upper March. Zurich endeavoured to gain for herself Gaster and Sargans, which were divided by disputes among themselves, and made an alliance with the countess, who bequeathed the domain of Uznach to the town. On the refusal of the leading people of Uznach to acknowledge the bequest, and to do homage to Zurich, Stussi exclaimed, in order to intimidate them, " Know ye not your very bowels belong to us?" Arrogant treatment only rouses the spirit of those who are not utterly sunk in apathy; and the threats of Stussi served but to add strength to the decision of the people of Uznach. Similar results took place at Gaster and Windeck, whose inhabitants wished to be subjected to Austria rather than to Zurich. The Zurichers begged the friendly mediation of Schwytz; but the latter, instead of meeting their advances, entered into close alliance with the people of Glarus, who found it for their interest themselves to take possession of the territory claimed by Zurich. The projects of aggrandisement pursued by Stussi at Zurich were rivalled in Schwytz and Glarus by Ital Reding and Jost Tschudi; but the latter were discreet enough to keep their personal enmities subor-

dinate to worthier ends. On both sides, however, the
desire to aggrandise their own cantons and their own
persons induced forgetfulness of the common good of
their country and of concord, on which its strength and
happiness mainly depended.

In the early part of the year 1437, Zurich and Schwytz
had already posted troops on their frontiers, when the
confederates made haste to interpose their mediation,
and appointed a diet to be held at Lucerne. The delegates were incessantly employed during four weeks in
holding consultations, or in offering propositions to the
opposite parties. They separated at length without
having come to any conclusion; and it was agreed to
hold a new assembly of nineteen arbitrators, chosen
from the five neutral cantons and the town of Soleure.

The second attempt at arbitration failed as the first
had done, because the terms proposed appeared, not altogether without reason, to indicate on the part of the (so
called) impartial confederates something like a leaning
towards the side of Schwytz and Glarus, if not a
decided plan for the humiliation of Zurich. A third
meeting, attended by delegates from several of the free
towns of the empire, as well as by all those of the confederacy, met with no better success than the two former;
for by this time Schwytz would no longer hear of compromise of any kind, being exasperated by Zurich having taken into co-burghership the people of the count of
Werdenberg-Sargans, who had previously contracted a
common league with themselves and Glarus. Further
attempts to negotiate were to equally little purpose.
Zurich, more and more disposed to violent measures by
the sense of having suffered injustice, appealed to the
arbitration of the emperor, without, however, choosing
to comply with his orders, that they should open a free
market, and transit of goods to Schwytz and Glarus.
Still, however, a hollow truce was prolonged, and the
parties appeared at Berne, on the invitation of the neutral
cantons, where a general meeting was held by the
council and the delegates of the cantons, and a declar-

ation issued, which was afterwards communicated to the disagreeing parties. On receiving it, the Zurichers protested against the menace which it held out on the part of the neutral cantons, of intervention with their whole force in case of its rejection. The league of the confederacy, they said, did not include freedom of trade or transport; and amongst the ancient rights which had been reserved in its formation, one of the principal ones was the right of appeal to the emperor.

In a diet at Zug, in the spring of 1440, Zurich refused any unconditional recognition of the rights of the confederates, and renewed its prohibition of all exports, while Schwytz and Glarus renewed theirs in the articles of wood, hay, &c. • Moreover, Zurich blocked up the transmission through her territories to those cantons of all rents and dues, whether from monasteries or private persons. On the other hand, Schwytz and Glarus suddenly took possession of Sargans, where the formerly arrogant partisans of Zurich surrendered without even a show of resistance, and consented to renounce their rights of co-burghership with that town. Both sides gave notice to the confederates; and Zurich, ever disposed to rely on uncertain hopes and vague expressions, reposed too much dependence upon several of the cantons. Schwytz and Glarus now declared war against Zurich, and took up, with above 2000 troops, a position on the Etzel, while a superior force of Zurichers hastened to post themselves near Pfeffikon. Troops arrived from Uri and from Unterwalden, which had hitherto delayed to espouse either side in the contest. Their choice between the two contending parties was determined by a chance exclamation of one of their own comrades. " God forbid," said the standard-bearer of Uri, Werner der Frauen, " that I should bear my country's banner against those who have all along made their appeal to the judgment of the league, and in favour of the rebels who renounce it." Both these cantons now broke with Zurich; and thus the flame of war at length burst forth in the fifth year since the origin of civil dissen-

sion.   A sudden panic struck the troops of Zurich, who
fled over the lake to the town in the night of the 5th of
October, and thus completely lost the confidence of the
neighbouring population, which in several districts had
not been long subject to Zurich, and were now with ease
converted from her adherents to her enemies. The troops
of Zug, Lucerne, Berne, and Soleure, now advanced into
the territory of Zurich, and the whole Argovian nobility
made common cause with Berne; as Zurich had become
extremely obnoxious to them by her conduct towards the
heirs of count Toggenburg and Austria; and the cause
of the confederates seemed for once to be identified with
that of the nobles.   Such is the speedy punishment of
that grave political error committed by those who make
themselves many enemies at once, without secure or
sufficient aids and alliances.

Fire, slaughter, and depredation, now laid waste the
lands of Zurich, flourishing with the fruits of a long
peace, and so lately enjoying the highest consideration
in the confederacy.   The miserable peasantry sought to
save themselves, and the remnant of their property, in
the town. Zurich at length acknowledged the authority of
the league; but now Schwytz and Glarus claimed to retain
the conquests which they had made for themselves and
their confederates. At length, however, terms of pacification were adjusted under the presidency of the Bernese
leader, Henry of Bubenberg.   Whatever had been lost
by Zurich across the lake of Wallenstadt was to remain
in the possession of Schwytz and Glarus,— all other claims
to be settled in conformity with the common rights of
the confederacy,—freedom of traffic and intercourse re-
established,— Zurich making a reservation only in the
article of foreign wine.

The disadvantageous terms of this peace, above all the
territorial cessions to Schwytz and Glarus, which formed
the first example of conquests made by confederates over
each other, had filled the hearts of the Zurichers with
bitterness, while the dissolution of union among the confederates had revived the hopes as well of the Argovian

nobility as of all the other friends and adherents of
Austria. Stussi and his party at Zurich sought to retrieve their fallen reputation at all risks. They applied
to the Austrian margrave, William of Hochberg, offered
to cede Kyburg to the emperor, and finally entered into
an alliance offensive and defensive with the house of
Austria. Zurich, indeed, expressly reserved the rights
of the confederacy; but the incompatibility of those
rights with the objects of this new league was too obvious not too justify surprise and displeasure on the part
of the other confederates. To flatter the resentment of
Zurich, as well as to set up a new combination against
the hated league of the Swiss, a new confederation was
agreed upon, under the presidency of Zurich and the
guidance of Austria, in which the Austrian districts, the
bishoprics of Coire and Constance, the abbot of St. Gall,
several secular lords and towns, Appenzell and St. Gall,
should be included.

The confederates demanded explanations from the
Zurichers, with regard to their league with Austria; and
the latter sought to justify themselves by alleging the
restrictions contained in it, and the necessity under
which they lay of securing their foreign trade. Constantly shifting diets and decisions succeeded each other:
Schwytz, in disgust, refused to send her delegates to a
meeting at Baden; and Zurich refused to appear at an-
another, to account for her league with Austria. A
numerous division of her troops had already adopted the
red cross, the distinguishing badge of that power, and
many displayed the hated peacock's feather on their
crest. The troops of Schwytz now posted themselves on
their frontier, declared war on the Austrians and the
Zurichers, and repelled, though not without loss, an attack of their forces near Freyenbach. Without any
fixed plan, the margrave and Stussi advanced with
5000 men over the Albis towards Zug, burned Blick-
enstorf, and retreated over the hill again with at least
equal rapidity, when the banners of Lucerne, Uri, and
Unterwalden, unexpectedly came in sight.

All the confederates now united their forces against
Zurich; and 5000 or 6000 troops marched over the
Albis, on the town itself, on the 22d of July, 1443.
The garrison and burghers made an obstinate stand,
under the double disadvantage of surprise and want of
discipline. Thrown into confusion by a manœuvre of
the enemy, they retreated with considerable loss into
the town, which only escaped capture through the want
of order in the attack. Stussi died as a hero, if he had
erred as a politician; and contributed much, by the
stand which he made at the bridge over the Sihl, to the
rescue of his unfortunate native city.

From Zurich the confederates marched to Baden, and
to Rappersweil, and laid siege in vain to the latter place.
The stout defence of the town brought about an armistice; the bad observance of which, and ill-concealed aim
of gaining time, acquired for it the name of the *rotten
peace.* Both sides employed the interval of truce to add
to their forces. The emperor and duke Sigismund
sought aid of France and Burgundy. The confederates
compelled the district of Grüningen into allegiance. At
a diet at Baden, in March (1444), the clerical and lay
lords and free towns could bring about no compromise
between Zurich and the confederates. When the passions of men in power and of the multitude are excited,
there may be more danger in speaking truth to a countryman, than difficulty in conquering an enemy. Three
burghers of Zurich lost their lives in a popular tumult,
being charged with having shown some leaning towards
the cause of the confederates at Baden.

The confederates drew their forces together at Cloten
for a new campaign. They were now, moreover, joined
by the men of Appenzell. Greifensee was defended
for four weeks against their whole force by the steady
valour of Wildhans of Breiten-Landenberg, the commander of a small but faithful garrison. No diversion
was attempted from Zurich; and these undaunted men,
cut off from all succour, were finally forced to surrender
at discretion. The success of the confederates was

stained by the decapitation of sixty-two of the garrison, promoted by the landamman of Schwytz, Ital Reding. The honest captain Holzach of Menzingen was denounced as a friend of Austria, by that young but savage chieftain, for daring to plead the cause of common humanity. The conquerors, who, except on urgent emergencies, never left their hearths for any long period, returned homewards, but soon united again for the siege of Zurich.

But now was Switzerland threatened on the west by a new enemy, the dauphin of France (afterwards Louis XI.) at the head of a formidable body of Armagnacs. These were troops of the same description as those which, under Ingelram de Coucy, had already ravaged part of Switzerland. Bernard, count of Armagnac, had employed them in the service of the house of Orleans; and though their leader fell in a popular tumult at Paris, they retained his name, and continued to distinguish themselves as Armagnacs. On the tidings of the advance of the French upon Basle, 1600 men were sent by the Swiss to strengthen the place. This little band surprised a far superior force of the enemy on the banks of the Birs, and their fortunate rashness was crowned with success and booty. Spurred by this earnest of victory, and regarding neither the commands of their officers, nor the immense superiority of the enemy, they rushed headlong through the stream of the Birs, but were soon stopped by the enemy's heavy artillery and cavalry. Five hundred Swiss took their stand on an open ait in the stream; 700 behind garden walls, near St. Jacob, against the constantly renewed attacks of the thoroughly disciplined enemy. After ten hours of the most murderous conflict, only ten of the Swiss escaped; the rest were left dead on the field by the side of many thousands of their enemies. This was the battle of St. Jacob by Basle, which spread the renown of Swiss valour through the most remote regions, notwithstanding a victory dearly bought by France, and vainly boasted of on a medal struck by order of Charles

VII., representing two prisoners bound back to back, with the legend *Helvetiorum contumacia et temeritas ferro frenata* MCCCCXLIV. The dauphin afterwards showed that he knew better how to estimate the advantages derivable to his crown from the alliance and the arms of the confederates than his father had done. In the mean time he saw the folly of all attempts on a country, of which the borders were defended with such obstinacy. He promised not to march with his army through any part of the lands of the confederacy, and offered his mediation in order to terminate the war of the confederates with Zurich and Austria.

Our narrative cannot stop to notice many minor actions, and must even omit a whole series of diets and pacific overtures. In all affairs of any importance, the confederates had the advantage; but the districts which were the seat of war had been wasted to such a degree by their ravages, as to furnish them with no farther means of subsistence. They were, besides, heavily burdened with the garrisons which they had to maintain at Baden, Bremgarten, Mellingen, Grüningen, Pfeffikon, &c. Both parties, in short, were tired out; and the war continued not so much from hope of advantage on either side, as because too many obstacles to a compromise had been raised by the exorbitant pretensions of both. However, at length the full and entire conviction of necessity enforced on them the postponement of all other considerations. The intervention of the electors of Mentz, Trier, and more especially of Louis, the young elector palatine, resulted in a conference at Constance, where many neutral personages were present. Through Louis's indefatigable activity, and with the aid of other active and numerous mediators, the foundations of a peace were laid. In the midst of contradictory demands and allegations, the end in view was limited with admirable discretion to the establishment of tranquillity, oblivion of the past, and the division of the points in dispute. The league of Zurich with Austria was declared null and void, as contrary to the rights of the confederacy.

We find the state of intellectual progress in the first half of the fifteenth century scarcely more satisfactory than that in which the spiritual polity was left on the untimely dissolution of the council of Constance. Those cobwebs of the brain which were accredited as sciences, as little deserved the name as they did that of wholesome nourishment for the mental wants and appetites of the people; while ignorance of the languages of antiquity set a seal upon the highest productions of genius, and even on the original records of Scripture. What darkness must have still prevailed when a German monk could preach as follows: — "A language has been lately invented, called Greek. This Greek is the mother of all schisms; and in it a book hath been written, which is called the New Testament, and in which are many perilous passages. Another language also hath arisen, which is Hebrew. Whosoever learns the same becomes a Jew!" Till the foundation of the university of Basle, which took place in the year 1460, no effectual care was taken for learning in any part of Switzerland. A tolerably instructed man was rarely found at the head of the schools, even in considerable towns. A person was considered perfectly fit for the office of pastor, who could read with facility, translate a little, retain the simplest rules of grammar in memory, sing tolerably well, and had any degree of natural eloquence. The most precious relics of Greek and Roman literature lay in numbers in a dark tower of the convent of St. Gall, and were rescued from dust and oblivion chiefly by foreigners. The poetical art of the Minnesingers had vanished; and the science of music had fallen into a state of utter decay, till the council of Basle made some attempts to revive it. Felix Hammerlin, who bore the punning surname of *Malleolus*, a canon of Zurich, an upright, learned, and sensible man, a very voluminous writer, and possessor of the then enormous number of 500 volumes, was long the greatest light of the confederacy. Even he, however, in those times the most learned man in Switzerland, and whose acquirements made him pass for a magician with the multitude, cherished many superstitious fancies. He held it, for example, highly fitting to pronounce certain forms of benediction over diseased cattle, or to still a tempest raised through satanic art by similar artifices, and, as a general rule, in cases of necessity not by any means too scrupulously to wave the devil's assistance. He fully approved the proceedings of the bishop of Lausanne, who caused sentences of Scripture to be read against the horse-leeches, which, to the great disgust of that fish-eating prelate, killed all the salmon. He also acquiesced in the indictment of the glow-worms before the spiritual court of the bishop of Coire, who, when the insect-advocate pleaded that the creatures of God did well to seek nourishment for the sustenance of their bodies, pronounced upon them solemn sentence of banishment into regions uninhabited by man. In like manner, the eels in the lake of Geneva were banished by one bishop of Lausanne, the earth-worms, grass-hoppers, and field-mice, by another. Failure in the accomplishment of these and similar sentences was of course ascribed entirely to the sins of the nation.

If the people placed implicit faith in fooleries of this kind, they no less firmly believed in signs and wonders, preternatural phenomena of every description ; and even spiritual dignitaries, in these respects, were no whit more enlightened than the lowest of the laity. Many were supposed to have a compact with infernal spirits, and thousands were led to death at the stake on account of this delusion. Happy was the man who, by intensity of devotion, and still more by bequests to religious houses on his death-bed, could secure a good reception for his soul in the next world. But what were looked upon as the holiest of all holies were the body of Christ contained in the host, the bones of martyrs and saints, and other relics. Whoever could get any thing of this kind in an honest way, was regarded by himself and

others as a made man, body and soul. But whoever
came unfairly by such treasures, purloined them, or
cast scorn upon them, was struck by wrath from heaven,
and by God's judgments on earth.

Anna Vögtli of Bischoffzell conceived the evil thought
of working enchantments with the host, and stole the
same from the church of Ettiswyl, in the canton of
Lucerne, on the 24th of May, 1447. She soon, however,
shrunk from her own device, and cast the host behind a
hedge privily. Whereupon a white seven-leaved rose
sprouted instantly forth from the ground, and in its calix
lay the consecrated wafer. The beasts of the field came
and bowed before it. The surrounding radiance revealed
it to the eyes of an innocent shepherdess, who discovered
it to the people of the village. Whereupon the priests
came out with toll of bell, with cross and banners, attended by a multitude of believers, to bring the holy
thing back to its place. A chapel was built in memory
of the circumstance, where the host did itself credit by
working many signs and wonders. We scarcely need to
add, that Anna Vögtli was burnt.

Greater was the general consternation at Berne than
would have been caused by a surprise from the most
powerful of her enemies, when, in the year 1460, in the
cathedral church of St. Vincent, the host was missing
one fine morning! That no thunderbolt from heaven
should have fallen on the delinquent seemed a sign of
the Almighty's displeasure against Berne. Innocents
were put to the torture to force from them a confession
of the theft. Fasting and strict discipline were enjoined
by flaming ordinances; penitential homilies were fulminated from all pulpits. A new and costly receptacle was consecrated to the host, and veneration to the mother of God
was displayed by renewing her temples. After the lapse
of years, a priest confessed the theft on his death-bed.

Eleven o'clock one Sunday night, owing to the negligence of the monks of Einsiedlen, three strangers made
away with certain relics from that monastery. The sacri-
legious plunderers, seized with horror, let their spoil drop

in the highway at a short distance from Zurich. The intelligence reaches Zurich,— the powers spiritual and secular, with the whole town at their heels, hasten forth,— the treasure is brought reverently and solemnly into the great cathedral church, — and a season of extraordinary fertility is attributed to this holy acquisition. Poor Einsiedlen, shamed and sad, forsaken by her pilgrims, could only with great pains and expense recover her lost property; and even such men as Hammerlin regarded its restitution with a sigh, as the most serious loss to Zurich.

The dearth of real devotion amidst all this superstition was felt, and sought to be remedied by pomp of ceremonial. Zurich was particularly distinguished for splendour of church-service, even in the times of distress and indigence, which long wars had brought upon the town. The pope was viewed as the visible centre of God's power upon earth, as the infallible guide of all men in their spiritual concernments : but so soon as he and his priests stretched forth their fulness of power over temporal matters, they had to rue, as we have already seen, the instant disappearance of the last trace of reverent obedience.

CHAP. IX.

FROM THE FIRST ALLIANCE WITH FRANCE TO THE DEATH OF CHARLES THE BOLD OF BURGUNDY.

1453—1477.

FIRST ALLIANCE OF SWITZERLAND WITH FRANCE. — LOUIS XI. — CHARLES DUKE OF BURGUNDY. — HIS CHARACTER. — TAKES POSSESSION OF ALSACE. — APPOINTS PETER VON HAGENBACH GOVERNOR. — CONDUCT OF THE LATTER. — COMPLAINED OF BY THE SWISS. — OFFENSIVE AND DEFENSIVE ALLIANCE OF SWITZERLAND WITH FRANCE. — WITH AUSTRIA. — FATE OF HAGENBACH. — BERNE DECLARES WAR AGAINST BURGUNDY. — CHARLES INVADES SWITZERLAND. — DESCRIPTION OF HIS CAMP. — SIEGE OF GRANSON. — COLD-BLOODED MURDER OF THE GARRISON. — BATTLE OF GRANSON. — EXULTATION OF LOUIS XI. — CHARLES RE-APPEARS IN THE FIELD. — BATTLE OF MORAT. — LAST EFFORT OF BURGUNDY. — BATTLE OF NANCY. — DEATH OF CHARLES. — ITS CONSEQUENCES.

The long and severe struggle carried on by the confederates with Zurich and her powerful allies, if its effects had been in some respects mischievous, had yet unquestionably heightened the courage and confidence of the people, and had rendered their little territory respectable in the eyes of its more powerful neighbours. Meanwhile the newly vindicated spirit of independence was often apt to swell into presumption and violence. Wherever there was room for martial enterprise, the youth of Switzerland asked not what was the cause, but where was the seat of warfare; and even the authorities were too disposed towards making conquests to consult for the preservation of peace with any great solicitude. An anecdote remains of the youth of Zurich, which indicates the restless and exuberant flow of energies characteristic of the period before us. In the year 1456 the young burghers of Zurich were invited to a feast at Strasburg. They set out from Zurich in the

K

morning, taking with them a covered pot of millet broth
with warm loaves, took boat down the Limmat, the Aar,
and the Rhine, regardless of the dangers of their rapid
course, and on the same evening brought their broth and
bread, still warm, to the table of their friends, to show
with what despatch, in case of emergency, Strasburg
might expect aid from Zurich. After a few days spent
in manly exercises the gallant youths returned to their
native town; but left the pot behind them, which, as a
monument of their enterprise, was deposited in the
armoury of Strasburg.

The first alliance of Switzerland with France was
closed under Charles VII., in 1453, and had no other
end than to secure friendly relations between the two
countries. This league was renewed in 1467, by the
next king, Louis XI., who had already, as dauphin,
purchased some experience of Swiss valour on the bloody
day of St. Jacob, and who from that experience strove
by every means, direct and indirect, to fix his Swiss
allies on his side, and to turn their powerful arms
against his formidable enemies, especially against the
house of Burgundy. He contented himself, at first,
with the renewal of the simple league of friendship
formed by his father; but it was not long before he resorted to the arts of intrigue and bribery, in order to
employ the confederates in a more effective manner
for his own ends.

In the year 1467, Philip, surnamed the Good, duke
of Burgundy, died at Bruges, in Flanders. His dominions were inherited by his son Charles, appropriately
distinguished as the Bold, who mortally detested the
French monarch, and was hated by him mortally in return. In the trial of strength which soon took place
betwixt them, Louis evinced the ascendancy of prudence
and intelligence over powerful but unregulated energies.
He had succeeded to the throne of his father with extraordinary abilities for ruling, and with no inconsiderable experience; and he sat there as if he only looked
upon himself in the light of the first officer of the state,

whose life should be devoted to the functions of his
office.   The main object which he steadily placed and
kept before his eyes was the foundation of unlimited
monarchical power in France, and the humiliation of
the arrogant and restless feudal nobility, at the head of
which were the dukes of Burgundy, Normandy, and
Bretagne.   To the attainment of this object Louis proceeded without scruple by direct or indirect paths.   He
employed mildness and rigour by turns, divine and
human authority, flattery and bribery, — constantly
fraud,—rarely force.   Fidelity to his word he only
practised when it served his purposes.   So soon as profit appeared on the other side, he never scrupled to
violate the most positive engagements.   He was commonly then most dangerous to his enemies when he
seemed to be most utterly inactive; and pursued his ends
most eagerly precisely at the moment when all the world
believed he had abandoned them.   It was said of him,
" that he only slept with one eye in war-time, but kept
both his eyes open, day and night, in time of peace."
Such was Louis towards all his enemies foreign and
internal, and above all, towards his hated rival of Burgundy.   Between the latter power and France neither
peace nor war could be said to exist, but abundance of
faithlessness, changeableness, and irritation.   Cunning
at last carried off the victory, bought at the charge of
others; and Louis attained his ends by perseverance and
caution, and by the skilful use of many secret instruments.

Charles the Bold of Burgundy, the great rival of
Louis, though nominally his vassal, yet in effect was
not less powerful than the monarch himself, and was by
no means disposed to play a subordinate part to him or
to any other person.   The flourishing condition of his
territories, enriched by industry, commerce, and navi-
gation ; the accumulated treasures of his ancestors, the
attachment of his subjects, and the excellence of his
troops, seemed to secure him superiority over any rival;
and his position at the head of all the malecontents in

France completed his claim to be viewed as the king's most formidable enemy. Charles was of middle stature, strong make, brown complexion, black eyes and hair, with an aquiline nose, a broad forehead, and somewhat prominent chin. His whole physiognomy indicated a stern and martial temper. He had known, from childhood upwards, no pleasures more alluring than the excitements of the chase or the camp—no worthier scope of human undertakings than the glory of a second Alexander. Insatiable ambition formed the groundwork of his whole character. His brain teemed with projects of aggrandisement, of the possible realisation of which a doubt never occurred to him. Courage, generosity, and openness were amongst the brilliant qualities of Charles. When he once thought he had tried and proved the character of a friend, he treated him thenceforward with the most unlimited confidence; but towards enemies, or those who were indifferent to him, he was not always scrupulous in keeping his engagements. He took to himself the credit of unconquerable firmness; but good fortune hardened this quality into arrogance and obstinacy, so that his heart was closed in the day of disaster not less to the counsels of prudence than to the feelings of humanity. Such were the very opposite dispositions of the two princes, whose enmity was the chief cause of the most severe struggle which had ever been maintained by the confederacy.

Recent feuds had rather provoked than pacified those nobles who maintained the part of hereditary enemies of Switzerland. Duke Sigismund of Austria, too weak in resolution to withstand the constant promptings and persuasions of his council, and too weak in resources to undertake any thing against the Swiss confederacy singlehanded, was easily prevailed upon to look out for foreign aid. He first endeavoured to gain allies in Germany, and failed: next he turned his views towards France, which had so lately sent the Armagnacs to vex the Swiss borders; but the cautious Louis had not so soon forgotten the day of St. Jacob; and saw, besides, too well how useful Switzerland might be to him, to wish for its destruction, had he possessed the power to effect it. For these reasons he granted, indeed, a subsidy in money; but declined the duke's proposal that he should take into his hands, by way of mortgage, the Austrian territories bordering on Switzerland, under condition of protecting them against the Swiss confederacy. Sigismund addressed himself next, as some affirm, by advice of Louis, to Burgundy. Such advice appears extremely characteristic of the far-sighted, acute, and subtle policy of that prince. Knowing the duke's temper, as well as that of the confederates, and well aware that the former would embrace, without hesitation, so good an opportunity of extending his dominions, he could easily foresee that when such irritable characters as Charles and the Swiss became neighbours, the outbreak of a war of extermination could not be far off. Then he would have a glorious opportunity of gratifying his hatred to the duke, without any risk or exertion on his own part, at most by some expense in money, and perfidy, which cost him nothing. If the inevitable conflict turned to the ruin of the duke, then Louis had provided for his personal vengeance, and might safely trust to his cunning to secure him the lion's share of the booty. On the other hand, even if the duke should be victorious, Louis's own experience furnished sufficient grounds of certainty, that before the Swiss gave themselves up for beaten, they would exhaust the strength of Charles so completely, that he must fall into the king's hands in a manner disarmed and defenceless. Either event could not but be advantageous to Louis: the last, perhaps, he deemed the more desirable of the two, as it might possibly place the Swiss as well as Burgundy at his mercy.

With Charles of Burgundy, Sigismund's advisers had no trouble in inducing him to accept a mortgage of the counties of Pfirt, Sundgau, Brisgau, Alsace, and the four forest towns, in return for a considerable sum of money. How, indeed, could that ambitious prince, whose favourite scheme was the junction of his unconnected domains,

and, if possible, the erection of a kingdom extending
from the North Sea to the Mediterranean, — how could
such a prince reject so rich an acquisition, which placed
in his hands a key to Germany, Switzerland, and Upper
Burgundy, and lay contiguous to the latter, which was
already his own property? The voluntary cession of
lands so valuable to him he regarded as a signal piece
of good fortune: the reservation of a future resumption
appeared to him merely nominal, as Sigismund's expensive habits seemed to afford no prospect of it; and the
proviso for the maintenance of the ancient constitution
was regarded as an empty form requiring no observance. Thus had the Austrian nobles gained their
end, of giving a powerful and dangerous neighbour to
the confederacy: what did not, however, come within
the range of their calculations, was, that thereby they
had exposed the lands of the empire to great dangers,
and prepared (in the words of Bullinger) " a rod for
their own backs."

The government of the newly acquired lands was
delegated to the knight Peter von Hagenbach, a tried
and proved servant of Charles, who had raised himself
by his merits at the duke's court from the humblest
station: this man, who, like other upstarts, thought to
efface the discredit of his birth by domineering assumption acted rather as a tyrant than a governor. As he
leaned for support entirely on his patron, and treated all
the world besides with total disregard, he scrupled not
to deprive the nobles and commons of their franchises,
and transgressed his deputed powers with so little de-
cency or mercy, that he acquired the appellation of the
" scourge of God." His first employment, notwithstanding the express terms of the mortgage, was to regulate
every thing according to the laws and customs of Burgundy. No representations or remonstrances were attended to; nothing remained but silence and submission;
for Charles had known how to crush the independent
spirit of far more strong and powerful populations. The
confederates regarded these transactions, which were

ominous of no good to themselves, with a mind prepared
for all events, but not without anxiety. Relations outwardly amicable prevailed between them and Burgundy,
till Hagenbach went so far as to plant the colours of the
latter power on the Bernese territory of Schenkenberg :
this occurrence Louis instantly turned to his own advantage. The confederates had empowered Berne, whose
government was better versed in diplomacy, and acquainted with the French language, than those of the
other cantons were in general, to close a treaty with
France in the name of the whole league, in any case of
necessity or expedience : this was accordingly done. The
king and the confederacy reciprocally engaged to give
no aid to the duke of Burgundy : this arrangement deprived the duke of all hope of Swiss assistance in executing his projects against France. Charles, who did
not wish to bring the confederates still closer to the king
than they were already, commanded his vogt to desist
from farther encroachments. The enmity between Charles
and Louis increased ; and, but for Berne's prudent and
resolute conduct, the confederates might already have
been plunged in a war. Many had been won by French
gold, others were inclined to the cause of Burgundy, and
the state of affairs became more and more complex. The
barons of Heudorf, Eptingen, and other noble foes of
the Swiss, saw with dissatisfaction that the mortgaged
lands had now been for three years in the duke's possession, without the expected war with the confederates
having commenced : they therefore endeavoured, under
the shield of Burgundy, to embitter the Swiss by flagrant
violations of the last treaty of peace, and the law of
nations. Thus the Swiss had now incentives to war on
two sides ; a third was soon added : for the mortgaged
lands, which had formerly been ruled with mildness and
equity, now, oppressed as they were by a reckless tyrant,
looked for relief towards the Swiss league. Hagenbach had
made himself, in a short time, as detested as the Gesslers
and the Landenbergs had formerly been in Switzerland.
The imposts which he exacted, the regulations which he

introduced, were utterly unendurable to the people : his
merciless rigour, joined with haughty arrogance; his
boundless immoralities, extortions, and judicial murders,
filled up the measure of popular hatred ; which, moreover, laid to his charge all that was done by him in
performance of the will of his master. Charles, who
felt no enmity against the confederates, assured them
of his undiminished favour ; and procured, by intervention of Sigismund, a settlement of the feud with
Heudorf and others. But Louis's intrigues, and Hagenbach's recklessness, diminished the advantageous impression made by the duke's efforts ; and, not long afterwards,
Charles offended personally a highly respectable body
of Swiss delegates, who came to complain of the conduct
of his vogt.

Hagenbach, who could not conceal his hatred of the
confederates, seized every opportunity of outrage against
the whole people, or its individual leaders. He increased
the tolls, invaded the rights of Swiss owners of land
whose property lay in the new Burgundian territory, and
supported with his influence every enemy of Switzerland.
Swiss traders were robbed by the nobles with his knowledge and connivance, and made prisoners for the sake
of extorting ransom. Hagenbach himself tried every
method of reducing Muhlhausen under the power of
Burgundy ; and when the harassed town pleaded her
existing league with the Swiss, the vogt scoffingly promised to convert it from a cow-house to a garden of
roses.

About this time the sorely oppressed districts addressed the most urgent petitions for release to duke
Sigismund. That good but feeble prince sincerely deplored that he had put his land in more powerful keeping
than his own, from which it would not be easy to recover
it. The *lower union,* a league of the most considerable
towns of Alsace, had promised to advance the sum required to redeem the mortgaged estates. But the assistance
of the warlike confederates was likely to be requisite in
effecting the redemption ; as it was easy to foresee that

Charles would accept no pecuniary equivalent for domains which he now viewed as his own absolute property. Sigismund, therefore, made overtures of alliance to the Swiss.

Shortly after these transactions Charles entered Alsace with 5000 horse, and a numerous courtly attendance. Panic preceded him every where. Many left the country with their property. The peasantry sought refuge in the towns; the towns solicited aid of the confederacy. Several fortified places closed their gates. . Basle made a defensive alliance with Switzerland, in case of any sudden surprise, and received an addition of 800 Swiss to its garrison, with the promise that in case it were besieged the whole force of the confederacy should march to its relief. In the mean time the confederates conducted themselves as if they had no cause for apprehension. They sent a deputation to the duke to pay their respects, and to lay their complaints before him against Hagenbach. At a more auspicious moment Charles might probably have averted the impending storm from his head, by affording satisfaction for the grievances complained of; but now, surrounded as he was by the worst foes of Switzerland, he showed offensive pride and haughty coldness. The humiliating ceremony of falling on one knee before the duke was enforced on the reluctant republicans; and after they had followed in his train for some time, they were uncourteously dismissed from Dijon, without reply to their application.

From this time forward the confederates attached themselves decidedly to Charles's enemies, while Hagenbach, to the duke's own disadvantage, received encouragement in his mischievous proceedings. On the 10th of January, 1474, Berne closed, in the name of all the confederates, an offensive and defensive league with Louis of France, which could point at nothing else but war with Burgundy. In this alliance the eyes of the confederates were blinded to their true interests by a large immediate profit. True policy would certainly not have led them to annihilate a power which alone balanced that of France. But their measures were much more the

result of momentary impressions than of any systematic
plan or principle.   From this epoch first began the de-
moralising influence of French manners and money,
through enlistments and pensions.   The intelligence of
this alliance took the duke by surprise, and he left no
means untried to win the Swiss back to his interests.
An embassy was sent to the confederates to soften the
impression made by Charles's haughty deportment.
Their efforts seemed to meet with success.   But the emperor and the French king, convinced that a check must
be given to Burgundy for the sake of their own safety,
and that the confederates were the instruments best adapted for that purpose, plied them with such active intrigues,
that hostile steps were soon taken.   The alliance which,
we have already seen, Austria courted with Switzerland
finally took place.   It was long before the Swiss could be
convinced of the sincerity of the Austrian intentions.
The hereditary hostility of that house to Swiss freedom was still retained in too lively remembrance ; but
Joseph von Sillinen, provost of Béronmunster, succeeded at length in satisfying his countrymen of the honourable purposes of Austria.   One hundred and fifty-nine
years after the battle of Morgarten, eighty-eight years
after the defeat of duke' Sigismund's grandfather at
Sempach, that prince and the whole body of confederates,
contracted, under the guarantee of France, the *eternal
covenant*, a treaty transmitted almost uninterruptedly
to our own times.   All wars and disputes were to be
ended by it.   Austria abandoned all claim to restitution
of her losses in Switzerland, whether early or recent.
Freedom of trade and intercourse was restored. Neither
party should favour or support the foes of the other ;
but stood pledged to afford each other reciprocal aid.
Hardly had this treaty been concluded, when Sigismund
hastened to demand the release of his land from the
duke of Burgundy.   The towns of the lower union advanced the sum, which in a few days lay in readiness at
Basle.   Sigismund, whose first intention had been to
humble the Swiss by aid of the Burgundians, was now

well pleased to find the former disposed to take his part against Burgundy. He made a visit to Switzerland in person, and won the hearts of the people so completely, that all remembrance of ancient enmity vanished, and the Swiss vied with each other in cordial welcome of their new ally.

When Hagenbach was informed of these transactions, he resolved to take all possible means to secure the duke his master in possession of the mortgaged lands, as he knew that Charles affirmed himself to have purchased them, and had no idea of making restitution. In this view, Hagenbach aimed at securing the fortified town of Breisach, entered the place on Good Friday, at the head of some hundred Lombards, disturbed divine service, committed various acts of violence, and drove matters so far with an already disaffected people, that a tumult arose. in which his Lombards were driven out of the town, he himself taken prisoner in the name of duke Sigismund, and his life rescued with difficulty from the fury of the people. Hagenbach was thrown into a dungeon, and Sigismund sent a new vogt to replace him in his territories thus regained without stroke of sword. Charles threatened loudly, and marched one division of his army to the frontiers. Hagenbach, in the mean time, lavished promises in vain to procure his liberation. He still entertained hopes from his master; but Charles was not magnanimous enough to interfere in the behalf of an old servant, whose death would give so welcome a pretext for revenge. Four weeks after Hagenbach's imprisonment he was brought to trial. The archducal councillors, the delegates of the mortgaged lands and the towns of the Lower Union assembled, surrounded by innumerable multitudes, brought together by curiosity or malice. The prisoner had often been awaked from uneasy slumber by the clatter caused by new arrivals of delegates, as they rode through the city gates, under the cell where he lay in confinement. His terror may be imagined when the keeper announced the arrival of a troop of tall and strong, though grey-headed, strangers,

coarsely clad, and indifferently mounted. " Those must
be the Swiss !" he exclaimed : " God help me; for they
have much to bring against me !" His gloomy antici-
pations did not deceive him. He was doomed to death ;
and no less than eight candidates disputed the honour of
executing the sentence.

Hagenbach's execution was the signal for war ; and
Charles swore he would lose his life rather than his
revenge. His revenge he was, however, compelled for
the moment to postpone, being entangled in a war of
some importance in another quarter. This interval was
employed by the confederates in providing for their
security on all sides. Friendly relations were established with Milan and Savoy. Duke René of Lorraine,
whose territories excited the cupidity of Charles, as they
very inconveniently severed his southern from his northern possessions, was taken into the union against Burgundy. Hostilities were commenced in the Sundgau,
in the autumn of the same year, by a division of troops
under the command of Hagenbach's brother. Berne
appointed a diet of all the confederates at Lucerne, and
was invested with discretionary powers to take measures
for the general good. Vain were the representations of
those who saw clearly, and said loudly, that the confederates were placing themselves as tools in the hands
of the French king, and that, so soon as they had done
his work, he would rob them of the profits. On the
2d of October, 1474, an alliance with France was concluded at Berne in the name of all the confederates.
The Swiss engaged to supply the king with 6000 fighting men whenever he might need their assistance : on
his part he should only be summoned to aid in case of
necessity ; and in all wars with Burgundy might contribute his contingent in the shape of a pecuniary subsidy.
Thus the crafty Louis called the Swiss confederacy to
arms for the promotion of his own ends against Burgundy, while he turned away the ravages of war from
his own territories. On the 9th of October, an embassy
from the emperor summoned the confederates to attack

the duke of Burgundy, with the promise, that while
they advanced on the south-east of his territories, the
emperor would assail them on the side of the Netherlands. The confederates hastened to Lucerne to complete their deliberations; but before these had been closed,
Berne, on the strength of the full powers which were de-
volved on her, declared war with Burgundy. Many,
indeed, did not consider these powers as warranting, in
their true sense, a measure so decisive; but regarded
them as merely having been given for the conclusion of
the necessary treaties with France. But the murmurs
of those unseduced by French pensions and promises
were shortly to be drowned in the shouts of victory.

The foregoing declaration against Burgundy brought
out the confederates more boldly than ever on the theatre
of events beyond the circle of their compact. In the
preceding age they had struggled against Austria in
defence of their national existence; in the war of the
Aargau they merely obeyed the summons of the empire;
they engaged in the war with Zurich first from passion,
then for their own protection. But now Berne had
drawn the other confederates, with the prospect of
but limited assistance from abroad, into mortal strife
with the mightiest of their neighbours, whose dominions
stretched from the coasts of the North Sea over the
greater part of the rich and populous Netherlands, over
the duchy and free county of Burgundy, and many other
lordships besides.

The army of the confederates, amounting in all to a
force of about 18,000 men, appeared before Hericourt,
a strong-hold of Diebold of Neufchâtel in the Franche
Comté. It was in vain that a strong body of Burgundians, under the command of Jacob de Romont, count de
Vaud, made an effort to effect a diversion. On the 13th
of November he was routed by the avoyer of Scharnachthal and Felix Keller of Zurich. Hericourt was
surrendered, and taken into possession in the name of
duke Sigismund of Austria. The army returned homewards; and the discontent which had arisen among

many of the confederates on account of the precipitate
declaration of war on the part of Berne was put an end
to by the victory, and still more by the plunder.   The
confederates, however, renewed at Lucerne the regulations of their old martial law, on account of the disorders
which had taken place through the stimulus of wine and
love of plunder; considering, moreover, that disturbers
of discipline are less deserving of mercy than open enemies.   It was resolved that a division of the rear-guard
should receive orders to cut down all who engaged in
plunder before the battle was over; and that then whatever booty was made should be fairly shared in common.
Louis XI. lavished flatteries; begged aid of the lords
confederates, in case the duke should attack him, and
promised to participate with them all the hazards of
warfare.   If his subsidies to the cantons suffered occasional delays, his pensions to their leading men at least
were paid punctually.   On the 6th of April, 1475, the
account of the disbursements to those magistrates and
officers, who had in effect sold themselves to France, was
regularly settled between Louis's commissioner and the
Bernese avoyer Diessbach.*

Republican venality was soon repaid by royal faithlessness.   The first of their august allies who forsook
the Swiss was the emperor Frederick, who, equally regardless of them as of René and duke Sigismund, concluded a dishonourable peace with the duke of Burgundy
in order to win the daughter of the latter for his son.
Actuated by similar delusive expectations, Louis closed
a nine years' truce with Charles, in which he sacrificed,
without scruple, the interests of Switzerland, as well as
of the lower union of Burgundy.   In the perilous position of the confederates, the margrave Rudolph endeavoured to mediate a truce for them with Burgundy.
His conciliatory labours did not prosper, as the former
would not abandon those allies which were still true to
them.   Charles had now achieved the complete conquest
of Lorraine; and from thence marched through Be-

* Müller, iv. 725, &c.

sançon in mid-winter, in order to chastise the confederates, above all, the Bernese, for their audacity. Flames and other incendiary devices on his banners gave a sufficiently graphic announcement of his intentions. At Besançon he was joined by his corps of artillery, and by reinforcements from Italy and Burgundy, which brought his force up to about 60,000 men. This army, though numerically imposing, consisted in a great measure of raw and hastily levied troops, and advanced as if the object of its meeting were the joyous celebration of some festival, instead of mortal strife with the descendants of the victors of Morgarten, Sempach, and Laupen. Charles drew in his train the greater part of his court, the whole splendid cortège of his attendants, all his treasures and valuables, a crowd of cooks and tradespeople of all descriptions, with whole stores of their several commodities, and a multitude of light and loose companions; so that his camp, including all its useless followers, might contain perhaps 100,000 persons.* This motley host inundated the land like a mountain torrent. Charles formed an encampment, which, in display of wealth and magnificence, resembled a luxurious capital city more than a place of arms. It was regularly laid out in wide streets. The richest and the most diversified articles of convenience and of ornament were displayed in tents and booths. But for the sullen roar of artillery, the scene would have appeared a fair rather than a camp. An artificial mount was raised in the midst, on which stood the magnificent tent of the duke himself. From the oriental pomp of this pavilion Charles might gaze with gratified pride upon the glittering lines beneath him, little imagining that he looked on all his glories for the last time.

On the 19th of February Charles laid siege to Gran-

---

* " A grand chevauchée," says Philip de Comines, "venoit le duc Charles, avec moult gens d'armes, de pied et de cheval, répandant la terreur au loin par son ost innombrable. Là étoient cinquante mille, voire plus, de toutes langues et contrées, force canons et autres engins de nouvelle facture; pavillons et accoutrements tout reluisants d'or, et grande bande de valets, marchands, et filles de joyeux amour."

son, a little town on the lake of Neufchâtel. He attacked
the place in his usual manner, by storm—by which all
that he gained was the possession of an untenable town,
while the garrison withdrew into the well-fortified castle,
on which the duke's artillery kept up an incessant fire.
Unhappily the powder magazine in the castle exploded;
the master gunner was killed, and a dearth of provisions
began to be felt in the garrison. Nevertheless their
courage did not abandon them, and no thought was entertained of surrender, till a Burgundian made his
appearance in the castle, by name Ronchant, who had
already at a former period wandered about Switzerland,
and acquainted himself with the character of the people.
This knowledge he employed with sinister skill in prac-
tising on the garrison with fabricated intelligence. He
assured them that Freyburg was already in ashes, Berne
had surrendered at discretion, and the troops of the
confederates were disbanded. He spoke alternately of
the dreadful wrath of the duke, and of his gracious dispositions towards the garrison, and was seconded so well
by a strong party in the castle, that the bolder spirits
were forced to yield to the cry for capitulation. Accordingly the castle was evacuated, and its recent defenders brought into the camp before Charles, who
contemptuously asked, on their appearance, " Who are
those people ?" and affected to know nothing either of
Ronchant or his promises. Persuaded by his councillors that a signal example was necessary, the terror of
which would throw all other fortified places open to him,
misled, moreover, by pride of power, the quality most
opposite to any thing like true greatness of soul, Charles
gave up the garrison of Granson to execution. Most of
them were stripped naked and hanged on trees the same
day; the remainder drowned in the lake on the following morning. The silent intrepidity with which they
met their death extorted respect, mingled with awe,
from the enemy; and the fortune and honour of Burgundy sunk from the hour when that atrocious crime
received its consummation.

On the very day when these proceedings took place, the main body of the Swiss army, 20,000 strong, was drawn together near Neufchâtel. The news of the mas-sacre filled them with deep rage and thirst for venge-ance, while the duke gave himself up to idle dreams of renown and conquest. When informed of the approach of the confederates, he made his preparations for imme-diate action. His army was entrenched behind Granson, in an admirable position, well fortified by art and by nature, with the lake on the right, the chain of the Jura on the left, in front the Arnou, the banks and approaches of which were covered by a formidable artillery. It was evident that the Swiss, whose whole force hardly amounted to a third of that of the duke, could not attack him in this secure position with any chance of success. They therefore resolved to draw him out by stratagem, and directed an attack upon the castle of Vaumarcus, which lay between Neufchâtel and Granson, and in which, by the account of several writers, some of Charles's favoured counsellors and courtiers had tem-porarily taken up their residence. The confederates hoped that Charles's pride would render it impossible for him to remain a quiet spectator of the action. They had calculated rightly, for Charles, sooner than they an-ticipated, and before they had made their assault upon Vaumarcus, quitted, against the advice of his best counsellors, a highly advantageous position; and, in order to protect a fortress utterly insignificant, marched to meet the Swiss upon ground where he could neither deploy his forces, nor make any important use of his artillery and cavalry.

On the 3d of March, the vanguard of the Swiss, the men of Schwytz and Thun, accompanied by nu-merous volunteers, advanced from Neufchâtel. It was early in a dull and misty morning. Having ascended the heights in the neighbourhood of the castle, they saw to their astonishment, when the vapours cleared from the low grounds, the whole force of the enemy drawn out into the valley before them. The Burgundians advanced. The Swiss sent back to hasten the march of their slowly advancing main body, and then fell on their knees to pray, according to the custom of their fathers. The enemy, unacquainted with this pious usage, and imagining that the whole confederate army was before them, and had fallen on their knees to implore mercy, raised a simultaneous shout of derision. A troop of cuirassiers dashed forwards to trample down the supplicants, but was indifferently received by the long spears of the confederates, and effectually repulsed by their advance in close order. After a discharge from the Burgundian artillery, which was pointed too high to take much effect, Charles endeavoured with his best troops to break the line of the Swiss in front, while count Louis of Château Guyon, a personal foe of the confederates, charged them in flank, at the head of 6000 horse. Now was the hottest rage of battle. The Swiss were hard pressed. Twice had Château Guyon seized with his own hand the banner of Schwytz ; when he was struck down. His troops wavered, dismayed by the fall of their leader. At this moment, a new and fearful sound arose from the heights in the rear of the confederates, and drew thither the eyes of the Burgundians. A fresh array of combatants covered the ridge. The horn of Uri blew the note of death, which was caught up and re-echoed by that of Unterwalden. And when the whole body of Swiss, after discharging their pieces with deadly precision, came down, man upon man, while new bands issued continually from the hollow ways and the thickets, that inexplicable sort of panic came on the Burgundians, which occasionally seizes the most resolute. They gave the battle up for lost. A feint of their own cavalry, who attempted by a retrograde movement, to draw the Swiss into a disadvantageous position, was taken by the infantry as a signal for flight. Vainly did Charles, at the head of his horsemen, throw himself across the swarm of fugitives. The whole host fell asunder; and instead of retreating to the fortified camp, where they might have rallied, took to flight, some towards Granson, some into the woods and fields, some over the Arnou or the mountains, and others again in boats across the lake. The unfortunate prince, with only five companions, directed his flight through the nearest pass of the Jura.*

When the spoil of the duke's camp came to be shared among the cantons, it was found to contain 120 pieces of ordnance, 600 standards, and about 10,000 pack-horses. These and an infinite quantity of other munitions of war, the whole of the ducal ornaments and valuables of every description, his golden seal, a pound in weight, his decorated prayer-book, the treasures of his generals and courtiers, remained in the possession of the victors. The rich hangings and pavilions were for the most part cut to pieces. Gold was shared by hatfuls; diamonds, which now adorn the most magnificent crowns in Europe, were first ignorantly thrown aside, then sold for trifling sums. In the division of this booty the least part came to the common stock. Many subsequent diets were engaged on the subject; and one of the great diamonds was sold in 1492, on the public account, for 5000 guilders. In imitation of foreign usages, the most distinguished leaders were created knights on the field of battle by the avoyer, Nicholas of Scharnachthal, as the oldest knight present. The town and castle of Granson were speedily retaken, and the exasperated youths of Berne and Freyburg hung part of the garrison up by the same ropes from which they had taken down their slaughtered brethren. They remained three days on the field of battle, and Granson was left occupied by a Swiss garrison.

Perhaps even greater pleasure was given by Charles's defeat to his evil angel Louis XI. than that which was experienced by the victors themselves. Indeed the battle was fought as much in his cause as in theirs, without having cost him any thing more than money and dupli-

---

* " A bien dire la vérité," says Comines, "je croy que jamais depuis il n'eut l'entendement si bon qu'il avoit eu auparavant cette bataille." — Liv. v. ch. 3.

city. On the first breaking out of war he had hastened
to Lyons, in order to be nearer the scene of action. From
thence he sent spies in various disguises into Switzerland,
and waited with impatience for decisive intelligence. The
Swiss, justly indignant at his treacherous conduct, had
alarmed him with the idea that they meant to close a
treaty of peace, if not actually of alliance, with his rival.
At length, however, arrived the tidings of Granson, on
the reception of which, the only alloy to Louis's satisfaction was, that more Burgundians had not been left
dead upon the field. However, he contrived to conceal
his pleasure, and did not omit to send the duke a message of condolence. The richest of his presents, and the
strongest of his assurances, were lavished on the Swiss,
to engage them in the farther prosecution of the contest;
for the day of Granson had neither sufficed to still his
apprehensions, nor to satisfy his thirst for revenge.

Charles, in the mean while, rallied all his resources:
every sixth man was enlisted, every sixth penny was
exacted; only a single iron vessel was left to any cook;
the bells were taken down from the church-towers to be
cast into cannon, and new artillery was brought from
Lorraine. Fresh troops were levied in Savoy and Italy;
and thirteen days after the rout of Granson, Charles
re-appeared in the Valais, and remained for seven weeks
at Lausanne, where he found himself again at the head
of an army still superior in numerical force to his former
one. The confederates, on the other hand, showed no
eagerness to comply with Berne's summons to the field.
They discovered, or fancied, projects of aggrandisement on
her part; expressed dissatisfaction with the division of
the plunder; and did not hold themselves bound to cross
the limits of the confederacy. A conference of their
delegates took place at Lucerne, where new regulations
were adopted with regard to plunder, &c. Finally, a
thousand men, with a newly arrived body of German
cavalry, were despatched to Freyburg, who, supported
by the citizens, engaged several divisions of the Burgundian army with vigour and success.

Berne detached 1500 men to garrison Morat on the lake of that name, under command of the ex-avoyer Adrian of Bubenberg, a man such as extraordinary emergencies demand, although they do not always supply. He had strenuously opposed the war with Burgundy at the outset, and therefore had been thrown into the background by the dominant party; but a man of his character never dreams of avenging on his country the wrongs which he may have received in his own person from his countrymen. He exacted of the garrison under his orders an oath to inflict immediate death on any one who should speak of surrender, himself the first, in case he should be guilty of such a proposal. On the 9th of June the Burgundian troops appeared before Morat. Attempts to take the place by storm were repelled with signal loss to the enemy, and the breaches made on the walls were all repaired during the night. Wherever danger appeared, Adrian showed himself. He sent to Berne to dissuade his fellow-citizens from exposing themselves by precipitately attempting to relieve him, until they should be reinforced by the rest of the confederates : in the mean time, he should know how to maintain his post without assistance.

Berne renewed, with earnestness, her summons to the confederates, some of whom had regarded Morat merely in the light of a point of aggrandisement for Berne, not as an important advanced post of the confederacy. But at length they took a larger view of the circumstances, and hastened to assist the besieged. Louis XI. remained inactive, having betaken himself to Lyons, on pretence of a pious pilgrimage, in order to observe the march of events, and be prepared to act according as his interest should dictate. He pretended friendship alternately to both sides. All the force which Berne could muster, with the aid of her out-burghers, reinforced from the other cantons, from Basle, the lower union of Burgundy, and a strong body of Austrian cavalry, drew up on the high grounds stretching on the south-west of Morat; and the young count René hastened through an enemy's

country to join them.   A Swiss council of war in those
times was not wont to deliberate whether or no an attack
should be made, but what was the most effectual mode
of making it.   Hans of Hallwyl led the van and the
right wing ; Waldmann, jointly with Wilhelm Herter
of Strasburg, the main body ; Hertenstein of Lucerne
commanded the rear.   For the first time the confederates
formed in widely extended lines.   They overlooked the
whole Burgundian army, entrenched behind quickset
hedges in close order of battle, with formidable batteries
in their front.   When the Austrian cavalry officers advised the confederates to ensconce themselves behind a
fence of baggage-waggons, and await, in this position,
the attack of the enemy, Felix Keller of Zurich made
reply, that the confederates were wont to be beforehand
with their enemies.   " God with us against the world !"
cried Hallwyl to his followers.   At this instant the sun
broke through the heavy clouds which had veiled it.
" Heaven lights us to victory !" he exclaimed, waving
his sword.   " Forward ! think of your wives and children : youths, think of your loved ones; yield them not
up to the lewd and godless enemy ! "

They rushed without hesitation on the terrible artillery, which galled the cavalry more than the foot-soldiers.
The garrison of Morat made a sally simultaneously with
the general charge of their countrymen.   The body guard
of the duke and a free company of English maintained
their ground gallantly for some time, but were driven in
at length, and all was lost.   The flying troops of Burgundy were pursued as far as Wiflisburg, with the
shouts, " Remember Brie ! Remember Granson !" Fifteen thousand corpses strewed the wide extent of the field
of battle ; thousands sunk in the neighbouring lake and
morasses.*   The plunder, in arms, valuables, and forage,

* The ossuary at Morat, which received the bones of the slain Burgundians, exhibited the following inscription, till its destruction by the French
in 1798 :—

Deo Opt. Max.
Caroli inclyti et fortissimi Ducis Burgundiæ,
Exercitus, Muratum obsidens,
Hoc sui monumentum reliquit.
M.CCCC.LXXVII.

though it could not be compared to that of Granson, was considerable; but in this, as in former instances, the rules of division were not adhered to. Charles fled, without once halting, to Morges. Notwithstanding the desire of Berne to follow up the victory, the confederates, for the most part, hastened homewards from the field of battle.

The emperor, the pope, and the king of Hungary, offered their mediation for a peace; but Charles could not be brought to renounce his pretensions to Lorraine. Too late he made approaches to his people in his misfortunes, and sought to inspire them with ardour for his cause. The Burgundians and Netherlanders received his advances coldly; and while he yielded up his mind to gloomy discouragement, René had again made himself master of his capital, and a considerable portion of his territory. Charles now collected all the force at his command, and prepared to besiege Nancy, while count René went to solicit aid of his friends the confederates. He presented himself in tears before the council of Berne, who, mindful of the reproaches they had incurred on a former occasion, would now conclude nothing without taking the sense of the other cantons. A diet was convoked at Lucerne, before which René renewed his pressing entreaties. It now occurred to every one, that a struggle with their enemy in Lorraine, and in the pay of count René, was preferable to gratuitous blows impending on their own frontiers. Count René was enabled to return to his own territories at the head of 8000 Swiss, of numerous reinforcements from Germany, and of such of his own subjects as adhered to his cause. In point of numbers Charles's force was inferior to that of René: he was surrounded, indeed, by his bravest and his most devoted warriors; but discouragement pervaded the mass of his followers. His faithful adherents earnestly implored him to retreat, to collect his strength, and harass his antagonists with delays; but a Neapolitan favourite of Charles, Campo-Basso, who had already long betrayed the trust reposed in him, unhappily still retained his entire confidence ; and, under this man's guidance, Charles blindly rushed on destruction. On the onset of the enemy, this wretch would have gone over to them, but was repulsed by the confederates with horror; Charles was left exposed in flank, and surrounded by the enemy; his bravest fell; his disheartened troops were soon scattered; and the duke himself, resolved to stake all upon a last throw, received a random death-stroke in the *mêlée*.

So soon as Louis was certified of his hated rival's death, he exerted himself to appropriate his succession, with an eagerness which seems to have got the better of his habitual cunning and caution. The princess Mary, daughter of the deceased duke of Burgundy, might possibly have been gained in marriage, by skilful negotiations, for Louis's younger son, the duke d'Angoulême; but as Louis attempted to exercise his authority over Mary as a crown vassal, *demanded* her hand for the dauphin, and developed too precipitately his plans of union with Burgundy, he alienated the princess altogether from his house. Soon afterwards a marriage treaty was closed for her by the states of the Netherlands with the archduke Maximilian, son of the emperor, in whom they hoped to find a protector against the threatened encroachments of Louis, and a ruler not too powerful for the safety of their liberties.

Immediately on the fall of Charles, the states of Upper Burgundy endeavoured, through the agency of delegates, at the head of whom stood the archbishop of Besançon, to establish for themselves either a sort of independence, or a league on equal terms with the Swiss. The Bernese alone perceived advantage to the confederation in accepting the alliance of these districts; the other cantons preferred receiving 100,000 Rhenish guilders, in consideration of granting a treaty of peace, and leaving the land to its own disposal. They argued that a ransom would be shared amongst them equally, while a distant domain or alliance would advantage none but the towns. In the midst of these discussions, French troops took possession

of the district in the name of their master, as feudal
sovereign. Terms of peace were at length arranged
between Louis and Maximilian, on condition of France
ceding Upper Burgundy. Convinced of the importance
of cajoling the Helvetic body, Louis granted extraordinary privileges to Swiss settlers in France; and not
only gave high appointments to those in his actual service, but, moreover, retained numbers in his permanent
pay, and dazzled the eyes of the multitude effectually,
by sending mule loads of gold to glut the avarice of his
Swiss allies.

CHAP. X.

ÆRA OF THE COVENANT OF STANTZ.

1477—1481.

EFFECTS OF THE BURGUNDIAN WAR ON SWITZERLAND. — IN-
CREASE OF CRIME. — FEUD OF URI WITH MILAN. — BATTLE
OF GIORNICO. — CLAIMS OF SOLEURE AND FREYBURG. — DIS-
SENSIONS. — NICOLAS OF THE FLUE. — COVENANT OF STANTZ.
— SURVEY OF THE STATE OF THE HELVETIC BODY UP TO THIS
PERIOD.

THE death of the duke of Burgundy, which excited such
surprise among the members of his house, and in his
more remote provinces, that for the space of several
weeks they disbelieved the intelligence, changed at a
blow the whole relations of southern and central Europe.
The renown of Swiss bravery rose higher than ever;
since, in collision with it, that mighty power was broken, in the presence of which the greatest kings had
trembled. But their glory was too dearly bought by
deep pervading evils: Swiss valour became from thenceforwards a marketable commodity, the value of which
had effects the most destructive to a free state. Foreigners came to purchase adherents amongst them: the

influence and the gold of France, of Austria, of the papacy, of Milan, and of other powers, bore every thing down before them in the diets, in the council chambers, and general assemblies. The uncorrupt defenders of their country's cause, where any such were still to be found, were derided or defamed by party leaders; the sober republican spirit disappeared almost entirely; obedience ceased to be rendered to ill-regulated authorities, which themselves transgressed their own laws and limits. The sudden wealth diffused by plunder and pensions excited its possessors to profusion and extravagance; while amongst others it inflamed the desire of procuring themselves, at any price, the means for the like indulgences. Love of labour was too often superseded by the taste for a loose rapacious idle life; domestic virtues became rare; immorality made public progress. Disbanded soldiers, and idle vagabonds of every other description, threatened the public security to such a degree, that a diet, held in 1480, decreed the punishment of death to all thefts and robberies, the amount of which would pay for a rope. Accordingly in a very few months, 1500 wretches were despatched by the hand of the public executioner, although the dean of Einsiedlen Bonstetten gives the number of Swiss at that time capable of bearing arms no higher than between fifty and sixty thousand. A surprising state of security for a short time followed these rigours; but similar causes soon reproduced similar effects.

Since the powerful duke of Burgundy, in his first collision with Swiss valour, had lost his treasures; in the second, the flower of his army; and in the third, his life, no enemy seemed any longer formidable: there was, accordingly, no end of provocations to war on the part of the Swiss.

Some timber had been felled by subjects of Milan, in a wood of the Val Levantina belonging to Uri; whereupon the youth of that canton instantly crossed the St. Gothard, and retaliated by robbery and ill treatment of the Milanese subjects in the neighbouring villages.

Uri, instead of inflicting condign chastisement on these young people, took them under her protection, proclaimed war on the Milanese, and applied for aid to the rest of the confederates. The latter saw the injustice of the proceeding, endeavoured to mediate, but at the same time were not willing to desert Uri in this emergency; they therefore despatched troops to act according to the circumstances.

On this the duke of Milan sent considerable forces under the command of count Borelli up the Ticino. At the village of Giornico lay the Swiss vanguard, consisting only of 600 men from Uri, Lucerne, Schwytz, and Zurich; the other confederates, nearly 10,000 strong, were as yet far behind. Borelli marched upon Giornico with a picked body of troops. It was mid-winter. The Swiss flooded the meadows in their front from the Ticino, and the surface freezing rapidly, they accoutred themselves with *skates*. As the Milanese cavalry and infantry advanced over the slippery field with difficulty, they were met by the Swiss, who sallied forth from Giornico firm on their feet; and, few as they were, were more than a match for the staggering ranks of the numerous enemy. Frischhans Theilig, the leader of Lucerne, was, with his good sword, the angel of death to the Milanese; 15,000 of whom fled panic-struck from 600 Swiss. This almost incredible victory spread the fame of the Swiss through all Italy: Milan purchased peace, paid indemnities, and consented that Uri should retain in fee for ever the Val Levantina, and the Val Brugiasco, on the tenure of paying annually a waxen taper three pounds in weight to the cathedral of Milan.

The results of the Burgundian war were very prejudicial to the internal connection of the cantons, and gave a powerful shock to their already imperfect union. Besides the jealousy entertained towards Berne by all the others, the rural cantons cherished a distrust of the towns: it seemed to them that the latter maintained a better understanding with Freyburg and Soleure than with them, and they complained of being postponed in

consideration and in influence. It could not be concealed
from them what enormous sums had flowed into the
towns from foreign sources : not less were they dissatis-
fied with the unequal division of plunder.

The towns of Soleure and Freyburg had stood stoutly
by the confederates in most of their wars, especially in
the late war against Burgundy : Berne took pains to
procure their admission into the confederacy. On the
other hand, the people of Uri, Schwytz, and Unterwalden,
offered strenuous resistance to the measure : they feared
lest the towns, which far surpassed them in mental cultivation, might in time become exclusive lords ascendant
in the confederacy. This jealousy induced them to resist
the augmentation of the number of the leading towns in
the league. On the other hand, the towns cherished suspicions of another kind with regard to the free rural
population. It was suspected that the people of the small
cantons aimed at establishing *equal freedom in all Switzerland;* and thus seducing the subjects of the towns to
throw off the dominion of the burghers, and erect an
administration of rural communes. This was a consummation not devoutly wished by the citizens : they had
acquired their subjects by purchase or by conquest, and
were determined to preserve what they called their rights
over them.

Thus arose reciprocal distrust in the confederacy ; and,
unfortunately, chance confirmed the suspicions of the
burghers. Peter of Halden, a stout old soldier, had
reasons of his own (besides those which he professed to
partake with the public) for discontent with the landvogt
of Entlibuch, and the lords of council at Lucerne. He
and his kinsman, the ex-landamman Heinrich, burgher
of Obwalden, and his brother-in-law Kühnegger, were
occasionally apt to wax warm in their cups on the subject of their country's degradation : they spirited each
other up at length to adventure a bold stroke in the town
on St. Leonard's day. The men of Obwalden were to
attend the feast in numbers : the avoyer, the council,
and the rest of their opponents, were to be summarily

despatched, and the fortifications pulled down. Lucerne was to be hereafter a petty village, and Entlibuch a free state. Such were the high-reaching views of the conclave. Unluckily the burghers of Lucerne became acquainted with them, as Peter had betrayed himself in his pot-valiance: he was arrested, confessed all, and was condemned to decapitation.

About the time of this insurrectionary episode, the confederates were holding a diet at Stántz, in the canton of Unterwalden: it was there that distrust and anger broke out openly amongst the cantons on the subject of division of the Burgundian booty, admission of the towns, &c. &c. The three democratic cantons uttered such threats against the towns, while the towns were so exasperated against the rural cantons, that the delegates of Soleure and Freyburg voluntarily and modestly refrained from the enforcement of their claims; and nothing less than an instant appeal to arms, and the total dissolution of the confederacy, appeared impending.

A pious hermit, Nicolas of the Flue, had lived in solitude many years in the district of Obwalden, absorbed in prayer and in holy contemplation. He was reverenced in the whole land on account of his devotion. It was said, that he had lived for many years without food, except his monthly partaking of the sacrament. He slept in a narrow cell upon hard boards, with a stone for his pillow; while his wife, who had brought him ten children, lived on their lands in the neighbouring valley. He had formerly served his country in the war of the Thurgau, with a high reputation for courage and humanity.

When this venerable man was made acquainted with the discord which prevailed among the confederates, he instantly left the hermitage for Stantz, and entered the hall where the diet was assembled. All rose from their seats to greet so unexpected an apparition. The solitary addressed the assembly with the dignity of a messenger from heaven, and admonished them to maintain peace and concord, in the name of that God who had given

so many victories to themselves, and to their fathers
before them. " You have become strong, he said, by the
force of union, and now will you sever that union for
the sake of a wretched booty ?   Far be it that surrounding lands should ever hear such things of you.
Let not the towns insist on claims injurious to the old
confederates.   Let the country places remember how
Soleure and Freyburg fought at their sides, and freely
receive them into the confederacy.   Beware of foreign
intrigues, confederates ! beware of internal discords !
Far be it from any to take gold as the price of their
father-land ! "

  " It is seldom," says an intelligent Swiss historian *,
" that truth comes off victorious in the conflict of passion, unless its assertor stand out as a being of other
mould from his hearers.   If he seems but a man like
the men around him, his words will be little heeded."
The solitary's strange and solemn warning found re-
sponsive chords in the hearts of the whole auditory.   In
a single hour the affairs at issue were settled.   Freyburg and Soleure were received into the confederacy.
The proposal of the venerable Nicolas, that territorial
conquests in war should be shared according to cantons,
but all other spoil, according to population, was acceded
to.   It was also resolved, that no one, without permission of the authorities, should assemble popular meetings, or make dangerous propositions.   If the people of
any canton offered resistance to their legal authorities,
the rest of the confederates should combine to bring them
back to obedience.

  The covenant of Stantz, under which title the decisions of this diet have come down to us, is remarkable
as the first solemn occasion on which the cantons collectively fixed and defined their federal constitution.   It
therefore presents a fitting opportunity to pause in our
narrative, in order to take a review of the Helvetic body
up to this period, in its principal points of political,
social, and military developement.

* Ludwig Meyer of Knonau.

The original idea of the confederation was that of a family, in which all possessed an equality of rights. Places of honour were given but for a short term: the burgomaster or avoyer (the highest rank in towns) might one year preside in the Helvetic diet, and vanish the next in the crowd of burghers, or sit as a common member of council. The whole body of burghers was assembled to name public officers, decide upon war and peace, and enact laws. It was, however, in the rural cantons only that this practice continued to exist. The increasing population, wars, and treaties of the towns, rendered the constant convocation of the body of burghers impossible, who, therefore, elected delegates to the councils; without, however, yielding the rights of sovereignty in the last resort.

The mode of procedure in all transactions was simple. If any thing seemed too weighty for the little council, the great one was convoked, which consisted of numerous popular delegates. In cases of dispute about the *meum* and *tuum*, or in which the honour or property of a burgher came in question, the judges (commonly members of council) sat in the open air on the highway. The accused and accuser could speak for themselves, or choose advocates from amongst the judges. In cases unprovided for by the laws, the court decided either according to precedent, or on principles of equity. All severities inflicted upon criminals were regarded as allowable and salutary. Torture was in general use; and any one would have been ridiculed who expressed a fear lest innocence might suffer. The pain of death was enhanced by all imaginable torments; such as nipping the flesh with red-hot pincers, trailing at the tail of a horse, or breaking on the wheel, as gentle preludes, or substitutes, to death by the means of fire, sword, or rope. Blasphemy, murder, robbery, and theft, were punished capitally: lesser offences with banishment, branding, slitting of ears, &c.

For security against attacks, whether from within or without, the several cantons joined themselves in a federal league, which regulated their relations to each other, and the amount of contribution incumbent on each for the common defence. The *Pfaffenbrief*, and that of Sempach, mention of which has already been made, were the only records of this league since the period of its first formation. The provisions made by the latter of these documents were ratified and extended by the covenant of Stantz. These regulations, prompted by the circumstances in which they were made, were intended to direct the efforts of all to one end, to limit the sphere of selfishness, and to curb reckless licentiousness. They might, perhaps, have answered their purpose, had simplicity and sincerity continued to be cherished in Switzerland, while the old confusion still prevailed throughout the rest of Europe; but they proved too weak against the inroads of moral corruption in the interior, and the general advance of civilisation in other countries.

The confederates still did homage to the emperor as their liege lord; but held themselves bound to little else than not to bear arms against him, and to obtain from him, as matter of form, the sanction of their liberties. Common interests were consulted upon at the diets of the confederation. The presiding canton, or any other in cases of emergency, called together the delegates of the rest of the Helvetic body, though it was not very clearly defined to whom belonged the right of sitting and voting. The inequality of rights amongst the confederates had an injurious effect on their deliberations, by keeping up a constant disposition to distrust and envy, and disadvantageous above all was the condition of the free bailiwicks.

The military skill of the confederates stood in the highest repute during the infancy of the art of war in Europe. Levies of men were made in the towns by guilds, in the country by communes and bailiwicks. Exceptions from service were rare, and only allowed on condition of finding substitutes: those who were unable to provide themselves with arms and food were supplied at the expense of their communes. The principal weapons were spears, halberds, arquebuses, and cross-bows. In addition to these, battle-axes and swords were considered necessary: knives and daggers came by degrees into use. The body was sheathed in armour; the head was covered with a helmet, or a strong felt hat, adorned with a cock's or ostrich feather. A white cross, stitched on several parts of the clothing, served as a badge, for which a key of the same colour was substituted in later times. The confederates had become familiar, not only with the use of guns, but also with that of pieces of heavy artillery. Their cavalry, such as it was, was formed by noblemen and church vassals.

The warriors of each canton, however scanty their number, took the field under a leader of their own, who, as well as the *Venner* (banner-bearer or banneret) was chosen by the government. The election of captains was trusted to the communes; twenty or thirty men formed a troop. The highest authority, after that of the general and banneret, was enjoyed by the commit-tees of the council and burghers, who formed the council of war with the above-mentioned officers. All matters of consequence were laid before the assembled troops, by whom the question of peace or war was often, in fact, decided, and who considered themselves invested with a power at least co-ordinate with that of the council and commonalty at home. The most express orders of the civil authorities often received the following laconic reply: " That a contrary decision had been formed by a majority of votes in the army."

A declaration of hostilities preceded the invasion. of an enemy's territory. The Swiss held it dishonourable to assail any one without having given him notice of their intentions; they knew not, or despised, the feints and manœuvres adapted to mislead the foe, or force him to give battle. Their troops were drawn up for action in close column, or in solid squares; after several ranks of spearmen came halberdiers; then again spearmen; in front or in flank arquebusiers; in the centre were the

M

banner and standard bearers. (It may here be observed, that the banner of a canton had more importance attached to it than an ordinary flag, which indeed might be inferred from the high rank in the army which, as we have already said, was held by its guardian.) The troops were exhorted to valour by their officers in the presence of the enemy, and then, having invoked on their knees, with outstretched arms, the aid of the Deity, they rushed with alternate animating cries upon the hostile ranks.

No prisoners were allowed to be made; none were allowed to retreat though wounded; each was ready to cut down his comrade, rather than see him take to flight. The Swiss regarded wounds and death so little, and obeyed the word of command with such precision, that the close mass of their combatants was moved with the utmost facility, sometimes forming a wedge, sometimes contracting, sometimes extending their lines. The Swiss did not distinguish themselves in the siege of fortified places. If they failed in the first onset, their zeal cooled with marvellous suddenness. They were better skilled to provide for the defence of their native country. For that end they collected munitions of war of all descriptions, barred the passes, announced the approach of the foe by beacons, shots, and alarums, and gathered all who could move so much as a stick on the point of danger.

The occupation most congenial to the temper of the free Swiss, next to that of a soldier, was that of a shepherd. In the pure air of their mountains, with their easy charge of cattle, the longest summer day seemed to pass rapidly. The more arduous toils of husbandry were comparatively neglected, no branch of trade or manufactures acquired leading importance, and the insecurity of the roads created serious impediments to the transport of commodities through Switzerland from Venice and elsewhere.

Though no description of privilege was acknowledged, yet a difference of ranks came to prevail. Those nobles who had settled in the towns, and who had sacrificed some advantages in order to secure the rest, maintained

in many respects a higher footing than the burghers.
Some were in possession of riches, others of experience
and knowledge of mankind, all had been from youth
upwards accustomed to the use of weapons. Beside this
old nobility, a new sprung up. Men who had enjoyed
a high reputation on account of their wealth, abilities,
or achievements, bequeathed consideration to their offspring. Their very name awakened advantageous reminiscences; their descendants were chosen willingly by
the people for its leaders, and had various means of
maintaining and augmenting their wealth and influence.
On the other hand, in families of a humbler grade, husbandry, the life of a shepherd, or some mechanical craft,
descended from generation to generation. But the different ranks were separated by no impassable chasm:
the knight of the empire did not shrink from mixing his
blood with that of the burghers, and hardly aimed at
higher polish of manners. If instances of collision sometimes occurred, they were seldom dangerous: the assumptions of the nobles were met not only with serious
checks, but with coarse and homely ridicule,—the most
formidable of all weapons in a state of society stamped
by familiarity and openness. The homely monosylla-
bles *thee* and *thou* remained in general use, and were
even employed by governments in their missives to their
functionaries. The burghers expressed their opinions
freely on all affairs of a public nature; and the highest
members of government might be seen at their doors on
fine evenings, exchanging greetings with all who passed,
hearing complaints, and imparting counsel.

But these traces of an earlier æra disappeared by degrees. Simplicity, sincerity, a sense of honour, and love
of country, daily became of more and more rare occurrence, until at length the all-engrossing thirst for gold
left no room for any other feeling. Indulgences were
relinquished with reluctance, to which the Swiss warrior
had accustomed himself in the course of his campaigns:
remembrance of past jollities, and disgust at present pri-
vations rendered his heart of easy access to temptation.

What could inspire those with dread, who feared neither death nor wounds — who valued protracted existence little, and only lived for the moment? War was
their watchword; war afforded full swing to their appetites; and decay of domestic happiness, neglect of
education, in short, universal disorder came in its train.

Those warriors who would while away the interval
between one campaign and another agreeably betook
themselves to Baden in Aargau. Here in a narrow
valley, where the Limmat flows through its rocky bed,
are hot springs of highly medicinal properties. Hither,
to the numerous houses of public entertainment, resorted
prelates, abbots, monks, nuns, soldiers, statesmen, and
all sorts of artificers. As in our fashionable watering
places, most of the visitors merely sought to dissipate
ennui, enjoy life, and pursue pleasure. The baths were
most crowded at an early hour in the morning, and
those who did not bathe resorted thither to see acquaintances, with whom they could hold conversation
from the galleries round the bath-rooms, while the
bathers played at various games, or ate from floating
tables. Lovely females did not disdain to sue for alms
from the gallery-loungers, who threw down coins of
small amount to enjoy the ensuing scramble. Flowers
were strewn on the surface of the water, and the vaulted
roof rang with music, vocal and instrumental. Towards
noon the company sallied forth to the meadows in the
neighbourhood, acquaintances were easily made, and
strangers soon became familiar. The pleasures of the
table were followed by jovial pledges in swift succession, till fife and drum summoned to the dance. Now
fell the last barriers of reserve and decorum; and it is
time to drop a veil over the scene.

But what horror seized the dissolute crowd when
intelligence suddenly reached them that the plague
was spreading its ravages over the land ! Instant flight to
the farthest mountain-recesses hardly baffled contagion;
youth and strength afforded no security; even love and
friendship yielded to the universal panic, and the sick

were left to die without consolation or attendance. The wrath of God was traced in this visitation; the churches filled with penitent and penance-performing sinners, and pilgrimages were made with all contrition and humility. Yet scarcely had the scourge ceased to be felt, when the old mode of life was resumed as eagerly as ever.

Notwithstanding the foregoing statements, Switzerland was perhaps less degraded than the other states of Europe; where the princes carried on warfare at discretion, over-ran the lands which they conquered, plundered the owners, and fired their dwellings; while even in peace the insecure state of the roads impeded intercourse. In most other states, the habits of the soldiers, chiefs, and clergy, were even more immoral than in Switzerland: public functions were venal; inhumanity was encouraged by the cruel inflictions visited upon criminals; and even palaces were disgraced by the most disgusting want of cleanliness.

CHAP. XI.

LEAGUE OF ST. GEORGE AND SWABIAN WAR.

1489—1501.

ADMINISTRATION, ARREST, AND DEATH OF HANS WALDMANN AT ZURICH. — COMPROMISE BETWEEN THE BURGHERS AND PEASANTRY. — PETTICOAT LEAGUE. — DIET AT WORMS.—FRENCH INTRIGUES AND INFLUENCE ON THE HELVETIC BODY. — CARELESSNESS OF THE LATTER WITH REGARD TO PAPAL BULLS AND THE PERSON OF THE EMPEROR. — ALTERCATIONS WITH THE IMPERIALISTS. — COMMENCEMENT OF THE SWABIAN WAR. — SUCCESSES OF THE SWISS AND THE GRISONS. — EMPEROR MAXIMILIAN ENTERS THE ENGADINES. — RETREATS INTO THE TYROL. — TREATY OF PEACE. — RECEPTION OF BASLE AND SCHAFFHAUSEN INTO ALLIANCE WITH THE CONFEDERACY.

THE transient restoration of concord could not restore the primitive moral habits of the people. Rapacity and ostentation flourished in the towns, corruption in all seats of civic authority, immorality and idleness in the people. Young men often marched in troops of hundreds and of thousands, headed by bands of music, over the Rhine and over the Alps, to follow royal standards in quest of booty or a grave. Nor was there any lack of fuel for their ardour. In one year, on the side of Italy, four wars were raging. Internal strife and uproar soon recommenced. The noble lords and priests of Zurich, who hated Waldmann the burgomaster, because he sought to impose bounds on their arrogance, inflamed the town and country people against him by their discourses. Hans Waldmann was the son of a peasant of Zug, and had come to Zurich first in the humble character of a tanner, had distinguished himself at Morat and at Nancy; and had at last attained to eminence by sheer force of courage and intellect. But it was now whispered against him, that he favoured Milan and Austria; and the Zurichers accused him of abuse of power through pride and passion. The burgomaster gave himself no concern about secret murmurs; and woe to those who dared to speak or act against him openly! When Theilig of Lucerne, the hero of Giornico, who had offended him, came into Zurich, bringing bales of cloth for sale, the burgomaster caused him to be taken into custody and beheaded, though his native town made urgent solicitations for the life of her illustrious citizen.

Such tyranny, notwithstanding his great qualities, brought universal hatred, and at length ruin, on Waldmann. His enemies took advantage of the tumults of the peasantry, and a revolt of the rural communes on the lake of Zurich. The country people advanced in arms up to the walls of the town, complaining of the injustice of the laws, and of other grievances. Delegates from the other cantons offered their mediation, and at length a proclamation was agreed upon by the council, that the complaints of the communes should be investigated, and satisfaction given to the people. But Waldmann, who thought fit to regard the honour of the town as being compromised by such a declaration,

caused the town-clerk to alter parts of the wording, as
if the country people had only alleged *supposed* grievances, and only obtained thus much by their humble
supplications, that those grievances should be looked
into on the first fit opportunity.

As soon as the falsification of this document became known, a new revolt took place against the town,
which, moreover, was disturbed in its interior. The
burgomaster no longer went out without armour, and
usually slept at the town hall. Authority is tottering
when it protects itself by any other panoply than the
popular attachment. The burgomaster Waldmann was
tumultuously arrested, put to the torture, and finally
decapitated, on the 6th of April, 1489.

On the day of his death, the subjects and authorities
of Zurich presented themselves as parties before the bar
of the confederacy, who brought about a permanent
agreement between them. It was enjoined upon the
peasantry, in the first place, to be faithful and obedient
to the great council of Zurich. On the other hand,
the privilege was granted them of bringing their commodities to what market they pleased, of exporting them
wherever they chose, of exercising arts and trades in
the villages, planting vines and purchasing lands at
pleasure, electing a sub-vogt in the lake-district, &c.
If at any time the town attempted to exercise a lawless
power on their subjects in the rural communes, the latter should send delegates to the diet of the confederacy,
that justice might be done to their complaints. This
instrument was signed on the 9th of May, 1489, for
the seven cantons of the confederacy, by their delegates.

New matter of mistrust occurred to revive the old
ill will subsisting between the confederates and Austria,
on the refusal of the former to join the new league of
St. George, otherwise called the Swabian, and derisively,
the Petticoat League, from a sort of kilt at that time
worn by the nobles, which, at a later period, came into

people, and   a time.

petticoat, in the sumptuary laws of Thurgau, dated 1530.
To this league the princes, counts, and knights of the
empire, and the towns of the Franconian, Swabian, and
Rhenish circles, acceded, partly of free will, partly on
compulsion.   Its ostensible object was to put an end to
the still existing system of club-law, and the prevalent
abuses of the right of self-defence.   Its secondary and
secret intent was to overawe the Bavarian dukes, and
other turbulent members of the empire, who made themselves obnoxious by opposing the will of the emperor, or
disturbing the tranquillity of their neighbours.   The
confederates, who clearly saw that a league of this description threatened themselves as well as others with
subjection, declined all accession to the compact.   These
considerations, however, did not prevent most of the free
imperial towns and trading corporations from joining the
new project of alliance, which held out hopes of increased security for trade and communication.   They
stigmatised those who refused concurrence as partisans
of anarchy.   " So frequently," says an eloquent Swiss
annalist, " does the love of freedom yield to the love of
profit!"

The grand diet of 1495, at Worms, where Maximilian
called for the aid of the empire against France and the
Turks, where private feuds were prohibited under pain
of the ban of the empire, and the court of the Imperial
Chamber erected for the general administration of justice,
was attended, indeed, by delegates from Switzerland;
but the proposal of taking 6000 Swiss into the pay of
the empire was without effect.   So were not the largesses
and intrigues of Bailli of Dijon, the indefatigable French
agent in Switzerland.   This man, who was familiarly
nicknamed *the Baillie*, explicitly declared to the Bernese
delegates, that if his purposes were thwarted by the few,
he should know how to effect them through the many.
To such a pitch may things come in a country, where
once foreign influence is permitted to establish itself.
More than 20,000 Swiss were soon under arms for France
in Lombardy.   Berne was so completely forced to tem-

porise with the French party, that she sent envoys to
welcome the troops returning from that service, depressed
as they were by the losses they had suffered, and dis-
figured by the loathsome aspect of many among their
number, who returned from Naples infected with a formidable malady, which was then supposed indigenous
in that city, and was naturalised too speedily all over
Europe.

Renewed demands of the empire on the confederates,
and renewed warnings against the intrigues of France,
remained equally ineffectual with all former ones; though
Berne was still devoted to the emperor, and exerted
herself vainly to prevent enlistments for France. The
pope was now called upon to support the imperial dignity
against all who should continue recusant; but, on mandates being issued by the papal legate at Lindau, which
threatened with excommunication all who should refuse
to quit the service of France, the confederates replied by
simply appealing to a better informed pope or to a general
council. The elector of Mentz, who acted as high-
chancellor of the empire, showing his pen to the Swiss
delegates, gave them to understand how serious evils
that little implement might draw upon their commonwealth. They replied, that what halberts had failed in
doing, goose-quills were not likely to do. And when
the emperor declared, that he himself, if they should
still refuse compliance, would stand foremost against
them, Conrad Schwend, the burgomaster of Zurich, returned for answer, " Our people are so ignorant and
rustic, that I fear they might not even spare the imperial
crown itself."

Though many who had joined the Swabian league
were discontented with it, and many feared the loss of
that degree of independence which had hitherto been preserved among the members of the empire, yet the number
of the foes of the Swiss confederacy increased in a still
greater proportion. Many powerful lords retained hereditary aversion to it. Many towns and subjects envied
its privileges, and many Germans were scandalised at

y. Cow-houses a...
appellations most commonly be...
...e Swiss and their country. " Spare me, spare
ear good bull-heads!" cried an unlucky Swabian whe...
made captive by the Swiss in the ensuing war; and his
curious cry for mercy having only procured him worse
treatment, he solemnly swore he had never heard any
other name applied to the Swiss. Numerous satirical
songs enhanced the mutual embitterment.

If the emperor and princes of the empire regarded
the confederates as rebels, the latter, on the other hand,
appealed to existing treaties; and to much that these
might not expressly contain they considered long possession as having given them a prescriptive right. During
the absence of the emperor in the Netherlands, his Ty-
rolese councillors, who distinguished themselves beyond
the rest in prompting the most arbitrary measures, resolved to delay hostilities no longer against the Grisons,
whom they viewed as the most recent revolters. About
the middle of January, 1499, they marched a force of
4000 men into the Munster-thal, on the border of the
Engadines. On this, Uri, and soon afterwards the six
other cantons, despatched reinforcements to the Grisons.

Berne still had hopes of preserving peace, and the
bishops of Constance and Coire effected an armistice.
But a series of provocations from the Austrians soon
brought about the commencement of that contest to
which history has given the name of the Swabian war,
without any declaration of hostilities. Meyenfeld was
given up by treachery to the enemy, who massacred the
garrison, and occupied the town and the neighbouring
mountain passes. Even before the reinforcements arrived
from the other cantons, the men of the Grisons carried
away the honour of the first victory, in which 400 of
the enemy were slain: the rest retreated into the castle
of Gertenberg.

The enemy marching from Constance had succeeded

in surprising the Swiss garrison of Emmatingen in their sleep, and killing seventy-three defenceless men in their beds. But they paid for it severely in the thickets of Schwaderloch, when 18,000 of them were routed by barely 2000 Swiss, so that they found the gates of Constance all too narrow to receive them in their flight, and reckoned a greater number of slain than there had been of Swiss arrayed against them.

A body of Swiss on the Upper Rhine marched into the Wallgau, where the enemy was entrenched near Frastenz, 14,000 strong. Heinrich Wolleb of Uri encouraged his men to disregard these odds against their own comparatively scanty numbers: they rushed under the roar of the artillery on the ranks of Austria, and strewed the plain with thousands of hostile corpses. The rest of the Austrians, panic-struck, made their escape through wood and water; " for then," says a native historian*, " every Swiss fought as if the victory depended on his single arm: for the glory of his country every one rushed with cheerful countenance on danger and death, and never counted the numbers of the enemy." The men of the Grisons fought with no less vigour, as was testified on the Malserheath, in the Tyrol, where 15,000 Austrians were attacked in their entrenchments, and completely routed, by a band of only 8000 men from the Grisons.

When the emperor Maximilian, in the Netherlands, heard of battles upon battles being lost by his armies, he addressed himself to the princes of the empire for aid against the Swiss boors, "in whom there was no virtue, noble blood, or moderation." Eager for revenge, he marched in person at the head of 15,000 men, to attempt once more the subjection of the Grisons. The inhabitants of the Engadines, with noble self-devotion, burned their huts, and retired into the mountains. They annoyed the enemy by rolling fragments of rock on them from the heights; and in two days' time the army was reduced to such a condition, as to be well pleased to effect its retreat back into the Tyrol, although not without considerable loss.

Peace was at length negotiated, and finally concluded, on the 22d of September, 1499. The emperor confirmed the confederates in the possession of their ancient rights and conquests, and ceded to them, besides, the jurisdiction over the Thurgau, which had hitherto been a privilege of the town of Constance. Thenceforward the emperors never again entertained the idea of attempting to dissolve the confederacy, or annexing its domains to the German empire.

" Thus ended," says a Swiss historian, " the last war of the old confederates in the cause of their own freedom and independence. They came out of the struggle in which they had defended their hereditary rights against the empire and the emperor more renowned, more respectable, than ever. But notwithstanding all the favours of fortune, which crowned confederate valour with its well-earned rewards, the period of this war has much matter of distressing meditation for the true friend of his country; who may draw from it too plain prognostications of the following universal tide of corruption."

The reception of the towns of Basle and Schaffhausen into a closer league with the cantons followed immediately on the Swabian war.

Basle, an ancient free town of the empire, distinguished by its advantageous site and growing magnitude, the seat of an university, of a bishopric, and an extensive trade, and the market of the whole surrounding region, had long adhered, without any positive compact, to the confederacy, and had often received its friendly aid in cases of emergency. During the Swabian war, the town was torn by intestine divisions. The burghers took the confederate, the nobility the Swabian, side; and both parties, openly and secretly, afforded every service in their power to their respective friends. The confederates hereupon marched into the district of Basle, made threatening demonstrations towards the town, and demanded to know whether they were to look upon its citizens as friends or as enemies. On this the nobles fled, and amused themselves, during their self-inflicted exile, in committing highway robberies on the merchants of their native town. The latter applied for aid to the confederates, who gladly embraced the occasion of forming a closer alliance with Basle, which was formed in 1501, to mutual satisfaction, though with some opposition from the rural population. There was never a more joyous day in Basle than that of her reception into the league of the confederacy. The magistrates rode in solemn procession to meet the Swiss delegates, who entered the town on the festival of its patron saint, the emperor Henry. The procession of the delegates, the council and the burghers, first visited the cathedral, and from thence, after attending the holy office, went to the corn-market. The treaty of alliance was here read from a scaffolding, and reciprocally sworn to by the contracting parties.

The flourishing town of Schaffhausen had been leagued with the confederacy more closely even than Basle since 1454, and had always shown unimpeachable fidelity. Its reasonable desire to become a member of the confederacy was therefore at length gratified in 1501. Thus was the league of the Thirteen Cantons completed nearly two centuries after the deed of William Tell. The Valais and the Grisons were also allied with the confederacy; and the free towns of St. Gall, Mühlhausen, and Rothweil in Swabia, were joined with it in a league of mutual defence.

CHAP. XII.

ITALIAN EXPEDITIONS.

1499—1522.

CORRUPTION OF THE HELVETIC BODY. — LOUIS XII. — LUDOVIC
SFORZA. — FRENCH OCCUPATION OF MILAN. — CLAIMS OF THE
CONFEDERATES ON THE MILANESE AND BELLINZONA.—ENLIST-
MENTS OF SFORZA IN SWITZERLAND. — OF LOUIS. — SFORZA
BETRAYED BY THE SWISS. — IMPRISONED BY THE FRENCH FOR
LIFE. — TREATY OF THE EMPEROR WITH THE CONFEDERACY.—
FRUSTRATED BY FRENCH INTRIGUES. — LEAGUE OF CAMBRAY.
—BATTLE OF AGNADELLO. — CHARACTER OF SCHINNER BISHOP
OF SION. — ALLIANCE AGAINST THE POPE BETWEEN THE
FRENCH KING AND THE EMPEROR. — HOLY LEAGUE AGAINST
FRANCE. — GASTON DE FOIX. — FRENCH EXPELLED FROM
ITALY BY THE POPE, SWISS, AND VENETIANS. — DUCHY OF
MILAN RECONQUERED BY THE FRENCH — WHO ARE DEFEATED
BY THE SWISS AT NOVARA. — EXPEDITION OF THE LATTER TO
DIJON. — PEACE WITH FRANCE. — FRANCIS I. INVADES PIED-
MONT. — BATTLE OF MARIGNANO. — PERPETUAL PEACE BE-
TWEEN FRANCE AND SWITZERLAND.

AFTER having viewed the Helvetic body in the first and
brightest epoch of its freedom, then engaged in civil and
intestine commotions, afterwards exalted to the pinnacle
of martial glory, and finally triumphant in its latest
struggle for independence, we have now to regard its
members in a state of rapid decay, selling their victorious
arms by auction to the highest bidder, and shamefully
staining their former fame for constancy and honour.
It is impossible to trace without a feeling of repugnance
the relations, whether foreign or domestic, in which
Switzerland was engaged during a period which, in spite
of martial achievements, must be deemed the most
deplorable and disgraceful of her history. Neither
honourable connections with foreign powers, nor salutary
arrangements in the interior, will henceforth yield the

materials of our narrative. It became the only object
of state policy in Switzerland to drive a lucrative traffic
with the blood of its inhabitants ; and though the article
must be acknowledged to have fetched a high price, it
is not the less a scandalous blot in the history of the
country, that so vile a trade should so long have remained
the only one pursued with any energy by the people and
its leaders. It is true, that the Helvetic seats of government were surrounded with more outward splendour
than ever. Ambassadors crowded thither from the emperor, from the pope, and from many other monarchs,
princes, nobles, and free towns, soliciting, with emulous
zeal, their friendship and alliance, and bidding against
each other for the iron arm of Switzerland, by offers of
absolution, special privileges, rich presents, large pensions, and high pay.

This state of things, which was looked upon by the
many as the very acmé of glory and prosperity, a few
regarded, on better grounds, as pregnant with the worst
evils ; for even a superficial view was enough to reveal
the misery which was ill disguised by tinsel decorations.
The social mischiefs generated by foreign bribes and
foreign service were so obvious, even at the very times
we are treating of, that the governments of the cantons
were compelled, however reluctantly, to issue repeated
prohibitions of pensions and enlistments, and to threaten
severe penalties against the transgressors. Unfortunately,
however, for the effect of these regulations, while the
members of successive diets raised their right hands in
solemn abjuration of the receipt of foreign pensions, the
left palm was secretly extended to receive them. This
melancholy period is delineated as follows in the energetic language of old Bullinger : — " In these times it
stood ill with the confederates, whom many princes and
lords solicited secretly and openly, proffering and pro-
mising moneys, and misleading simple people who had
heretofore known little of such dealings. Moreover,
the confederates were divided amongst themselves, —
some being for the papacy, some for France, and some

for the empire,—whereby the old simplicity and brotherly love were extinguished, and the bond of the confederacy loosened. A lewd and wanton life was commonly practised, with gluttony, gaming, dancing, and
all manner of wantonness, day and night, especially
where diets were held, as at Zurich, Lucerne, and Baden.
The common people in town and country were drawn
away from honest labour to idleness, lewdness, and warlike undertakings, — and reckless and abandoned habits
thus prevailed every where."

The king of France, Louis XII., and the duke of
Milan, Ludovic Sforza, surnamed Moro, or the Moor,
from his dark complexion, had co-operated zealously in
mediating peace between the confederates and the emperor ; not that either of them cared for the welfare of
Switzerland, but because they both stood in need of the
stout arms of the Swiss to combat with each other for
Milan, which the latter ruled *de facto,* while the former
set up claims to it. This was the second enterprise prepared by France against Italy ; but it differed from the
former, undertaken by Charles VIII., in being primarily
directed against Sforza (the very man whose alliance had
principally occasioned the Italian expedition of that monarch), and in pointing against that former friend of
France the arms of Italian powers which till then had
ranked with her enemies.* An alliance had been formed
against Sforza between the pope, the king of France, and
the republic of Venice, which made his position one of
extreme danger, and compelled him to take every means
for procuring the aid of Switzerland, which seemed to
afford his only hope of rescue. The confederates long
hesitated which side they should choose. The voice of
reason, urging to remain neutral, was heard in vain.
The majority maintained that the Swiss, the resources
of whose territory did not suffice to nourish all its
offspring, must of necessity seek foreign sources of revenue. These were alone to be found in foreign alliances; and the only point for careful consideration was

* See Sismondi, Rép. Ital. vol. xiii. c. 99.

from what quarter the greatest amount of profit was to
be looked for. Duke Sforza had already found the gold
of France an obstacle in the attainment of his views on
the confederates, and its magnetic influence once again
attracted the majority. Moreover Sforza, in 1496, had
refused recognition of the privileges acquired by the confederates in the Milanese, and when the Swabian war
broke out had assumed a hostile attitude towards them.
All this had very naturally estranged them from his
interests, and tended to frustrate his latter attempts to
engage them in his alliance. Louis, on the other hand,
spared neither gold nor promises, closed a defensive
alliance with them, aided them in the Swabian war, and
thus acquired the attachment of the great mass of the
people. Both princes commenced active preparations
for hostilities. No prohibitions, not even the threat of
capital punishment, could deter Swiss soldiers from de-
serting their country's service, and from going over to
that of France or Milan, even before the conclusion of
peace between Switzerland and the emperor.

Sforza's situation became more and more critical.
How, indeed, could he enter the lists, with any hope
of success, against the power of France and of her
warlike allies? He therefore hastened anxiously to cooperate in the conclusion of peace between Austria and
the confederates, in order to conciliate the latter by his
good offices, and acquire claims on their subsequent
assistance. But even before the close of that peace,
Milan was in the hands of France by the aid of a large
body of Swiss troops, who had engaged in the French
service in defiance of their governments. Sforza, who
was detested by his subjects, found himself abandoned
by all on the approach of the French army, and only
succeeded with difficulty in placing himself and his
treasures in safety, under the protection of the emperor.
In August, 1499, the French were in possession of the
whole duchy excepting the Valteline.

The confederates, on receiving the intelligence of these
events from Louis XII., immediately resolved to prohibit

all engagements in the service of Sforza, to send the
king an embassy of congratulation, to demand the restoration of their rights over the Milanese, as well as the
town and domain of Bellinzona for Uri, and to recall
to recollection the remaining arrears in the subsidies.
The confederates received friendly treatment and royal
largesses, but their claims were only answered with
empty words. This, with the indifferent treatment bestowed on the Swiss soldiers, alienated numbers from
France. Sforza gladly seized the opportunity of winning the confederates back to his interests. The diet
showed itself now disposed to listen to his proposals;
but even before he had time to make them, 5000 Swiss
had joined his standards, consisting principally of those
who had been ill treated by France. The duke advanced
rapidly upon Como, with these and other troops from
the Valais. The French had rendered the people of
Milan averse to them by their arrogance and utter contempt of discipline, and had reduced that people to long
for the return of their old master, whom they now found
infinite reasons for preferring to their new one. Popular revolts prepared the restoration of Sforza. With
the exception of a few fortified places, he reconquered
his whole duchy not less rapidly than he had lost it. He
was welcomed back with joyous acclamations into his
capital; reinforced his army, and advanced upon Novara, which surrendered, with the exception of the citadel.

It was not before Sforza had succeeded in regaining
the good will of the confederates, that Louis was aware
of the impending danger. He demanded instant aid
and reinforcements from the confederation. These were
promised, on condition that the subsidies in arrear were
paid, and that all legitimate claims of the confederates
were conceded. The envoys of Milan and Austria co-
operated with admirable skill against France. Sforza
in the mean time had reconquered Milan. In these
circumstances, Bailli of Dijon, whose merits have already
been alluded to as a member of the French embassy,

employed the only infallible expedient to arm the Swiss in the interests of France. He travelled from one place to another; distributed gold in handfuls; did not hesitate to gratify the most impudent demands; and by these methods, with or without consent of the cantonal governments, he had soon levied a force of 24,000 Swiss. Freyburg was selected for the place of rendezvous. The troops were soon in motion for Italy, joined the French army, marched upon Novara, and for the first time, Swiss stood against Swiss in the pay of foreigners.

The news of the advance of this army had reached Sforza; but relying on the promises of the diet, he refused to believe it, and rejected the advice of his more clear-sighted Swiss officers to fall back upon Milan, where men and money, provisions, fortifications, in a word, all the requisites for withstanding the French, lay at his disposal. In the mean time, a diet at Lucerne decided that the Swiss engaged on both sides should be ordered home, and resolved, besides, to offer its mediation to the belligerent powers; but all was already decided before the arrival of its delegates. The overwhelming force of France had shut up the duke in Novara; and the castle was, moreover, in their hands. These material advantages were, besides, aided by treachery. The Swiss officers on both sides came to a secret understanding. Many deserted from the duke; a few, perhaps, prompted by indisposition to fight against their countrymen, but most from a more tender care for their gold and for their booty. Those who remained clamoured for their pay, raised disturbances, and threatened to disband and return to their homes. The duke was in a manner constrained to a vigorous resolution by the greatness and the imminence of his danger. He resolved to cut his way through the besieging force to Milan; marched his troops out, and charged with his cavalry. At this critical moment, the Swiss in his service wheeled round, declaring that they would not fight against their countrymen in the French army. This movement decided the fate of Sforza. The

Swiss, without his consent or knowledge, treated with the French, and stipulated free egress for all except the duke and several Milanese nobles. The only point they yielded to the entreaties of their betrayed employer was the permission to accompany their march in disguise. He joined their ranks accordingly in the garb of a common soldier, or, by the account of some authors[*], of a Cordelier monk, but was betrayed by Rudolph Turmann, a native of Uri, and languished out the remainder of his days in a French dungeon. His mercenary Swiss, on their return to their country, were received as the reports which had preceded them well warranted: not only had they entered foreign service at a moment when their country was endangered by a war not yet concluded, but they had taken gold from both sides at once, had deserted from the one to the other, and had robbed foreign merchants within the peaceful borders of Switzerland. Strict investigation and severe animadversion were enjoined by the diet on the several cantons. Some of the delinquents in effect were punished; but illicit enlistments were too closely connected with the pensions and emoluments of leading men to allow that results of any great consequence should ensue. Rudolph Turmann, whose offence was at least one of the most flagrant, was executed at Uri by way of atonement for the common guilt.

The Swiss reputation for valour and rapacity had become diffused so widely by their mercenary victories, that their services were sure to be solicited wherever martial work was on hand; but all other demands were disregarded, so soon as the rival powers of France and Austria entered the field. France, indeed, had played them false on many former occasions, yet France continued still the general favourite, through her well-timed liberality in pecuniary largesses. On the other hand, the recent reminiscences of the Swabian war had revived the old distrust against Austria; yet the emperor, too,

---

[*] Mémoires de Louis de La Tremouille, cited by Sismondi, Hist. des Rep. Italiennes, tom. xiii. p. 64.

had many friends in Switzerland, whom he partly owed
to political considerations, and partly to the slights and
affronts of France. In 1501 the rival potentates took
the field against each other; and both renewed their
active applications to the confederates. Maximilian
claimed their escort, as members of the holy Roman
empire, in his coronation-progress to Rome, and justified
the Italian nickname bestowed on him of *Massimiliano
pochi denari*, by humbling himself so far as to offer
mortgages of part of his land as securities for the pensions which he promised them. This roused the competition of the French, who were secure of winning the
day with Swiss cupidity, as the envoys of Maximilian
could only plead their cause in words and writings,
while those of France employed the stronger rhetoric of
ready money. In November, 1505, the existing prohibitions against pensions were repealed; and the council
and burghers of Berne were released on the authority of
the bishop of Lausanne, from the obligation of the oaths
which they had taken on that subject. Nor did the
diets affect much longer hesitation, when Louis desired
leave to levy 4000 men under the titles of a body-
guard and guard of honour. The labour-loathing youth
of the cantons flocked in numbers to meet the summons: 8000 were enlisted by the French, — many rejected. It was not until the actual march of the
troops that the affair seemed to inspire the diet with
scruples. The new recruits were accordingly ordered
not to cross the Po. But the French dollars spoke to
their apprehensions more conclusively than any declaration of the diet: they crossed the Po; assisted in the
conquest of Genoa, and were shortly after dismissed by
the king with abundance of pay and flattery. Louis
returned triumphantly through Milan into France.

Maximilian was divided between anger and apprehension, when he found that the confederates had attached
themselves to his enemy. Yet he did not despair of
ultimate success in his designs. He convoked a solemn
diet at Constance in 1507, at which delegates from Swit-

zerland attended, and were received with high honours
and rich presents. They acceded to the decisions of the
diet, and promised to escort the emperor's Roman expedition with a body of 6000 men; providing only'that
nothing should be undertaken hostile to France. Maximilian exhausted his store of flatteries and favours to
secure the duration of these good dispositions.   On the
return of the Swiss delegates from Constance, the cantons confirmed the treaty with the emperor; but French
intrigues soon changed the aspect of affairs. The French
ambassador, Rocquebertin, kept open house in Zurich,
and was friendly and accessible to all comers. In Baden,
where crowds of military adventurers and easy fair ones
assembled, rather for pleasure than for health, he often
paid the score for whole parties, and threw gold into the
baths, and among the women.   His colleague, Pierre-
Louis, acted the same part at Lucerne as he had done
at Zurich and Baden.   The effects of this expenditure
were to render the confederates more and more lukewarm
in the service of the emperor; and every successive
meeting of the diet subtracted from the number of the
promised escort.   The disposition to fulfil their recent
engagements had entirely disappeared in most places;
but Uri, Schwytz, and Unterwalden, still offered their
services, and promised to send 8000 men to support the
imperial army.   Parties became more and more heated,
and threatened to produce a civil war.   It came under
discussion at the diet by what means this calamity could
be averted; and several of the cantonal governments
found themselves compelled to make regulations against
the proceedings of the French embassy.   Happily for
the peace of the confederacy, the ardour of the Germans
cooled along with their own; and the Roman expedition was abandoned.

To retrieve the ill success of this abortive undertaking,
and to revenge himself on Venice for having contributed
to its failure, Maximilian eagerly caught at the scheme
for the ruin of that republic contained in the so called
League of Cambray of 1508, planned by pope Julius II.,

in alliance with France and Spain, for the partition of the Venetian territory. To this alliance also acceded Savoy, Ferrara, and Mantua. It was whispered that the league was directed not only against Venice, but against free commonwealths in general, and would consequently endanger the confederates. This apprehension for once procured a hearing to the warnings of the true friends of their country. Strong measures were proposed against enlistments ; but as soon as the tempting dollars tinkled, the drums beat, and the flags waved, —all was forgotten,—and numerous bands of confederates rushed into the field. An embassy from Venice arrived too late in Switzerland, for the purpose of directing the attention of the diet to the common danger, and effecting between the two republics a useful and sincere alliance. Already, on the 14th May, the French, supported by 6000 confederates, had won the battle of Agnadello over the Venetians, which would have assuredly sealed the doom of the latter, if the jealousy and disunion of the allies, and especially the altered views of the pope, had not rescued from ruin the then mistress of the seas. After the battle of Agnadello, Julius II. began to apprehend the preponderance of the French, whom he hated ; and his rancour against Venice yielded at length to more cool-blooded political calculations. Accordingly, he made overtures to the latter, and did every thing in his power to break the league, and, if possible, to arm most of its members against France. His views were chiefly directed towards the confederacy. His confidential counsellor, Matthew Schinner, bishop of Sion, entered Switzerland with a good store of gold and absolutions ; and on the 13th March, 1510, a league *"for the defence of the church"* was closed betwixt the pope and the cantons ; the confederates engaging to supply 6000 men, while the holy father pledged himself to the distribution of various ghostly and worldly benefactions.

The extraordinary man who brought this alliance to pass, who impressed thereby a direction altogether unexpected on the whole political system of the confederates, and became thenceforwards the soul of all their enterprises against France, claims our attention on account of the influence exercised for a considerable time by him on the destiny of Switzerland. His parents were of humble station in Mühlebach, in the Upper Valais. His destiny brought him in contact during boyhood with an old priest, who knew how to excite his pupil's soul to high endeavours. Schinner gained distinction as a scholar at Zurich and Como, by assiduity and versatile talent. He exhibited an early predilection for the study of the ancient Roman writers; his pittance was devoted to the purchase of their works, for which he willingly paid the price of every convenience, and almost every necessary of life. His learning, spirit, and eloquence, combined with his ascetic mode of life and rigid morality, attracted great attention to his preaching, while he was yet only a parish priest in the Valais. The bishop remarked him, and favoured his rise, which soon became so rapid, that in 1500 he himself obtained the episcopal office, and with it a sphere commensurate to his activity and ambition. From thenceforward his hand might be traced in all affairs of importance. His energy in word and act, his overpowering eloquence, his intrepid zeal in the cause of his native country, his immovable fidelity to the papal court, together with his bitter hatred of France, excited and enabled him to arm all Europe against that power, and to spread his own renown throughout the civilised world. He possessed, in a high degree, the art of veiling his acute views with the semblance of extreme simplicity; had friends and connections every where; and was initiated thoroughly into all the deepest mysteries of statecraft, so as to give colour and countenance to the popular superstition, that a familiar demon disclosed to him whatever was hidden from others. Most means appeared legitimate to him in furtherance of his ends; but all became allowable when the object was to gratify his hatred of France. It was sympathy in this point which procured for him the confidence of the similarly disposed Julius II.; and the services which he rendered towards the gratifying of that pontiff's resentments, and his own, procured his nomination to the dignity of cardinal.

The ten years' alliance which Louis had closed with the confederacy in 1499, came to a conclusion, without either of the contracting parties showing any desire to renew it. France stood on the most amicable footing with the emperor, and in the most favourable situation with regard to all other powers; so that Louis thought himself able to do without the purchase of Swiss blood. He was besides induced, by ill-timed motives of parsimony, to prefer the cheaper services of the Landsknechts; and he thought himself sure, in any case of emergency, of obtaining as many Swiss as he chose, without consent of their governments. The cantons were as little disposed as the king to protract the alliance. As soon as the French had gained their own purposes, they had treated the confederates with their customary insolence. After the victory of Agnadello, to the gaining of which Swiss soldiers had so powerfully contributed, they were dismissed from the French army without their pay, and loaded with insults. Louis himself, when the confederates, in the course of negotiation, demanded higher pensions in return for their services, is said to have replied, that he was not accustomed to let mountain-boors like them prescribe laws to him. He proceeded to connect himself more closely with Maximilian; and the two princes resolved to attack the pope, and to deprive him of his spiritual and secular prerogatives; of the former by a council of the church convened at Pisa, of the latter by the force of arms. The first scheme was frustrated by Julius, who thundered his anathemas on the council of Pisa, and convoked an opposition-council at Rome. The former body, moreover, was compelled by a popular revolt to fly to Milan. The secular arms of the royal allies had, however, better fortune. The papal army was soon driven back on all points; and Rome

would, in all probability, have fallen into the hands of
Louis, if some inexplicable scruple had not withheld him
from desecrating by military violence the residence of
God's vicegerent on earth. The French army fell
back again upon Milan; and its departure relieved the
pope from a severe illness, the effect of disappointment
and anxiety.

It was not, however, long before Julius contrived to
engage Spain, England, and Venice in the so called holy
league against France; even Maximilian wavered, and
his ambassadors secretly hinted at the diet of the confederacy, that if the latter meditated any attack on
France, they need not be deterred by fear of hostilities
from the emperor. At the same time Maximilian
showed himself willing to recall the German Landsknechts from the French service. But Louis did not
let himself be intimidated. Troops of Germans, Italians,
even of Swiss, joined his army; and the excellence of
his general Gaston de Foix, duke of Nemours, seemed
to offer a secure guarantee of victory. Events for
a while justified his confidence. In February and April,
1512, Gaston forced the combined papal and Spanish
army to raise the siege of Bologna; from thence marched
upon Brescia, routed the Venetians; and on the 11th of
April won a no less bloody than brilliant victory over
Spain and the pope, in the neighbourhood of Ravenna.
The day was dearly bought by the young hero with the
sacrifice of his life and the flower of his army. With
him expired the fortune of France in Italy.

From the extremity of danger which again menaced
the holy father, he saw himself unexpectedly saved by
the aid of the confederacy. King Louis had attempted
to renew his connection with the latter, and the itching
felt by many a palm for the touch of French dollars
augured a favourable issue to his overtures: but the
high demands of the Swiss deterred the frugal mind of
the monarch, and after the victory of Ravenna the
French broke off all negotiations. This was highly advantageous to the cause of the pope. A Swiss embassy

negotiated with cardinal Schinner at Venice, while at Zurich the papal legate, Philomardo bishop of Veroli, distributed plenary absolutions, plentiful blessings, and some little of the gold which he had previously collected from the Swiss for the remission of their sins. The Swiss embassy at Venice was completely gained by the courtesies of the Venetians and the cunning of Schinner. On one occasion the cardinal surprised them with two sumptuous presents made them by the pope, consisting of a red silk hat with rich trimming, and decorated with gold and pearl embroidery representing the descent of the Holy Ghost in the shape of a dove, and a golden sword in a sheath of gilded copper, of which the hilt was adorned in like manner with pearls. The value of these presents was enhanced by the cardinal's exposition of their mystic meaning, and of the privileges annexed to them by the hand of the holy father. The over-joyed ambassadors returned home; and though many places broke with France unwillingly, war was at length decided on by the diet.

In May, 1512, a force of 20,000 confederates assembled at Coire, under the command of Ulrich von Hohen Sax, the experienced leader of Zurich. The Grisons, too, who considered their alliance with France as dissolved by acts of violence and injustice on her part, and their old league with the confederates as more binding, joined their party. Their combined forces marched on Verona, and the town was deserted by the French. On the 30th of May, they began their march from Verona, and effected a junction with the Venetians at Villafranca. From thence their march resembled an uninterrupted triumphal procession, and overflowed with plunder and pleasure. The already inadequate forces of the French, which besides were daily weakened by the emperor's recall of the Landsknechts, abandoned even fortified towns without attempting serious resistance. On the approach of the confederates to Milan, the fathers of the Pisan church assembly, who had betaken themselves thither, and who had just deposed the pope from all his spiritual and secular dignities, were the first to seek their safety in flight. A popular insurrection, marked by horrible atrocities, wrested this metropolis from the French. Important troubles also took place in Genoa and other towns. At Pavia the French army vainly attempted some defence. From thence it fled in disorder over the mountains. The king retained in the whole of Italy hardly any other place than the fortresses of Milan and Cremona. At the former place the confederates pulled down the splendid monument of the hero of Ravenna, and even dragged his corpse from the grave, that one who had been anathematised by the pope might not rest in consecrated ground.

After the expulsion of the French, disputes arose betwixt the Swiss, the confederates, and the cardinal, with regard to the allotment of their conquests. The Venetians decamped in one night unexpectedly, and without any previous notice. Disorders threatened to break out in the Swiss army; and at length it was resolved to return home, well paid and enriched as they were with plunder. The pope rewarded the seasonable aid of the confederates, by bestowing on them the title of " Defenders of the Freedom of the Christian Church," and solicited an embassy to be sent to Rome from the diet; in order, as he pretended, that his trusty and beloved sons might take a part in all affairs of importance, but in truth that he might entrap them more completely by means of pensions, flatteries, and presents, and show the whole world how devoted to him was the valiant and formidable Helvetic body.

Now came the important question, into whose hands the conquered duchy of Milan should be delivered. This query could not possibly be indifferent to any of the allied powers—least of all, perhaps, to the confederates, whose trade must be in some degree dependent on the favour or disfavour of the ruler of Milan. The Milanese themselves wished for the son of their late ruler, the expelled Ludovico Moro. This choice pleased the pope, as coinciding with his plan for purging Italy entirely from foreigners. It also pleased the confederates, who wished for a prince in Milan not powerful enough to do without their friendship and alliance. The emperor and Spain, on the other hand, hoped to see the ducal crown on the head of a younger branch of the imperial family. At an assembly in Mantua, the pope and the confederates carried the day; and it was resolved to invest with the dukedom Maximilian, the eldest son of Ludovico Moro. The confederates fixed their relations with the new ruler by formal deeds.

Apparent quiet was now restored in Italy; and it was thought that Louis, embarrassed as he was from all quarters, would be compelled to abandon hope of reconquering Milan. But a new and fearful conflagration soon blazed up from the embers. The country wasted, impoverished, and depopulated by the consequences of war, depredations, and banishments, had expected of the new government cures for its many and deep wounds. The easy-natured prince gave ear to the wishes of his subjects, and formed the most benevolent intentions; but his womanish weakness allowed him to put nothing in execution; and what little good might have issued from his irresolute and powerless hands was intercepted by the rapacity of the imperial, papal, and Swiss embassies. Hence arose a wish for the return of the French, who had subjected the people to less grinding oppression. This change of sentiments did not escape the penetration of those who were its principal objects. They had still retained connections in the Milanese, and only watched a favourable moment to re-enter into possession of the land. That moment seemed to have come; for they succeeded in opening negotiations with the Swiss,— and the king expected great effects from the tried power of his gold. But an offended people is not so easily reconciled. Before the French embassy could even obtain its safe conduct, certain sums were to be paid, the castles of Lugano and Locarno evacuated, and solemn

engagements taken to make no secret levies.   The conditions imposed by the Swiss during the course of
negotiation, and especially the entire renunciation of
Milan and Asti, appeared to the king so rigorous and
unbearable, that the whole transaction failed, as neither
promises nor even bribes could bend the determination
of the confederates.   Though there were many who
preferred the French crowns and fat pensions to the
consecrated banners, hats, and swords of the pope, his
copious benedictions, and his frugal gifts; yet ill will
against France was so prevalent, and Schinner employed
alternately words and gold with such dexterity, that the
French embassy not only were very roughly treated,
but, their intrigues having exposed them to suspicion,
were threatened with immediate dismissal.

The death of Julius II. seemed to open better pros-
pects for France; which soon disappeared, when cardinal
John of Medicis, who had just escaped from French
captivity, succeeded to the papal chair by the name of
Leo X. On the other hand, the king succeeded in
forming a close alliance with the Venetians, who had
felt themselves affronted by the allies.   The disunion
of the confederates, the defenceless state of the duchy,
and the possession of the fortresses of Milan and Cremona, seemed to ensure success to any new attempt on
the part of France.   Sixteen thousand picked troops,
with a band of traitorous Swiss, were collected under
the most eminent French generals, and directed their
march across the mountains towards Asti.   Ten thousand Venetians, under command of count Alviano,
moved on Verona, and captured several places.   A revolt in favour of France took place in Genoa.   Duke
Maximilian, on the other hand, with neither men nor
money, was surrounded by a disaffected people, and was
within the range of the French artillery, even in his
own palace.   His position was by no means enviable,
though 4000 confederates had already joined him, and
more numerous forces were expected.   He found himself betrayed by one of his generals; his city of Milan

opened its gates to the French; and the rest of the country soon followed the example set by the capital. Novara and Como only preserved their allegiance to the duke. Into the former of these towns Maximilian threw himself, with the Swiss in his pay, and a few hundred Lombard horsemen, and was soon blockaded there by the French army. He looked forward to a fate like that of his father, who, thirteen years before, in the same circumstances, had been betrayed by the same confederates in whose hands his destiny now lay. The hostile leaders confidently anticipated the same issue. But the fidelity of the Swiss for once deceived their expectations. In vain the French heaped promises upon promises ; the only reply was a sally from the garrison. In vain the French artillery battered down the fortifications; the resolution of the Swiss was so far from wavering, that the gates of Novara were constantly kept open in defiance. On the second day, when the garrison was reduced to the last extremity, the enemy's discharges unexpectedly ceased. The French had raised the siege with precipitation, on intelligence of the approach of a Swiss army, which, however, was detained on its advance by many difficulties. At length the main body was collected at Arona, and waited there three days for the rest. On their non-arrival, it was finally resolved to advance and provoke an engagement. The French were not to be found before Novara, but had formed an encampment half a league from the town. Their great superiority, not only in number, but in cavalry, artillery, and in the advantage of their position, might have dissuaded the confederates from attacking them until their whole number should have come up ; but they nevertheless resolved to engage.

Before daybreak on the 13th of June, the Swiss army, 9000 strong, made its onset. Each single discharge of the French artillery stretched on the ground fifty or sixty of the assailants, who pressed forward in close column. Nothing, however, could stop them ; and it soon came to a conflict between man and man, with knives and daggers. The French cavalry had long kept off attacks in flank, and even fallen on the rear of the confederates. Every thing yielded at length to the obstinate courage of the Swiss. In five hours they had gained a complete victory, and covered the field with 8000 of the enemy; but their triumph was bought with the blood of 1500 of their countrymen. The remaining divisions came up on the same evening and the following morning. Plunder and forced contributions in Piedmont, Montferrat, and Saluzzo, indemnified the victors for outstanding arrears of pay.

In order to give the people new occupation, and in compliance with the emperor's summons, the confederates now undertook an expedition into France. Against that power, an alliance which had been formed between the emperor, pope Leo X., Ferdinand of Arragon, and England, and which called itself by the name of the Holy League, already had commenced open hostilities. Ostensibly, this league was only formed against the Turks; but France was aimed at also by it, in a manner not to be mistaken. The act of adhesion, subscribed by the confederates and the duke of Milan, stated the holy league to have been closed against tyrants, the Turks, and specially for the defence of the Italian nation. Its duration was fixed for the lifetime of the high contracting parties.

The emperor sent artillery and cavalry under the command of duke Ulrich of Würtemburg, with whom several of the cantons were in alliance. The combined forces appeared before Dijon in September, 30,000 strong instead of 16,000, the number which had been called out by the diet. The French general La Tremouille could hardly gather 6000 men round him, and panic unpeopled the open plains of France; but the Swiss force, although adequate to the greatest undertakings, was, at the moment, without guidance or order. So early as the 13th of September, a peace was effected in spite of the duke of Würtemburg's remonstrances, through flatteries, insinuations with regard to the views of the emperor, and the most seductive assurances of all kinds. The king was to concede whatever belonged to the pope, the duke of Milan, or the emperor, and give up the castles of Milan, Cremona, and Asti to the confederates. Four hundred thousand crowns should be paid to the latter; half within eighteen days, the other moiety before the 11th of November. Conditions were also made in behalf of duke Ulrich and his followers. Four splendidly clothed hostages remained with them as securities, and the army returned homewards as if beaten out of the field.

It was soon perceived that the king had no intention of confirming this treaty. The only man of importance among the hostages escaped from an inn at Zurich, where he ought to have been carefully watched. The proposal made by several men of honour and courage, immediately to renew the invasion of France, was frustrated by the party in the French interest, which now began to raise its head anew. The duke of Milan more and more betrayed his incapacity, and excited discontent among his protectors: nothing, however, at last remained for him but deference to their will, and avoidance of whatever might displease them.

Through the pope, who was playing fast and loose with the confederates, king Louis now sought to renew his friendship with them; but he did not succeed, as he would not renounce his pretensions upon Milan. On the other hand, though well aware of the faithlessness of Leo, they renewed with him the league which they had formed with his predecessor.

On the death of Louis XII., Francis I., his successor, proposed terms of alliance to his " dear and honoured friends" the Swiss. The bearer of these was reprimanded for coming without having made previous application for safe-conduct; and the only answer vouchsafed to him was, that peace had already been closed at Dijon. But the youthful monarch was not to be diverted from his purpose; and the delegates of his uncle the duke of Savoy employed every possible means, at suc-

cessive diets, to gain the Swiss over to his interests without renunciation of Milan. All was in vain; and the
efforts made to turn their distrust towards other powers
only confirmed its direction against France. The French
had in the mean time occupied Genoa; and pope Leo,
in whose policy the interest of the house of Medicis took
precedence of all other considerations, prevented the
confederates from anticipating their movements. Maximilian Sforza, whom the great preparations of the new
ruler of France had filled with anxiety, renewed his
applications to the confederacy, who sent him 24,000
regular troops in three divisions, who were followed by
6000 volunteers. There was but little union or discipline in this army; yet it obeyed the decree of the diet
for occupation of the mountain passes, marched towards
Piedmont under Prosper Colonna, an experienced Milanese general, and took up a position between Susa and
Saluzzo. Unexpectedly the French army appeared in
the district of Coni, accompanied by an hitherto unprecedented force of 20,000 Landsknechts, and by the then
notorious black band of Gueldres, and furnished with
eighty pieces of artillery. Colonna was surprised at
Villafranca by the French, before the bulk of the Swiss
force could come up to his assistance: moreover the
inaction of the emperor inspired distrust, and retreat
was at length decided on. The men of Berne, Freiburg,
and Soleure, marched homewards through Arona; the
troops of the other cantons, and the volunteers, towards
Milan: the heavy artillery was carelessly left at Novara.

The cantons, in the meanwhile, with the exception of
Uri, Schwytz, and Glarus, were engaged in negotiation
with French envoys; and though the proposals of the
latter were less advantageous than might have been looked
for from the duke of Savoy's assurances, yet terms of
peace were finally agreed between the parties. Immediately on its conclusion, that division of the Swiss troops
which had reached Arona, accompanied by the Valaisans,
pursued its march homewards; but the Bernese volunteers, and the Argovian reinforcements, remained behind

with the rest of the Swiss army. They were now upon
the point of disbanding, when, on Schinner's persuasion,
the body-guard of the duke, and part of the Swiss troops,
provoked an action with the French in the vicinity of
Marignano. Schinner soon succeeded in moving the rest
to support their countrymen; and the French army
double the Swiss in numbers, found itself unexpectedly
attacked in its strong position, protected by sixty-four
pieces of heavy artillery, a deep trench, hedges, and
walled enclosures. Regardless of the fearful execution
done by the cannon, the Swiss pressed forwards, and
soon compelled the black band to retreat; every thing
gave way before them: the king fought in the murderous *mêlée*, surrounded by his nobles; and nothing but
darkness put an end to the struggle. The French leaders
employed the night in recovering their order. Early on
the 14th, the main body of Swiss renewed their onset,
with Uri and Zurich at their head; and the French at
least sold their lives dear to their antagonists, who rushed
upon them under the well-pointed fire of their guns.
But the fortune of the day was reversed about noon by
the Venetians, who fell upon the rear of the Swiss, already exhausted by this *battle of the giants* (as it was
called by the old general Trivulcio). Nevertheless the
latter repulsed the first charge; but the obstinacy of the
new assailants at length decided the victory. The confederates, compelled at length to yield to the unwonted
necessity of retreat, retired slowly, carrying off as many
as possible of their wounded, as well as the guns, standards, and horses captured from the enemy. The Swiss
had lost from six to seven thousand men, and neither
prayers nor promises could keep them in Milan, whither
they had betaken themselves at first: they hastened homewards, without any great anxiety being exhibited by the
enemy to pursue them. And thus ended the last expedition on Lombardy undertaken by the confederates in
their own name and in that of their country.

The king of France, astounded by a victory which
rather wore the aspect of a defeat, closed the so called

perpetual peace with the confederacy in the following year; a treaty which did justice to its title by a duration almost uninterrupted for three centuries, and formed the basis of all subsequent negotiations between the Swiss cantons and the kings of France. Francis was thus enabled to hire the aid of the confederates against the emperor, the pope, and the duke of Milan; and their soldiers bled in his service for some years without success or advantage to their country, unless we should except an invitation to Paris in the quality of godfathers to his new-born son. On this occasion every canton sent a delegate thither, each with a baptismal present of fifty ducats. A present on which Francis set a higher value was that of 16,000 Swiss soldiers, who were sent to aid his Italian expeditions: but when 3000 of these troops had fallen at Bicocca; and when, out of 15,000 others who had marched into Lombardy, hardly 4000 ever returned, the taste for such expeditions became by degrees less general in Switzerland.

CHAP. XIII.

ÆRA OF THE REFORMATION.

1519—1531.

GENERAL RESULTS OF THE ITALIAN EXPEDITIONS. — CORRUPTIONS
OF THE CATHOLIC CHURCH. — CASE OF JETZER. — LEO X.
EXTENDS THE SALE OF INDULGENCES. — SENDS AN APOSTOLICAL
COMMISSIONER INTO SWITZERLAND. — ULRICH ZWINGLI
APPOINTED PREACHER AT ZURICH. — RESOLUTION AGAINST
COURTISANS. — FIRST DISPUTATION OF BADEN. — COUNCIL OF
ZURICH. — ITS REFORMS OPPOSED BY THE OTHER CANTONS —
ANABAPTISTS — AND OTHER SECTARIES. — LEVIES OF TROOPS
IN SWITZERLAND BY FRANCIS I. — BATTLE OF PAVIA. — CAP-
TURE OF THE FRENCH KING OCCASIONS CONSTERNATION IN
SWITZERLAND. — SECOND DISPUTATION AT BADEN. — CAUSE
OF REFORM ESPOUSED BY BERNE. — THOMAS MURNER. — ANA-
BAPTIST EXCESSES. — IMBITTERMENT OF RELIGIOUS PARTIES
— CHRISTIAN LEAGUE. — ATTACK ON CAPPEL. — DEATH OF
ZWINGLI.

THE Italian expeditions had for some time contributed
to maintain the Swiss military character; but by degrees
it became evident, that the changes in the art of war
attendant on the general use of fire-arms, and on the decline of the heavy cavalry of the middle ages, had placed
other nations in possession of an infantry not inferior to
their own.   The rays of power, refracted from two centuries of victory, could not linger very long after the loss
of real pre-eminence.   The latter campaigns in Italy had
not tended to retrieve the consideration of foreigners,
whose faith, if not in the courage, at least in the conduct
of the dreaded mountaineers, was at length completely
shaken.   Through the effects of these campaigns, too,
the character of the people had been rendered more
intractable than ever; the bond of the confederacy had
been still farther loosened; domestic virtue and useful
activity banished, and the vital juices drained from the

o 3

nation by slaughter, or dried up by contagious disorders. All these too perceptible and prevalent evils must have tended, in no small degree, to prepare the minds of many for those new religious impulses which were soon to set the world in motion.

Christianity had been more and more perverted, and employed for purposes foreign from its origin : this had been effected the more easily, as almost all knowledge was confined to the clergy; while the ignorance and implicit faith of the people rendered it mere brute material in their hands. Though the princes of Europe, after a long struggle with the popes, had been able to maintain their most important prerogatives ; and though even the confederates had restrained within certain limits the manifest assumptions of the hierarchy, yet in spiritual concerns the civil governments of Europe had become mere subdivisions of the ecclesiastical empire.

When the bishop of Rome had brought the people of Christendom so far as to revere in him a delegate of the Godhead, and had thereby become a legislator and judge in matters of faith, the original records of that faith of course sunk in importance. The popular religion came to consist in implicit adoption of whatever was prescribed by the priesthood ; and, above all, in superstitious veneration of its head. Arrayed in forms of constantly increasing outward splendour, it ceased to aim at an inward elevation of the soul, and became, with most, a mere amusement of fancy and of the senses. The appropriate destination of man to the active use of his mental and corporeal powers was forgotten ; while renunciations, pilgrimages, penances, donatives to consecrated places, observance of innumerable holidays, were held infallible methods of salvation. Prayers were addressed no longer to the Deity, but to the dead who had been raised by the pope to saintship ; and this veneration became by degrees a species of actual worship, which extended itself to lifeless things, to images, and symbols. To these, and to the relics and the rags of the saints, to the sound of bells, to holy water, &c., miraculous and divine powers were attributed. When misfortune came upon either individuals or communities, it was sure to be ascribed to the neglect of some ecclesiastical precept or observance; and reconcilement with the Deity was to be sought by one or other of the above-mentioned appliances.

Instruction, whether moral or religious, had become in a manner closed against the people: the use of the Bible was wholly withdrawn from laymen; and the select few of the clerical order who did or could read it, used it only in the study of scholastic theology, and in the propping up of canonical and hierarchical pretensions. Ignorance and dissoluteness prevailed among the lower clergy: the higher, in particular the Italian, gave themselves up to every species of licentiousness; and their crimes went for the most part unpunished, as they had managed to exempt themselves from the civil jurisdictions. Ever since the cessation of the schisms which had been caused by rival candidates to the papal chair, it was occupied, after brief lucid intervals, by men who gave themselves up to the most execrable vices, or who pursued the most perfidious policy.

If the attempts of Arnold of Brescia, Huss, and others. and the measures of the councils held at Constance and Basle, had failed of their anticipated effect, they had, however, introduced a very general conviction of the necessity for some sweeping church reform. But this reform, instead of being sought by any rational means, was expected to proceed, as it were, spontaneously from the very men whose dignities, wealth, and influence depended on the corruption of religion. In the mean time, the invention of printing, the newly-revived acquaintance with the writers of antiquity, and the diffusion of a more profound study of the Scriptures, accelerated the coming of the mighty change.

The indolence and vices of the clergy had occasioned discontent even in Switzerland. The rivalship of the several monastic orders, in their claims to saintship, miracles, and relics, was productive of innumerable deceptions. Four Dominican monks were burnt at Berne in

1509, who, in order to maintain, in opposition to the Franciscans, the doctrine of their order on the immaculate conception, had endeavoured to manufacture a new miracle by deluding a simple brother of the order. There is something horribly ludicrous, if the phrase may be permitted, in the details of this iniquitous transaction; and as the whole affair is a tolerable sample of the means of *moral influence* used by the rival confraternities, the recital of it may not be entirely without interest.

In a chapter of the order held at Wimpfen on the Neckar in 1506, it was resolved, after general condolences on the growing influence gained by the Franciscans, and the poverty and contempt into which their own order was falling, to venture one bold stroke for winning back their hold on public opinion. After long deliberations on the place and mode of execution, the sub-prior Franz Uelschi offered his monastery at Berne as the theatre, and promised his best aid in getting up the intended drama. He described the population of that town as simple and valiant, and, therefore, easily moved to attest, by force of arms if necessary, the truth of any miracle worked in honour of their native place. The proposal was accepted with alacrity. On his return to Berne, Uelschi confided his purpose to the prior Johann Vater, friar Bolshorst, and the steward of the monastery, Steinegger, as well as to the other principal monks. He himself undertook the arrangement of the plot, and soon found a fit subject for deception in a simple-hearted tailor, Jetzer by name. The plotters reckoned securely on the credulity of this poor wretch, from the air of earnest devotedness with which he had sought admission as a lay-brother, offering them in return for that privilege all that he possessed, which consisted in fifty-three florins and a few pieces of silk. They began their operations upon him as soon as he entered the cloister, first by nightly noises, then by visual apparitions of St. Barbara, and a soul out of purgatory. The superstitious fears of this poor fanatic were thus by degrees worked upon so effectually, that he threw himself for spiritual assistance into the arms of Bolshorst, who had purposely been assigned as his father-confessor. The artful betrayer encouraged Jetzer's faith in the foregoing appearances, and in the promise of a visit from the Virgin, which it seems had been made him by St. Barbara. By these means he was easily persuaded to perform perpetual penitential exercises, and, in short, to act the part of a saint for the popular edification, whereby shoals of curious visitors were attracted to the Dominican convent.

The eclipse of the Franciscans was, however, incomplete, unless they could be deprived of the monopoly of the five prints of our Saviour's wounds, which had drawn the adoration of a barbarous age to the emaciated body of St. Francis. One step was made towards the attainment of this end by Bolshorst, who approached our unlucky tailor's bed in the character of the Virgin, and with lofty strains on the grace which was thus vouchsafed to him, drove a sharp nail through one of his victim's hands. The cry of pain put forth by the latter hindered his betrayers from finishing their work on that occasion; but on the following night, after giving him a strong sleeping-draught, the requisite marks were produced by means of corrosives on four other parts of his person. When he awoke, the monks took advantage of his amazement to expatiate on the miracle which had taken place, and persuaded him to regard himself as a favourite of the Virgin, if not actually as the Saviour of mankind. They took him into a room hung with pictures of Christ's sufferings, which the deluded fanatic set himself to imitate in looks and gestures: he wrung his hands as if he were in the garden of Gethsemane; he drooped his head as if it were encircled by the crown of thorns; sometimes he fell into strong convulsions, aided by the potions administered, and sunk down as one struggling with the agonies of death. The people streamed in greater crowds than ever to the monastery, supped themselves full of horrors on the spectacle set before them, and listened with implicit faith to the

homilies of Bolshorst, who enlarged on the glory vouchsafed by these new miracles to the Dominican order,
and on the evidence which they afforded of the errors of
the Franciscans.   It was now the turn of the latter to
be neglected; and respectable, even learned men, began
to partake the reigning delusion.   No question but that
the crazy tailor of Berne would have maintained to this
day a distinguished legendary station, had he been
quietly withdrawn from the stage at the zenith of his
glory.

But the betrayers had successfully reached the summit of effrontery only to suffer a more tremendous fall.
Secure in the blind credulity of his victim, Bolshorst
took less pains to disguise his voice on his next appearance in the character of the Virgin, and was recognised
by Jetzer, who railed at him till he was forced to leave
the apartment.   It fared no better with the prior, who
took his place the next night; and the sub-prior was
equally unsuccessful in supporting the part of St. Catha-
rine of Siena.   It was now resolved to still the rising suspicions of the lay-brother, by acknowledging the latter
deceptions; but, on the other hand, to persist in the
reality of the earlier visions, and persuade him to continue his fanatical exhibitions.   In this they succeeded
with some trouble; but growing fears of detection urged
them to hasten the closing scenes of their drama.   A
report was put about by old women, that an image
of the Virgin in the Dominican church had been seen to
weep.   A congregation of the curious was of course
attracted, who saw the tears, and moreover saw Jetzer
kneeling before the miraculous image in an attitude of
palsied immobility.   His four betrayers approached him
with an air of utter unconsciousness, and asked him
what was the reason of his presence there, and of those
tears; he affirmed that some invisible power had transported him thither, and held him there until he should
have disclosed all to the leading men of the canton.
Upon this the monks had actually the audacity to solicit
the attendance of the avoyer Erlach, and of several of

the principal members of council. Jetzer declared in
their presence that the mother of God wept because of
the ruin of the town, which would assuredly be caused
by the receiving of French pensions, and, above all, by
farther tolerating the errors and false doctrines of the
Franciscans. Amidst the general surprise at this announcement, several clear-sighted men tacitly combined
themselves to give the affair a thorough investigation.

At the same time, a suspicion awoke in Jetzer's mind
that his holy brothers meant to make away with him:
indeed they made no farther secret of this, on his refusal
to partake suspicious viands, after he had detected them,
on more than one occasion, engaged in preparing their
mummeries, or in enjoying their nocturnal orgies. They
forced him to swallow a poisoned wafer, the fatal effect
of which was, however, withstood by the strength of his
constitution. They next tortured their victim into a
solemn promise of silence; but he soon afterwards seized
an opportunity to escape, and reported in the town the
norrible tricks which had been played on him. The
Dominicans, backed by a powerful party, still dared to
deny the charge, and even despatched messengers to
Rome, whence they hoped to procure a sentence in their
favour. But it soon appeared that the council of Berne
had sent a similar message to the bishop of Lausanne
and the pope; in consequence of which Julius despatched
his legate, Achilles de Grassis, who, with the bishops of
Lausanne and Sion, and in the presence of several
members of council, commenced the investigation at
Berne, according to the usual mode of procedure at that
time in criminal cases. Poor Jetzer, who might have
been thought to have already suffered enough, was once
more put to the torture, but stoutly persisted in his former
story. The confessions of the monks, which were of an
equally dark and revolting nature, were likewise sent to
Rome, after the council of Berne, with some trouble,
had obtained communication of them to eight of its own
members. The only reasons given for the sentence,
which was published were, that the criminals had denied

the Godhead, coloured the sacramental wafers, and painted
false tears upon an image of the Virgin; and, moreover,
had mocked the sufferings of the Saviour, by the five
prints of wounds which they had made on the person of
Jetzer. The four monks were publicly divested of their
priestly functions, and delivered up to the secular power
for execution by fire, which accordingly took place, in the
presence of many thousand spectators; but in so clumsy a
style, that the popular abhorrence of the criminals was
forgotten in the feeling excited against the executioner.
Jetzer, who had still been retained in custody, contrived
to make his escape by the aid and connivance of com-
passionate souls, but was again arrested, several years
afterwards, and made some farther disclosures supple-
mentary to his former ones, which threw additional light
on the aim and plan of the conspiracy. Innumerable
versions of the whole disgusting history were spread
in several languages through all Europe, and deeply
wounded the credit of the Dominican order, while it
infinitely scandalised all simple believers. Meanwhile,
philosophical minds found pregnant matter of inference
from this case to a hundred others similar; and it gave
no inconsiderable impulse to the first steps of the infant
reformation. Besides which, the faith of the Swiss in
papal infallibility had been much undermined in the
course of the Italian expeditions, and the metropolis of
the Christian world became the butt of jests and proverbs.
The inconsiderate rapacity of the papal court at this time
conduced to plunge it in still deeper discredit.

Pope Leo X., whose love of splendour and warlike
undertakings kept him constantly in need of large revenues, extended the sale of indulgences beyond all former
limits, and sent an Italian monk, Bernard Sampson by
name, laden with them, as apostolic commissioner into
Switzerland. This man offered his wares to the poor at
the rate of a few pence, and drew from the rich whatever
they chose to bestow. Tariffs of the rates of absolution
were established, and married women encouraged to buy
against the will of their husbands.

When Bernard Sampson made his appearance in Schwytz, his first opponent was Ulrich Zwingli, the parish priest of Einsiedlen. This extraordinary man was born at Wildhausen, in Toggenburg, A. D. 1484 : he was distinguished even in boyhood by his ardour for knowledge, and studied at Berne, Basle, and Vienna. Being appointed to a curacy in Glarus, he attended its banner, according to the custom of those times, in the battles of Novara and Marignano. Here he learned to know, by daily examples, the causes and effects of dissolute morals, of pensions, foreign enlistments, and the prevailing neglect of religion. While thousands around him were not in the smallest degree sensible of the prevalence and extent of corruption, Zwingli implored remedial measures at the hands of bishops and prelates, when hardly past the period of extreme youth.

The trader in indulgences proceeded to Berne, which was then the seat of wealth and superstition. At the price of a stallion Jacob von Stein purchased absolution for himself, his soldiers, his ancestors, and his vassals, at Belp. The bishop of Constance openly declared against this traffic; and the dean of Bremgarten, Bullinger, distinguished himself so much in opposition to the seller of indulgences, that the latter launched the ban of the church against him, from which he could be released by nothing short of 300 ducats.

In Zurich, where corruption of morals had spread itself as widely as in any town of Switzerland, fomented as it was by the presence of foreign ambassadors, and by the frequent holding of diets, Sampson had hoped to make a lucrative haul, the rather as a diet was sitting on account of transactions with Würtemburg. But at the same epoch Zwingli was placed as preacher in the cathedral; and his exhortations soon had powerful effect, as they were backed by influential and respectable persons. The trader in indulgences was compelled to evacuate Zurich; and received emphatic hints from many members of the diet, that he had better not pursue his mission in Switzerland. Zwingli preached to crowded congregations

against the prevailing corruption of morals, foreign enlistments, and foreign luxuries. A general anxiety was
excited by his sermons for acquaintance with the biblical
writings; and, in the following year, the government
promulgated an ordinance that preachers should be guided
by the word of God exclusively. From the presses of
Amerbach, Froben, and Petri, at Basle, Bibles, classical
writings, and, at last, those of Luther and Erasmus,
were disseminated. The latter author, who visited the
Basle university in 1519, contended with success against
superstition, so long as the expression of his clear views
remained unchecked by the apprehension of hurting
himself with powerful persons and parties, and turned
monastic abuses into ridicule by his satirical powers,
while his Latin version, with notes, of the New Testament, awakened a disposition for the well-grounded
study of Scripture. When, at a diet in Baden, in 1520,
the legate Pucci demanded the destruction of all Lutheran
writings, his proposal was by no means met with alacrity;
and, in the same year, the confederates unanimously resolved that all *courtisans** who were not deterred by
the notice thus afforded them, should be put in sacks and
drowned.

Had Zwingli and his fellow-labourers only sought to
effect an ecclesiastical reform, they would have gained
their end more easily than by extending their aim to a
moral one, as they felt themselves bound to do. Their
attacks on foreign services and pensions made them
enemies among numerous and influential classes. With
these open or secret opponents in the laity were united
monks and other clerical personages—some from conviction, others from apprehension of the effects which
any radical change must have on their own interests.

* *Courtisanerie* was the name applied to one of the most impudent abuses
of the catholic church. Italian priests, and other vagabonds, made their
appearance in Switzerland, furnished with papal titles of succession to such
benefices, (named or unnamed) as should be vacant. Curacies, deaneries, and
prebends were invaded by the holders of these scandalous documents; and
not only were well-deserving candidates excluded by them from offices
which they had earned by the labour of years, but it often happened that
more than one of these letters patent were given for a single place or
benefice, whereby disorders, quarrels, and even bloodshed were occasioned.

So long as the new doctrines worked no visible alteration in the outward form and features of the ecclesiastical polity, the court of Rome and its legates paid but slight attention to them ; the more so, as the exhortations of Zwingli against French influence seconded the secret political views of Leo X. But when during Lent, in 1522, many neglected the ordinance for fasting, without having purchased dispensations for the use of forbidden food, the bishop of Constance issued a mandate against all innovations, and despatched to the council of Zurich a missive directed to the same purpose.

Zwingli and the majority of his followers had hitherto, for the most part, abstained from attacks on the outward forms of the church ; but the resistance which was now rising forced them to a more complete development of their system. Zwingli now inculcated the avoidance of all merely external observances in the service of the Deity. He diffused his doctrines in small pamphlets or treatises, which, like those of Luther, were eagerly read. He now demanded a public investigation of the charges brought against him by his accusers. Accordingly a disputation was fixed to be held on the 29th of January, 1523, at Zurich, to which the delegates of the cantons assembled at Baden were invited. All the preachers of Zurich, with many foreign prelates and men of learning, assisted at this disputation in the presence of the great council. The episcopal vicar, John Faber, endeavoured in vain to postpone investigation, and to defer it to a general council. Zwingli was not confuted by his opponents ; and the great council encouraged him by an ordinance to persevere in preaching the word of God ; and enjoined on the other preachers to advance nothing which they were not prepared to make good from the same source. A second disputation was held in the autumn of the same year, at which a decision was first pronounced against images and image-worship, and next for abolition of the mass. These decisions were communicated to the Basle university, the bishops of Constance, Basle, Coire, and the twelve cantons, accompanied with a challenge to produce their objections. In the following spring the delegates of the confederacy appeared before the great council of Zurich, admonished it to desist from all innovations, threatened the exclusion of Zurich from the diets of the confederacy, promised that rigorous measures should be taken against *courtisans,* and for the removal of all clerical abuses. The sentiments of the delegates were, however, far from unanimous; and Schaffhausen showed some disposition to approximate to the system of Zurich.

The great council of Zurich, which in a manner had assumed to itself the conduct of the affairs of the reformation, replied, that it would accept correction only from the word of God; and proceeded in its career of innovation. Processions, pilgrimages, and images were done away with,—relics, amongst which were discovered several gross deceptions, were buried,—the sacrament was restored to its original institution, and communicated in both kinds to the laity. The inmates of the monasteries received permission to leave them, and the monasteries themselves were turned into alms-houses, schools, and hospitals, while a great part of their revenues was applied to the support of preachers, charities, and gymnasia. In a short time all the ceremonies and services of the Romish church were abolished, without the slightest disorder, throughout the whole canton. Many members of the clerical order married; but so great is the force of ideas in which men have been brought up, that many of the bigoted adherents to the old system, who had connived at, or excused as unavoidable, the practice of concubinage by the catholic clergy, were the loudest in condemning the *marriage* of clergymen as a crime. Thomas Wyttenbach, and others of that order, who had entered into the holy state of matrimony, were fairly compelled to renounce their clerical functions altogether.

Though most of the Swiss governments and dignified clergy opposed themselves to the doctrines of the reformation, these doctrines spread in every quarter where entrance was not closed upon them. According as the

friends of one or the other creed in a canton gained
preponderating influence in the council, reform either
made rapid progress or suffered retardations. At Schaffhausen, St. Gall, Mühlhausen, Basle, in the Grisons,
and the Thurgau, it received alternate checks and en-
couragements. Constance decreed that teaching should be
regulated according to the word of God only. Several communes in Appenzell abolished the mass, retaining, however, the images over the altar. Berne, which, in 1523,
had allowed some nuns at Königsfelden to leave the
cloister and marry, in 1524, displaced preachers who did
likewise, and adhered in most of its measures to the majority of the cantons.

As Christianity, in its very cradle, afforded occasion
to schisms and false doctrines, even so the reformation
soon developed infinite varieties of principle. Long
before Luther and Zwingli had come forward, many
elements of disorder were fermenting in the bosom of
the German population; and now those whose enthu-
siastic wishes were unsatisfied with the doctrines of the
moderate reformers were joined by men whose ambition
was more worldly, and the existing discontents secured
them numerous auxiliaries. Confounding the condition
of the first Christian societies with that of modern empires and communities, they sought to level all the
existing forms of ecclesiastical and civil jurisdiction.
Some refused the payment of tithes, others complained
of feudal burdens and services; many denied the use-
fulness of a spiritual order, and others the necessity for
authority of any kind, except of such as suited with the
reign of the saints. As many of them only allowed the
baptism of adults, and consequently bestowed the rite a
second time on their followers, they acquired the name
of *wiedertäufer* (anabaptists). In many places they not
only withdrew themselves from divine service, and taught
their doctrines in forests and retired places, but threw
off all allegiance to the temporal government: Zurich,
Soleure, Appenzell, the district of St. Gall, and the

P

bishopric of Basle, were especially infested by them.
Without reflecting that no new idea ever warms the
human heart without exciting human passions, timid
people joined chorus with the enemies of the reformation
in attributing entirely to its principles the fever in the
brain of a set of enthusiasts.

Another occurrence, which stood in no connection
with these movements, did nevertheless contribute not a
little to give rise to apprehensions of a similar kind. The
Swiss land-vogt, Amberg, in the Thurgau, carried off in
the night a protestant preacher of Burg, near Stein. This
occasioned a tumult among the populace, who attempted
to free their pastor; and failing in the attempt, plundered and burned the monastery of Ittingen. Spectacles
like these alarmed the governments, as well as many
powerful individuals. The subtle and accomplished
Faber, episcopal vicar at Constance, exerted himself to
increase their apprehensions; and many former friends
of reform in Berne and other places had now become its
declared and open enemies.

Although at Zurich the authorities, as well as the
reformers, did their utmost to avoid the imputation of
scandalous or violent measures, yet they could not
always succeed in checking the zeal of individuals. Not
only were reciprocal provocations exchanged betwixt
their own and the neighbouring cantons, but in Zurich
itself some of the clergy denounced with more than clerical zeal ideas to which they had not been accustomed.
A shoemaker, Nicholas Hottinger, and others had overthrown a·crucifix even before the disputation, and the
subsequent prohibition of idolatry. After an imprisonment of several months, Hottinger was banished for two
years; but being afterwards arrested for indiscreet expressions at Klingnau, he was carried to Lucerne, and
there illegally condemned to death. Thither, too, a
preacher of the name of Oechsli was carried, put to the
rack, but at length restored to liberty. Frequent diets
were held, at which the necessity was acknowledged of
leading Zurich back from her errors into the bosom of the

catholic church, and of arresting the march of heresy in the undecided cantons.

While the leaders of the government of Berne concurred with the other cantons in maintaining the old system, the new doctrines still continued to gain a firmer footing. In the Grisons, the loose and scandalous deportment of bishop Ziegler occasioned much agitation among the people. In consequence, without any secession from the Romish see, regulations of church discipline were made, which show how much may be done by a catholic government even in spiritual matters.

During these proceedings, foreign influences had been active in most parts of the confederacy. Many warlike spirits had already forgotten the lessons of the last campaign in Italy: 6000 Swiss, and 4000 men from the Grisons and the Valais, joined the French army, which, in the autumn of 1523, marched under Bonnivet through Piedmont into Italy. It was only because the French general did not take advantage of the circumstances that Milan failed to be captured by his army. His slighted fortune soon changed for the worse. The Swiss were so embittered by the loss of several hundred men, surprised and cut to pieces by the enemy, that for some time they spared none of the prisoners, even when the French brought them in. 6000 troops from the Grisons were compelled to retreat by the skilful movements of their antagonist, John of Medicis, and a new Swiss reinforcement of 6000 or 8000 men, after affording many proofs of valour, only served to facilitate the retreat of the French out of Upper Italy. The confederates themselves had been obliged to advance pay for their troops, and not much more than the third part of those who had marched ever returned; and these returned, stripped of every thing over the Great St. Bernard.

Francis I. now put forth his whole strength and resources. Fear of the increasing power of the emperor, Charles V., had engaged pope Clement VII. on the side of the French; and, in order to win the support of the confederacy, the new allies agreed that the duchy of

Milan, when it was conquered, should belong to the third son of the king, whom they had carried to the baptismal font. The king weakened his army by marching one division against Naples, and by the harassing siege of Pavia, undertaken during the winter. He found himself unexpectedly attacked, on the 6th or February, by the most experienced generals of the emperor; whose army had gained strength, in the same proportion as that of Francis had lost in number and in confidence. He received an utter defeat, and was made prisoner, notwithstanding all the exertions of his personal intrepidity. The leader of the Swiss, John of Diesbach, threw himself into the thickest of the battle, in order to escape surviving dishonour; and, with few exceptions, the other leaders fell in a similar manner. The fugitives returned home by the way of Como, almost in rags; and the general consternation caused by their tidings was equal to that occasioned by the disastrous day of Bicocca. The lessons of experience, however, did not suffice to hinder about 8000 Swiss recruits from joining Francis again on his return from Spanish captivity.

Even the friends of the old system in Switzerland were, at length, compelled to propose a disputation; but, mindful of the consequences of those which had been held at Zurich, they chose a theatre fitter for their purpose, and adopted regulations, by which they hoped to secure the victory. Berne's proposal of meeting at Basle was negatived by the magistrates of that town themselves: Baden was preferred as a place standing under the safeguard of the eight orthodox cantons. The disputation was fixed for the 16th of May, 1526; and the bishops of Basle, Constance, Coire, and Lausanne, were invited to assist at the meeting. Zurich was coldly and formally admitted to send delegates; but Zwingli received timely warnings not to make his appearance. Besides the delegates of the cantons, many lay and clerical personages of note attended the sittings. Dr. Eck of Ingolstadt, and the celebrated Œcolampadius, were the most distinguished champions of the opposite parties. The catholic majority of the meeting, without publishing any report of their proceedings, declared themselves to have triumphed in the controversy, and prohibited the works of Luther and Zwingli. But Berne, Basle, and Schaffhausen, issued a counter-declaration, that they would consider nothing as proved, until they had minutes of the evidence. Glarus, and Appenzell also refused acquiescence.

The cause of reform was now espoused by Berne: it was announced to the four bishops in that canton, that their authority was no longer to be recognised, and the same arrangements were made about church property as at Zurich. Notwithstanding the opposition of many members of the government, a solemn engagement was entered into against foreign pensions and alliances, and the league with France was limited to the observance of the perpetual peace. Great was the effect of so complete a revolution, in the councils of this most important member of the Helvetic body.

Thomas Murner, a friar of Lucerne, and one of the most vehement opponents of the reformation, wrote, in the most offensive manner, against Berne and its measures. The anabaptists had found numerous adherents in that canton, and excited some disturbance in the district of Schenkenberg; commotions also took place in the vicinity of Interlachen, where the peasantry regarded the suppression of the monasteries as including the cessation of all payment of dues and offerings. These disorders were soon composed by the aid of the men of Thun; and Berne discovered her strength in the adherence of her faithful people. New disturbances next broke out in the Oberland, where the men of Hasli carried the restoration of the mass by a majority of forty voices. Uri and Unterwalden sent thither a party of priests to foment disaffection, and the repeated admonitions of the government were fruitless. The revolt soon extended over the Grindelwald, and as far as Untersee; and many districts refused to contribute their aid

against the insurgents.   Moreover, 800 Unterwäldners
marched over the Brünig, and, in conjunction with the
men of Hasli, took possession of Untersee.   The wise
and prudent policy of Berne was now rewarded by the
devotedness of by far the greater number of her subjects.
The Unterwaldners hastily retreated, and a general submission took place, without shedding of blood.

The national sympathies, momentarily revived by the
disaster of Pavia, soon expired in the bitterness of controversy.   Men who had been taught from their youth
upwards, that beyond the pale of the church there was
no salvation,—that all dissenters ought to be forced back
into the orthodox creed, and that no engagement with
heretics was binding,—were capable of the most atrocious outrages, when personal passions added their
venom to that of religious hatred.   A priest of Zug
suffered severe punishment for having eaten in company with Zwingli at Zurich.   Two men of the March
were burnt in Schwytz.   Such occurrences sufficiently
showed the reformers in what light they were looked
upon by the opposite party, and forced them on the
most decisive measures in self-defence.   Nor did they
abstain from sanguinary reprisals: Marcus Wehrli of
Frauenfeld, a zealous foe of the new doctrines, was arrested in his passage through Zurich, in company with
the land-vogt of Unterwalden, and beheaded on the
charge of persecutions and false accusations of heresy.

About this time Zug and Lucerne stamped a small
cross on the new coinage of Zurich, to signify that
church plate had entered into its composition.   Five
cantons required the people of Bremgarten to deliver up
their new books and Bibles, a demand to which Zurich
and Berne alone openly opposed themselves.   These two
cantons now set on foot a so-called Christian league, to
which they declared themselves compelled by the attempts of eight of their colleagues to suppress the reformation among their subjects.   Into this alliance all
confederates espousing the reformed creed were admis-
sible; and so sacred was the bond of the empire still

esteemed in Switzerland, that its rights were made points of express reservation, as were those of the confederacy itself.

The opposite persuasions were first brought into hostile collision by an attack made by the Catholics on Cappel, where the defeat of Zurich was aggravated by the death of Ulrich Zwingli. The enemy found him lying on his back severely wounded; and, not knowing his person, asked if they should bring him a confessor. This being declined, by a faint motion of his head, they exhorted him to call on the holy Virgin and the saints. Rejecting this suggestion in a similar manner, he was saluted by the enraged foe with the names of dog and heretic, and despatched by the sword of a citizen of Unterwalden. " Thus," says Bullinger with touching simplicity, " thus was master Ulrich Zwingli slain in the midst of his own flock, with whom he remained even unto death." The body was not recognised till the day after the battle, when the fury of the enemy displayed itself by dishonouring it. In vain their leaders enjoined moderation and reverence of the dead. The multitude determined that the body should be quartered and burned by the public executioner of Lucerne. Even the ashes were purposely mixed with impurities, lest his friends should enjoy the last mournful solace of collecting them.

CHAP. XIV.

FROM THE ALLIANCE OF BERNE AND FREYBURG WITH GENEVA TO THE BORROMEAN LEAGUE.

1526—1586.

TOWN OF GENEVA. — ITS EARLY HISTORY. — OPPRESSED BY THE DUKE OF SAVOY. — MAMELUKES. — CRUELTIES EXERCISED ON THE BURGHERS — WHO COURT THE ALLIANCE OF FREYBURG. — DUKE CHARLES ENTERS THE TOWN. — EXECUTION OF BER- THELIER. — ALLIANCE OF BERNE AND FREYBURG WITH GE- NEVA. — IMPOTENT RESENTMENT OF THE DUKE. — SPOON LEAGUE. — TREATY OF ST. JULIAN. — ZEAL OF FAREL AND OTHERS. — ABOLITION OF CATHOLICISM. — EQUIVOCAL DE- PORTMENT OF DUKE CHARLES. — CONQUEST OF THE VAUD BY BERNE. — CO-BURGHERSHIP BETWIXT BERNE AND GENEVA. — CALVIN. — SERVETUS. — EFFECTS OF THE REFORMATION. — COUNCIL OF TRENT. — BORROMEAN LEAGUE. — CALENDAR CONTROVERSY. — ESCALADE OF GENEVA.

THE original foundation of Geneva is buried in obscure antiquity. It was already a considerable town under the Romans, in the age of Cæsar and Diviko. Under Charlemagne and the Burgundian kings it was possessed of many important franchises, through which it raised itself gradually to almost complete independence. Situ- ated on the banks of the Leman lake, at its southern extremity, surrounded by extensive suburbs and highly productive vineyards, the seat of a bishopric, the central point of the trade of France, Germany, and Italy, pro- prietress of a great fair, and acknowledging no lord paramount but the emperor, Geneva grew in prosperity through the industry, the enterprising and independent spirit of its burghers. Their rights were, however, con- stantly in danger from the counts de Genevois, who derived their title from the name of the town, and the bishops of Geneva, whose episcopal seat was within its walls. The preservation of the town was not less owing to the quarrels of the counts and the bishops than to

the native love of freedom in its burghers.   At a later
period the favour of the German emperors conferred the
principality of Geneva on the bishops, and the power of
the counts fell into decay.   On the other hand, the
ducal house of Savoy aimed, during the thirteenth century, at sovereignty in Geneva.   The burghers themselves had called in its assistance against the counts; but
when their new allies grasped at all the prerogatives of
their former masters, established themselves in the forts
of the town, and encroached on all its liberties, they
learned to lament their folly in expelling a weaker
enemy by the aid of a too powerful protector.   Even the
ambitious plans of Savoy were long frustrated by the
energetic stand made by the bishops combined with the
burghers, until towards the close of the fifteenth and the
commencement of the sixteenth century, when an almost
uninterrupted line of princes of the house of Savoy ascended the episcopal chair of Geneva.   The last of them,
a contemptible weakling, abdicated in favour of duke
Charles III. all the secular rights which he supposed
himself to possess in the town.   This illegal abdication
caused considerable disturbances.   The burghers almost
unanimously refused to accept the yoke of Savoy, and the
few who seemed inclined in its favour were stigmatised
with the name of *Mamelukes*.   The duke now had recourse to open violence to complete an undertaking which
he had begun in contempt of justice.   Burghers of
Geneva were imprisoned in the Savoyard territory, confessions of a conspiracy extorted from them by means
of torture, and employed as a pretext for their judicial
murder.   These proceedings struck the Genevans with
terror.   Many, dreading a similar destiny, banished themselves from their country.   Many turned an eye of hope
on the neighbouring Swiss confederacy.   Philip Berthelier, a Genevese exile, gained over the government of
Freyburg to the cause of his fellow-countrymen; and in
the year 1519 the municipality of Geneva resolved to
form an alliance with that town.   On this the duke took
up arms, as remonstrances were in vain with the Swiss,

and unexpectedly appeared with his army before the
gates of Geneva. The inexperience, indecision, and
disunion of the burghers worked in his favour not less
than the discipline of his own troops. He entered the
town, disarmed the burghers; and Geneva would have
undergone the extremities prepared for conquered rebels,
had not some moderation been forced on the duke by his
fear of the Swiss. Freyburg summoned the aid of the
confederacy, and the summons was answered from all
sides with alacrity. "Every one," says an old writer,
" who had any thing like heart in his breast, was resolved to aid in the rescue of Geneva, and in punishing
the duke's usurpations." Six thousand Swiss entered
the Savoyard territory, and threatened an unsparing
retaliation for every act of violence which should be
ventured at Geneva. The duke had prudence enough to
conceal his resentment, and to pay the war expenses of
the Freyburgers. Geneva thus remained in his hands ;
a general amnesty was promised; notwithstanding which
Berthelier's head fell on the scaffold, and the town was
obliged to give up its league with Freyburg. The latter
was persuaded with great difficulty, by the rest of the
Helvetic body, to accept the terms of this treaty.

Duke Charles now rioted without restraint in the enjoyment of his newly regained dominion. Wherever
his will met with opposition, it was summarily suppressed by the sword. All independence of spirit
seemed for ever crushed in Geneva. But when the
duke mixed in the grand contest for Milan, the town
employed the occasion to renew its struggle for freedom.
On this the duke passed sentence of death on the heads
of the popular party, who fled to Freyburg, and besieged the Helvetic body with their complaints. Freyburg again declared herself, with Berne's concurrence,
for the cause of Geneva. The duke hastened thither in
alarm, released the prisoners, and procured a declaration
of his sovereignty from an assembly of the burghers,
surrounded by his body-guard. Thereupon he left the
town, imagining that he had placed his dominion over

it on a new and permanent basis.   Formidable discontents broke out on his departure.   The council declared
those who had been banished "friends of their country."
The citizens called loudly for a league with Berne and
Freyburg.   Every street re-echoed the cry of " Long
live the confederates !"   The highest municipal functions were conferred on a friend of Switzerland.   The
exiles returned home, and brought along with them a
project of co-burghership with Berne and Freyburg.
The whole town, excepting six individuals, joined in the
shouts of congratulation with which the proposal was
received.   Even the bishop Peter de la Beaume, a partisan of Savoy, but rather a weak than an ill-intentioned
man, declared that he would oppose no impediment to
the measure.   On the 12th of May, 1526, a league was
sworn between Berne and Geneva, for reciprocal aid,
freedom of trade and intercourse, defence and protection
of liberty and property.   The allied towns answered
the duke's remonstrances with the threat that they would
secede from the alliance between Savoy and the Helvetic
body.   He was kept quiet besides by the apprehension
of losing the Pays de Vaud, which lay so well within
the reach of the Swiss, and which had been twice before conquered by them already.

The Genevans now laboured to consolidate their freedom, to appropriate the rights of the duke to themselves,
and to remodel the whole frame of their constitution.
The adherents of Savoy were driven out of the town,
their goods confiscated, and forty-four of them sentenced
to death in case of return.   The bishop was still tole-
rated, as long as he continued undecided, and appeared
to incline in favour of the town.   When he afterwards
betrayed his leaning to Savoy, his authority, too, was
speedily at an end.   These events were viewed by the
duke with powerless indignation; and the only signs of
hostility which he ventured in return were the closing of
all trade with the town, the reception of the exiles, and
the capture and imprisonment of prior Bonnivard, a
courageous and enlightened friend of freedom.   Fear

of the confederates deterred him from stronger measures. In the mean time a new enemy appeared against
the town, in the shape of a league of the Savoyard nobility. Some of them, carousing in a castle of the
Vaud, had boasted that they would sup the Genevans
up like spoon-meat. This sally suggested the formation
of a fraternity which took the name of the *spoon league*,
and the members of which mounted a spoon as their
badge in front of their hats. This league might probably meet with secret encouragement from the duke,
but he dared not openly sanction, and had neither the
power nor the will to prevent it. Shortly afterwards,
when the head of this association was slain by the exasperated burghers of Geneva, a struggle arose of a very
harassing nature for the town. On this the allies of
Geneva took the field with 10,000 men. The members
of the *spoon league* were no match for such a force:
their castles were burned, their soldiers scattered, and
nothing remained for themselves but submission.

Through Swiss mediation an armistice was concluded
at St. Julian. Reciprocal guarantees of trade and intercourse were agreed upon. The duke guaranteed peace
on the part of his subjects,—Berne and Freyburg stood
securities for the tranquillity of Geneva. If the treaty
should be broken by the duke or his subjects, possession
of the Pays de Vaud might be taken by the governments
of Berne and Freyburg. On the other hand, in case of its
violation by Geneva, the former towns should be bound
to take up arms against it. A considerable part of the
war expenses was imposed on the duke, and in return
his original rights over Geneva were restored to him.
Thenceforwards the situation of the town was very precarious. The duke for the most part only fulfilled so
much of the treaty as served his purpose, and scarcely
concealed his thirst for revenge, which he watched for a
safe occasion to gratify. On the other hand, the Swiss
were tired of the league, and wished to secede from it.
This determination was only altered by the most earnest
supplications of the Genevans.

The bishop excommunicated the town; the town threw off the authority of the bishop; and the triumph of the new creed was decided. The images were destroyed by a spontaneous popular movement; and the council was persuaded by one Farell, subsequently a colleague of Calvin, to do away with the mass. The expulsion of the bishop, by which his intrigues were rendered harmless, was the most important step towards the attainment of freedom, and the reception of the reformed creed was the best means of retaining it; as the constant friendship of so powerful a neighbour as Berne was thus secured, by the double bond of policy and community of sentiment.

In defiance of the treaty of St. Julian, the Savoyard nobility and the banished episcopal partisans continued their hostilities against Geneva. The town was closely blockaded, and reduced to severe extremities. Traitorous plans were discovered for its capture. The enemy showed themselves daily before the gates, and devastated even the suburbs. Duke Charles viewed these incidents in silence, if, indeed, he did not secretly encourage them. This equivocal demeanour was imputed to him by Berne as a breach of the treaty of St. Julian. Certain it was, he had closed that treaty reluctantly enough, and had fulfilled it as indifferently as possible; his inactivity, however, during the hostile proceedings against Geneva, admitted of excuse on two grounds. The town had provoked his anger by the expulsion of their bishop, and the curtailment of his own ducal rights, and had given him a plausible pretext for evading the performance of his engagements. He was himself, besides, threatened with an attack on the side of France, and certainly had not the power, if he had even had the will, to keep within bounds the turbulence of his subjects. These extenuating circumstances were utterly overlooked, and nothing was regarded but the outrages which had taken place; for Berne had resolved to turn the duke's embarrassments to her own advantage. All negotiations were fruitless; and Berne held a high and threatening

language, demanding that the channels of trade should
be opened; the banished Genevans expelled; the nobles
of the Vaud kept in check. A truce of six months,
desired by the duke in the consciousness of his weakness,
was refused him. Charles declared, with the energy of
despair, that he considered himself no further bound by
treaties. Several weeks later he sought vainly to retrieve
the effects of this precipitation by a special embassy, and
formal list of charges against Geneva. Berne was fully
determined upon war — the rest of the Helvetic body
strongly against it; but Berne relied on the favourable
sentiments of her own people.

On the 21st of January, 1536, 7000 Bernese marched
into the Vaud, and in a few days the whole district fell
into their hands. Even the lake of Geneva did not stop
their triumphant progress. They took possession of the
district of Gex, and, on the south of the lake, of a considerable portion of the dukedom of Chablais. Such rapid
and important conquests, in the worst season of the year,
excited attention and envy in the rest of the Helvetic
body. The confederates recommended the abandonment
of a war in which the emperor might so easily mix, to
the detriment of the whole league. Berne acquiesced
with facility in many of their demands; but in the main
business resolutely adhered to her own purposes. The
conquest of the Vaud was completed in 1554, by the
ruin of the once-powerful counts of Gruyères, who
found themselves compelled to cede their extensive landed
domains to Berne and Freyburg for a moderate sum of
money; and thus underwent the same doom which had
successively reduced to nothing all the ancient houses
within the bounds of the confederation.

The grasping spirit of Berne showed itself next in a
dishonourable manner towards the Genevans. The latter
had hoped for more than a mere transmission to her
powerful ally of a sovereignty grounded in usurpation.
It was death to their hopes, when Berne declared that
all the powers of the dukes and bishops had descended
into her hands by right of conquest! The main point

was, however, given up after long discussion. A co-burghership between the *free towns* of Berne and Geneva was closed for five and twenty years in 1536, which was afterwards converted to a perpetual league of the same description.

Hardly had political independence been asserted, when its enjoyment was disturbed by religious discord; and that ascendency which had been lost by dukes and bishops over Geneva was transferred to an itinerant preacher — JOHN CALVIN.

The second great reformer of the sixteenth century was born at Noyon in Picardy, on the 10th of July, 1509. His father, Gerard Chauvin, a cooper, devoted him at an early age to the clerical profession. Calvin, in a letter to Claude d'Hangest, abbot of St. Eloy at Noyon, avows himself indebted to the family of that prelate for early instruction and liberal education. When hardly twelve years old, he was appointed to a canonry in the cathedral of his native town; and, six years after-wards, to a parochial cure, which he soon exchanged for another. Thus Calvin had obtained several benefices, by aid of patrons, before his twentieth year, and before the termination of his studies at Paris. Here he made the acquaintance of a countryman, some years older than himself, Peter Robert Olivetan, from whom he received the first germs of the new religious doctrines, which had already begun to obtain diffusion in France: he was thereby induced to quit the field of theology for that of law, which he studied at Orleans and afterwards at Bourges. In this he made rapid progress; and instructed himself at the same time in Greek under Melchior Vol-mar, a German, who confirmed him in the tendency to adventurous speculation, which had already been excited in his mind by Olivetan. In 1532 he returned to Paris, and gave up his benefices. In the same year he pub-lished a Latin commentary on the two books of Seneca, *De Clementiâ*, under the name of *Johannes Calvinus*, lengthened and latinised from *Jean Chauvin*, according to the taste of the times. In the following year he was

forced to flee from Paris, having incurred suspicion, along
with his friend Michael Cop, the rector of the university,
on account of some discourses of the latter on the new
doctrine. Calvin next betook himself to Du Tillet, canon
at Angoulême, with whom he pursued the tranquil course
of his studies, and began to collect materials for his
work on Christian Doctrine. From thence he repaired
to the court of Margaret queen of Navarre, sister of
Francis I.; who, less from any decided attachment to
the new creed than to science in general, protected men
of learning whom their opinions had expelled from
France. Here Calvin was well received, and formed
the acquaintance of several men who in the sequel became useful to his party. He proceeded next to Basle,
where he published his work on Christian Doctrine,
Institutio Christianæ Religionis; the intention of which
was to clear his slandered brethren from the charges
brought against them, from political motives, of being
turbulent anabaptists, having nothing in common with
Luther. It would be quite beside our purpose to enlarge upon the points in which he went farther than
Luther, with regard to the topics of free-will, account-
ableness, and the merit of good works; we content
ourselves with indicating a few of the bold deductions
which he drew from his own principles. He not only
contested the supremacy of the pope, but the authority
of general councils. In his view neither bishop nor
priest could be visible head of the church; and he acknowledged no other vows than baptismal ones, no other
sacraments than baptism and the Lord's supper; nor
did he regard even these as indispensable to salvation.
Masses he deemed a desecration; saint-worship, idolatry.
The preface to the above-mentioned work, which was
addressed *Ad Christianissimum Regem quâ hic ei liber
pro confessione fidei offertur,* had no effect in putting a
stop to religious persecution in France; as the most
Christian king, Francis I., was totally devoid of all enthusiasm, and actuated wholly by political motives. Calvin visited Italy, where he was favourably received by

the duchess Renata, daughter of Louis XII. of France, and wife of Hercules d'Este; but was soon compelled to take to flight, and returned once more to Paris. Here, however, he could not remain in safety, and took his way to Basle through Geneva, where the reformed doctrines had now been established for some years, and where Farel was engaged in preaching them. Calvin united with this man; and soon received a commission from the government as a teacher of theology, to which he devoted himself exclusively, leaving pulpit oratory to Farel. But they speedily drew a host of powerful enemies on their shoulders, by some trifling deviations from the established ceremonial. Under their auspices leavened bread was used in the sacrament; the baptismal font was removed out of the church, and all festivals were abolished, excepting Sundays. These innovations were disapproved by the synod of Lausanne, and compliance with the decision of that body was enjoined on Calvin and Farel by the magistracy of Geneva: on their refusal, they were ordered to quit the town within three days, and took their departure accordingly in April, 1538. Thence they proceeded to Berne, from which place Calvin went to Strasburg, where admission had been gained by Bucer for Luther's doctrines ten years previously. Here he was appointed, through the influence of Bucer, to the professorship of theology; and, at the same time, obtained permission to establish a French church, which soon became considerable by the influx of refugees from France. It was here that he published his work on the Lord's Supper, in which he set himself as well to controvert Luther's opinion, who interpreted that sacrament in the literal sense, as that of Zwingli, who understood it figuratively. It was not till a later period that he declared himself, without reservation, in favour of the latter doctrine.

Meanwhile Calvin's views were still directed towards Geneva; and his friends at length succeeded in effecting his recall. A deputation was sent from thence to Strasburg, expressly for the purpose of soliciting the magis-

tracy of that town to restore their pastor to his flock.
On his return, he laid before the council a set of regulations with regard to church discipline, which were im-
plicitly adopted.   In accordance with these, a consistory
was permanently established, consisting half of clerical,
half of lay members, to watch over the conservation of
morals and pure doctrine.   By this body every one was
liable to be called to account for the most insignificant
words or acts ; and cases where ecclesiastical penalties
seemed inadequate were referred for animadversion to
the council.   Thus Calvin was, in some sort, made the
arbiter of every act, and almost every thought, of his
fellow-countrymen.   His spirit held exclusive sway in
the council as in the consistory ; and neither of these
bodies ever failed to punish any one who ventured to
oppose his measures.   Thus a member of the magistracy
was displaced and sentenced to two months' imprisonment, " because he was a man of irregular life, and
connected with Calvin's enemies."   In like manner Jacob
Gruet was condemned to the block, for having written
immoral verses and godless epistles, and for having con-
spired to overthrow the ordinances of the church.

The pious perseverance with which every excess and
disorder was prosecuted and punished at Geneva occasioned popular tumults, and at last a regular revolt,
which was followed by judicial executions.   However
great were the services of Calvin, in introducing republican manners and useful activity,— of which the effects,
after the lapse of ages, are still visible in the industry and
intellectual tone of Geneva, — yet he inflexibly enforced
the rigorous maintenance of orthodoxy, the idea of which
he transferred from the system in which he had grown
up to that which he had later espoused.   His influence
procured the exile of Bolsec, an ex-Carmelite, for having
dared to attack the doctrine of predestination.   A still
deeper disgrace was brought on the memory of Calvin
by the execution of Michael Servede (Servetus), who
suffered at the stake for holding anti-trinitarian tenets,
which, however, he had not attempted to disseminate

at Geneva. Calvin had, indeed, proposed a milder mode of death; but it is easier to set bigot zeal in motion than to moderate its subsequent violence.

The manners of the great Genevan reformer were marked by strict sobriety; his character was sombre and inflexible. His only idea of friendship was utility to his grand design; his only passion was centered in the triumph of his opinions. His temper was impatient, and endured no contradiction. " None of my struggles," he wrote to Bucer, " against my other failings, many and great as they are, are equal to those which I have to wage with my temper; over this devouring beast I have not yet attained the mastery." The tone of his controversial writings was almost always sharp and contemptuous; and he seldom succeeds in suppressing his full consciousness of superiority. As a theologian, Calvin stood second to none of his contemporaries in depth of learning, acuteness, and the art of setting forth his subject. His Latin compositions are distinguished for method, correctness, and dignity: he was, moreover, an accomplished jurist, and able politician. But none of these advantages singly, nor all conjointly, would ever have raised him to the head of a distinct religious party, but for his bold rejection of outward ceremonial. It was this that, on the one hand, gained the support of many instructed persons, who were disposed to regard as derogatory all appeals to the senses, while it furnished the uninstructed with a compendious method of marking out their difference from the opposite persuasion, independently of any essential ground of separation, to investigate which such disciples were neither willing nor able.

The effects of the reformation made themselves manifest in all the relations of private and public life. General attention was directed to the internal wants and welfare of the country; and the rising generation acquired taste for the arts of peace, and for the sciences by which the mind is most enlarged and elevated. The study of the ancients and of history had been revived by theological enquiries. If enlistments still continued to take place for foreign services, yet the venality of rulers and their subjects had ceased to be so prevalent as formerly. Improvements were made in agriculture, commerce, and manufactures; and the reception given to fugitive co-religionists introduced or furthered several branches of industry. Alms-houses and hospitals were instituted or improved. Strict regulations were made against prodigality, gambling, and usury; and rigid limits were set to public amusements.

Under the name of ecclesiastical discipline, the clergy in Geneva and the canton of Berne assumed a very extensive jurisdiction. The clergy possessed important weight and influence with the people; and when they interfered in word or in writing with the constituted authorities, their *dicta* were in general received as decisive. Their intervention, as might be expected, was not in all cases free from polemical passions, or sacerdotal arrogance; but it oftener took an aspect of beneficence, particularly when the secular authorities neglected their duties. The better part of the clergy themselves never lost sight of the evils engendered by an unlimited domination of their order.

The independence of the cantons, and the difference of their forms of polity, necessarily occasioned variations in their church discipline. These were taken advantage of by the enemies of reform to reproach its friends with the want of a sure foundation for their faith. The subsequent evangelical leaders, harassed by the virulent attacks of their opponents, imagined the production of explicit confessions to be requisite for their justification. The four evangelical cantons, Zurich, Berne, Basle, and Schaffhausen, and the three allied towns, St. Gall, Mühlhausen, and Bienne, agreed upon a common form of confession, to be laid before the general assembly of the church when convoked by the emperor. In the same year (1566) Geneva also issued a confession, composed by Farel. Finally, on the 1st of March, 1566, the so called Helvetic confession was promulgated at Zurich, which was also received by the reformed churches in

Scotland, Holland, and Hungary. Thus the successors of the first reformers, by holding fast the letter, often departed from the spirit of their great predecessors, thereby aggravating the schisms among protestants, and disgracing themselves and their cause by persecution.

The reformed cantons made frequent, but for the most part ineffectual, intercessions for their oppressed co-religionists in France and Savoy. Numerous refugees from these countries found protection and support in Switzerland. Geneva became a city of refuge for persecuted Italians, and Zurich for the English, who fled from the tyranny of queen Mary.

' The church of Rome, unable to withstand any longer the demands for reformation, even of catholics themselves, had at last consented to open a council at Trent. The selection of this spot, on the borders of Italy, and within the bounds of the empire, gave assurance to the emperor, as well as to the pope, that no third party could establish a predominance there, and each of them expected to confirm his own ascendency. Pope Paul III., with many expressions of sorrow that the Evil One had succeeded in enticing away a part of the confederates from the bosom of the church, exhorted them collectively to obedience to the council. The evangelical party replied that they had published their confession of faith ; that they could not regard a council as impartial, which was subordinated entirely to the pope ; but that, on the other hand, they were ready to conform themselves to whatever should be resolved in a free council, and according to the word of God. The absence of the protestants disappointed the hope of bringing them back to subjection to the Romish church by the sentence of the council, which was now forced to content itself with condemning all who rejected its doctrines. Many improvements of discipline were enacted by this body ; but at the same time it riveted the fetters of belief, confirmed the papal authority in ecclesiastical matters, and encroached so far on the rights of secular rulers,

that several catholic states refused to submit to its decisions. Its reception by the catholic cantons occasioned
the reformed ones to be regarded by them more than
ever as renegades and reprobates, while it served to increase the suspicions and imbitterment of the latter. All
sentiments of patriotism yielded to religious hatred,
which constantly found new food for itself.

In former times the confederates had always maintained a jealous vigilance with regard to the pope, considered as a foreign power, and with regard to the clerical order in general, as instruments of that power.
But now, the zeal of polemics, and the prevalent ideas
of the duty of submissiveness to the spiritual authority,
placed a part of the Helvetic body entirely at the command of their ecclesiastical superiors; and, by consequence, attached them to that line of foreign policy most
conformable to clerical interests. At this epoch, cardinal
Charles Borromeo exercised a distinguished influence in
spiritual and political matters. Elevated at the age of
three-and-twenty to the bishoprick of Milan, and the
dignity of cardinal, he felt an early vocation to the office
of reformer of the catholic clergy and church discipline;
but his mind was so thoroughly imbued with the spirit
of a dominant priesthood, that even the heads of the
catholic cantons were compelled to resist his proceedings.
He powerfully contributed towards putting in execution
the decrees of the council of Trent; he established at
Milan a college for the bringing up of Swiss youth to
the clerical profession; he induced the pope to keep a
permanent nuncio in the catholic cantons. His establishment of Jesuits at Lucerne was still more momentous
in its influence on the public mind, and on education :
while the effect produced by the Jesuits on the upper
classes, was rivalled by that which the order of Capuchins exercised over the lower.

The first permanent nuncio, the bishop of Vercelli,
a *protégé* of the cardinal Borromeo, brought about, in
1579, a league between the bishop of Basle and the seven
catholic cantons. This may be regarded as a sort of

catholic counterpart to the *Christian league* of Berne and Zurich, mentioned in a former chapter. The contracting parties promised each other aid in the affairs of religion, &c. The seven cantons engaged *to retain in the catholic faith such subjects of the bishop as had not yet abandoned it, and to use their endeavours in re-converting those who had apostatised.* In 1586, the so-called Borromean, or *golden league,* was sworn by the seven catholic cantons, the provisions of which were similar to those of the foregoing one, with the addition of the following clause: — *That, in case of individual members manifesting any inclination to desert the faith, the others should compel them to abide by it, and visit the promoters of defection with condign punishment.*

A ludicrous example of the length to which distrust of Rome was carried by the protestant party was afforded by the controversy excited on the occasion of the reform of the Julian calendar. Astronomers had reckoned that the Julian calendar, which, after every three years, each containing 365 days, introduced an intercalary year of 366, had produced, in the year 1582, a miscalculation amounting to ten days, thus gradually disturbing the uniformity and correctness of the measure of time; as, according to more accurate observations, the year contained about twelve minutes less. Pope Gregory XIII. commenced his reform of the calendar by striking off ten days from the year 1582. The catholic cantons adopted this arrangement, after Unterwalden had offered some objections to it. The protestants, on the other hand, conceived an apprehension lest the reception of a calendar decreed by the pope, and named after him, might pave the way for future papal encroachments; and lest their compliance might wear the appearance of deference to a papal mandate. The catholic cantons not only adopted the Gregorian calendar, but enjoined its observance on the free bailiwicks, and instructed the vogts to punish recusants. Irritated by this mode of proceeding, Zurich turned the affair into a question of religion: the greatest ferment, however, was in the

Thurgau. The two religious parties had now not only different feast days, but confusion took place on market days, and other civil arrangements. After the waste of much discussion on the matter at successive diets, the neutral cantons, in concert with the French ambassador, finally concluded an arrangement, by which the regulation of the calendar was committed to each canton within the bounds of its own territory.

Geneva continued still the object of undisguised abhorrence to the leaders of the catholic hierarchy, and of hostility more dangerous, because more concealed, to the reigning duke of Savoy, Charles Emanuel. The town reposed in false security, heedless of the warnings given from time to time against its crafty neighbour, whose policy rejected no expedient which could forward his purposes. Even the notices received of the near approach of the enemy were treated with contempt or carelessness. On the night of the 11th–12th December, 1602, 2000 troops of Savoy advanced unperceived on the town, and the duke himself hovered in the neighbourhood. Before three in the morning, the walls had already been scaled by 200 of them, who made an attempt to burst open the new gate from the inside, while estafettes were sent off to announce the capture of the town. The burghers, taken by surprise as they were, and half naked, nevertheless rushed to arms with alacrity, slew seventy-six of the Savoyards, and took thirteen prisoners, whom they afterwards hanged as brigands and assassins. The rest endeavoured to save themselves by leaping from the walls; and the discomfited troops hastened to Bonne, where the duke was awaiting their triumph. " *Vous avez fait là une belle cagade*" were the words he used to D'Aubigny, the leader of the expedition. A Savoyard embassy, sent to Berne to excuse this treacherous inroad, received an intimation from the government that they had better retreat as quick as they could from the popular indignation. Terms of peace were, however, at length negotiated by the neutral cantons, which provided for free intercourse betwixt Geneva and Savoy, and precluded the duke from stationing any garrison at a distance within sixteen miles from the town. This affair has preserved, under the title of *the escalade,* a memorable station in Swiss history.

CHAP. XV.

FROM THE BEGINNING OF THE THIRTY YEARS' WAR TO THE PEACE OF WESTPHALIA.

1620—1648.

DESCRIPTION OF THE GRISONS. — EARLY HISTORY. — FORMS OF GOVERNMENT. — INFLUENCE OF PARTICULAR FAMILIES. — SPANISH AND FRENCH PARTIES. — POPULAR TUMULTS — MASSACRE IN THE VALTELINE.—FRUITLESS NEGOTIATIONS WITH SPAIN AND AUSTRIA. — SUBJECTION OF THE GRISONS BY THE LATTER POWER. — RECOVERY OF THEIR FREEDOM AND INDEPENDENCE. — STATE OF RELIGIOUS PARTIES IN SWITZERLAND. THIRTY YEARS' WAR. — DISUNION IN THE CONFEDERACY. — INROADS OF FOREIGN ARMIES. — INTRIGUES OF FOREIGN AMBASSADORS. — PEACE OF WESTPHALIA. — DECLARATION OF SWISS INDEPENDENCE.—FOREIGN RELATIONS.—FRAGMENTARY STATE OF KNOWLEDGE IN SWITZERLAND.

" With the close of the reformation," says a respectable Swiss annalist *, " expires almost all that can animate and enliven the historian of Switzerland. He has now to wade through a dull period, equally void of original records as it is of events worthy to be recorded : under such circumstances, the task of writing the history of his country becomes as great a burden as it was previously a pleasure. It is true, that the age immediately preceding the reformation was by no means very honourable to Switzerland ; still it was an age of unexhausted national vigour. The æra of the reformation elevates the mind by the spectacle of the triumph of enlightenment over darkness ; but later times show little else than discord and degeneracy. The history of the Swiss, from the foundation of their freedom to the over-

* J. Conrad Vögelin.

throw of their old *eternal* league, may be said to resemble their mountain heights, the base of which exhibits smiling and fertile fields and valleys, the middle region wild but majestic ridges,—from thence to the summit lifelessness and ruin."

Without identifying our sentiments with those of the author here cited, we must agree with him that the history of the old Helvetic body (so far as progressive development is included in the idea of history) may in some sense be considered to close with the age of the reformation. And, perhaps, a gentle wish may unreproved escape the tip of our pen, that for the space of nearly two centuries ourselves, as well as our readers, might be allowed to indulge in unmolested slumber, till aroused by the first mutterings of a mighty social change, which (like the hollow sounds preceding the fall of the Rossberg) foreboded the first outbreak of the French revolution. True, the intervening space is occupied with warfare and diplomacy in abundance ; but diplomacy is a sharper's game, and war an inglorious squabble, save when sanctified by national feelings and interests. It will be some relief to deviate for the present from the main track of our history into those remoter regions which have hitherto received less of our notice, and to resume the course of events which raised the highlanders of Rhætia to the rank, first of allies, and afterwards members of the Swiss league.

The scenery of Switzerland Proper, with the exception of the lakes, does not bear away the prize of varied beauty from the vales of the Grisons, where nature has been lavish of her loftiest style of ornament. Rocky battlements frown upon the narrow path of the traveller, or indent the distant horizon with their fainter hues and outlines. Life or living thing haunts not their summits ; sound and motion there are none but of the glacier-stream from its icy reservoir, or the avalanche rolling in thunder over fissures and abysses, or the clouds that fleet or lower upon the breasts of the mountains, whose summits glitter high above their region in the sunlight. Lower down, the Alpine meadows, spotted with flocks and shepherds' huts, repose in primitive stillness and simplicity. No suspicion penetrates these pastoral solitudes of the progress of human intellect, or the arts of modern luxury. Lower still, lie smiling villages, half enveloped in thickets, cheerful country houses, with their pleasure grounds and vineyards, and scattered hamlets, seeming to mock the vicinage of the knightly towers whose ruins have frowned from their rocky site for centuries.

The modes of thought and degrees of civilisation in these highlands are as various as the features of their scenery. There are few countries of Europe in which circumstances have coincided to produce such a motley mixture of manners and of usages : the very form of the vallies, by which one set of inhabitants is divided from the rest as though in separate apartments, conduces not a little to the same effect. Local and communal rights oppose impediments to the settlement of strangers, and the natives themselves are counted strangers in every valley but their own. Marriages are rare between inhabitants of distant vallies ; and a certain set of habits and ideas, with their accompanying propensities and prejudices, are faithfully transmitted from one century to another.

But even if this insulated mode of life, together with varieties of climate, were not enough to stamp the traits of separate populations on the different inhabitants of these highland glens, that effect would be produced by their diversities of language, which in general draw the strongest lines of national demarcation. There is no doubt that the people of the Grisons sprung from several sources. First of all, some branches of the original Gaulish stem occupied these regions under the name of Lepontii and Taurisci: afterwards, the wars of the Gauls in Italy occasioned emigrations out of Tuscany. The valleys of the Lepontii and Taurisci afforded refuge to thousands from the horrors of war, and the rage of barbarians. According to the legend preserved by Livy, the fugitives were headed by one Rhætus, whose name

became transferred to the people.   Even at the present
day there are traces to be found which confirm the au_
thenticity of this legend.   Above all, the old Italian
language is traceable up to our own times under the title
of the *Romanisch* or Romaunsch.   This dialect is un_
questionably an offspring of the Roman language, not of
the days of Augustus, but of earlier times and ruder
districts.

A second dialect, spoken in the Engadines at the
present day, is the Ladin, which, though related to the
former, is more musical, and more nearly approaching
to the Latin or modern Italian.   This seems to have
been imported by a new body of emigrants, who are
said to have fled thither in the time of the second Punic
war.   Thus there are two languages in the Grisons,
unknown in any other part of Europe.   Both have been
used by preachers, writers, and poets ; and the districts
where they are spoken are precluded by that circumstance from intercourse with others, more than even by
their walls of rock.

A third language spoken in the country is the German, which has always been used exclusively, with the
exception of Latin, in courts of justice, and which has
already, in a great measure, superseded both the others.

A fourth is the Italian, which prevails on the borders
of Italy, and particularly in the valleys of Misocco,
Salanca, and Puschiavo.

The effects of the foregoing causes were aided by the
influence of political arrangements in converting every
valley of the Grisons into the residence of a separate
population, each having little in common with the
others.   After the revolution in the fifteenth century,
which gave freedom to these mountainous districts, the
people rose at once to absolute sovereignty from a state
of feudal bondage and subjection.   The highest possible
degree of individual freedom lay at the foundation of the
new constitution ; and the popular passion for unre_
strained free agency was favoured by the variety of languages and localities.

Thus arose the Rhætian league, a federative system without precedent or parallel in the history of the civilised world. Each individual member of it was a little lord in his own commune. He gave his voice on all public occasions; was capable of every public function; provided sparingly for the maintenance of his clergy and his schoolmasters, and generally not at all for that of the civil authorities. Every little knot of families formed a hamlet; every hamlet might be regarded as a small independent state, with its peculiar jurisdictions, rights, and privileges; each had its own local administration, under the presidence of a magistrate called *Cuvig.* Several hamlets together formed a *commune,* in which, however, the separate rights of each were made matter of reservation. At the head of it stood the *amman,* who presided over the council and courts of justice, conducted the general government in the name of the commune, and represented his little republic in the general diets of the league, after his commune had supplied him with the necessary instructions.

A circle of neighbouring communes, without prejudice to their separate rights, formed a higher and more extensive jurisdiction. A landamman, who in some places bore the title of Podesta, and in others that of Land-vogt, held the executive power with the concurrence of a council. Each of these districts formed a republic equally independent with any of the Swiss cantons, with this difference, that it constituted, along with other districts of like extent, a *league* empowered to negotiate with foreigners. Rhætia was divided into three such leagues in the fifteenth century, and from thence was derived its title of the *Three Leagues,* distinguished as the *League of the Ten Jurisdictions,* that of *God's House,* and the *Grey League.* Each of these was connected with the rest by special treaties. Each had its own general assembly, and all were represented in a grand assembly or diet. This only took place once a year, excepting in extraordinary cases. In the interim a

congress of the presidents of the three leagues conducted
the current affairs of minor importance.

Thus the art of man strove to outdo the plastic hand
of Nature in moulding the Rhætians into a number of
petty populations, which had neither climate, language
usages, laws, nor feelings in common. That no repul-
sive element might be wanting to complete disunion,
religion threw a fresh apple of discord into the motley
mass ; and foreign intrigue speedily took advantage of
the schism which arose here, as in Switzerland, between
the reformed and catholic churches.

Since the epoch of the battle of Pavia, which put
Spain in possession of Milan and all Lombardy, that
court aimed continually, though secretly, to extend its
dominion over the Grison territory of the Valteline, in
order to maintain through the Tyrol a closer and more
uninterrupted connection with Austria, from whence
Spain, in the existing state of things, could only receive
aids or reinforcements at Milan, through the territory
of Venice or the Grisons. With these views the Spanish
viceroy at Milan seized every pretext for mixing in
the transactions of the Valteline, where religious zeal
produced perpetual differences. For since the Grison
league had permitted the free exercise of the evangelical
persuasion in the Valteline, many of the communes had
espoused that persuasion, and much dissension and discord was the consequence.

The king of France, as the enemy of Austria and of
Spain, warned the Grisons of the secret views of the two
combined powers ; and these warnings were re-echoed
by the Venetians, who had reason to fear encroachments
from the same quarter. Venice, France, and Spain sent
ambassadors to the Grisons, who were lavish of fair
words and presents to the heads of the leading houses,
who, notwithstanding the nominal sovereignty and self-
government of the people, practically directed public
affairs by their personal influence. Of the two most
influential families, Planta and Salis, the former headed
the Spanish, the latter the French party. Each side

was accused by the other of treasonable practices, and
each endeavoured to spirit up the communes in its own
favour. These, at length, assembled round their banners, and set up a criminal tribunal at Coire, for the
trial of (so called) traitors to their country. Thereupon,
as commonly takes place in popular tumults, innocent
and guilty alike were imprisoned, exiled, or robbed of
their property; and two individuals, holding eminent
stations, brought to the block. The evangelical clergy
industriously employed themselves in blowing up the
sparks of civil discord to a flame. They spread the
report that the viceroy of Milan had sent large sums
into the country to promote the Spanish alliance, and
that, in case of ill success in that undertaking, he was
resolved to throw the Valteline into confusion, fall on
the protestants, and celebrate a new St. Bartholomew by
the massacre of the whole evangelical party. These
reports, which were too soon to be verified, produced
the desired effect throughout the country. Rudolf Planta
was compelled to fly from the Engadine into the Tyrol.
A criminal tribunal was erected under the auspices of a
set of protestant preachers, which pronounced numerous
sentences of outlawry and confiscation, banished some
from the country, and brought others to the block.

The banished party leagued itself with Spain, Milan,
and Austria in a treacherous plot for massacring the
protestants in the Valteline, and for separating that district from the Grisons. The subjection and oppression
under which it laboured, and the general aversion entertained by its inhabitants for the reformed faith which
was favoured by its rulers, held out hopes of a favourable
issue to the enterprise. The conspirators secured a numerous body of adherents in the Valteline, and even in
the Grisons, collected under various pretences on the
frontier, and awaited the auspicious moment for action.
On Sunday, the 19th of July, 1620, these bands, led by
Rudolf and Pompey Planta, fell by surprise on the unfortunate district. Alarums sounded from all sides, and
a massacre of many hundred protestants ensued, marked

with circumstances of exquisite atrocity. Some were
thrown out of windows, shot, strangled, or burned; many
were flayed alive; others had their eyes put out; others
again were beaten to death with sticks, torn to pieces,
beheaded, or mutilated in various ways. Neither beauty
nor youth, age, deserts, or dignity,—not even the ties of
friendship nor of family affection, — could mitigate the
rage of these savage zealots. One fellow is said to have made
it matter of boast that he had murdered eighteen persons
in one day. The head of an evangelical preacher was
brought into his own church, stuck on the pulpit, and
mocked, it is said, in the same words as the crucified
Jesus. At Teglio, the protestants having shut themselves
up in the church, the murderers climbed up to the
windows and fired on the wretches within: at length the
doors were forced, and those who had fallen were to be envied in comparison with those who came alive into the hands
of their enemies. The victorious zealots seized with
blood-dripping hands the reins of government, and declared the independence of the Valteline.*

It was the Austrian and Spanish policy rather to
prompt than repress these horrors, with the view of
taking advantage of the general confusion to possess
themselves of the Valteline, — perhaps of the whole
of the Grisons. Negotiations were opened with these
courts, in the vain hope of inducing them to part
with the posts and passes which they occupied in the
Valteline. They were found, however, less disposed to
part with what they had got, than to appropriate Chiavenna and Bormio, as well as the lower Engadine, in
order to keep a passage open between Milan and the
Tyrol, for mutual aid against the French in Italy and
Germany. As the negotiations soon became too tedious
for the patience of the people in many communes of the
Grisons, the peasantry took to arms in a tumultuary
manner, and marched on Bormio and the Valteline, to
conquer the land on their own account, but effected
nothing by their enterprise, excepting that they exas-

* For a full description of these scenes see Fox's Book of Martyrs.

perated the archduke of Austria, who, exclaiming, " If you *will* have war, you *shall* have it !" marched a body of troops into the Grisons. After an obstinate but fruitless struggle, the insurgents were compelled to yield to the overwhelming force of the Austrians, who reclaimed their old hereditary sovereignty over the league of the Ten Jurisdictions, while the two other leagues were forced to agree that the troops of Spain and Austria should in all future time be allowed free passage through their territory.

The French monarch could not acquiesce in an arrangement which allowed the Austrians entrance at any moment into Italy, and established their ascendancy so completely in that country. He closed an alliance, accordingly, in 1623, with the pope, Venice, and Savoy, and marched an army through Switzerland into the Grisons. Berne and Zurich allowed his troops free passage through their territories, and the emigrants from the Grisons formed the vanguard of his army. On its advance, it was joyfully joined by the mass of the armed population; the garrisons of Austria were driven out of the Ten Jurisdictions, and possession was taken of Chiavenna, Bormio, and the Valteline. These territories, which had formerly been subject to the league, were freed from its jurisdiction in the treaty of peace dictated by France, and shortly afterwards acceded to on the part of Spain and Austria. But so soon as peace was again broken between France and Spain, and hostilities were recommenced in Italy, the emperor marched 40,000 men into the Grisons so suddenly, that no defence was possible. A part of the army was detached to the aid of the Spaniards into Lombardy, while the rest remained to overawe the Grisons. The Ten Jurisdictions, along with the lower Engadine, became once more the subject land of Austria.

This apparently hopeless aspect of affairs was suddenly altered by the peace closed between France and the emperor at Cherasco, by the terms of which the latter engaged to withdraw his troops from the Grisons. So soon

R

as the Austrian garrisons were drawn off and their
works demolished, the whole people joyfully resumed
their ancient league, and posted 3000 men under arms
on the frontiers of the country. After the land had thus
been freed from foreign domination, the inhabitants
addressed humble petitions to France and Spain for
leave to retain peaceably their newly-recovered territory.
Accordingly, a treaty of perpetual peace between Spain
and the Grisons was closed in 1639, at Milan, in virtue
of which the sovereignty of the Grison league was fully
re-established in Bormio, Chiavenna, and the Valteline,
with the single proviso that the catholic church should
retain its exclusive rights in these districts—a proviso
which precisely coincided with the wishes of the catholic
communes. In this manner good neighbourhood was
restored with the house of Austria, while Gustavus
Adolphus furnished that house with fighting enough in
Germany; so that it was well content to retain its
allowed prerogatives in the Engadine and within the Ten
Jurisdictions, without further attempts to restore an an-
tiquated sovereignty. Ten years had hardly elapsed before
these districts purchased the jurisdiction which Austria
still retained in their territory. Thus the Grisons became
free and independent, along with the two other leagues
in Upper Rhætia.

Though the treaties and campaigns of the Grisons
had supplied the Swiss cantons with matter in abundance for discussions and discourses in diets and council-
rooms, they had given birth to no distinguished enterprise for the vindication of Rhætian independence.
This resulted from the state of continual discord kept
up between the several cantons. If the reformed cantons wished to act, they were thwarted by the catholics;
if the catholic would have been active, the protestants
were sure to oppose themselves : the former sided with
Spain and Austria, the latter with France and Venice.
The one took gold from one party, the other from
the other, and closed treaties and sent soldiers to

serve under the standards of those foreign powers to which they had attached themselves; a practice which, while it enriched particular families, impoverished and orphaned others.

In the free bailiwicks, where the power lay between catholics and protestants, the two persuasions quarrelled everlastingly. Although in the terms of the general pacification, both parties in these vogtships enjoyed equal freedom of worship; yet the enjoyment of this privilege was imbittered to the catholics by the reformed vogts, and, on the other hand, by the catholic vogts to the protestants. Ecclesiastics mixed themselves up, as usual, in the matter. The bishop of Basle, supported by the emperor, as long as his arms were victorious in Germany, demanded of Mühlhausen and Basle restitution of all the property of his monastery, which he had lost long ago. The abbot of St. Gall reclaimed larger jurisdictions in the Thurgau and the Rheinthal than could equitably be given him; the abbot of Einsiedlen maintained, in opposition to Schwytz, a right of taxing the forest lands; the abbot of Fischinger wished to erect a catholic altar in the reformed church at Lustorf. Each of these reverend dignitaries found partisans as well as assailants. And more than once it had nearly come to civil war in Switzerland, which was only withheld from breaking out by the fear of the advantage which would be taken of it by foreigners. For at this crisis the thirty years' war, which originated between catholics and protestants in Bohemia, had not only spread over Germany, but involved in the sphere of its ravages Sweden and Italy, Spain, France, and Hungary. This war had been begun about matters of faith; but it was carried on for the acquisition of territory. French and Venetians, Spaniards and Austrians, in turn, negotiated for passages through the mountain passes of the Grisons, or solicited the alliance of the confederates; and the armies of the belligerent powers, when they drove each other from battle-field to battle-field on

German ground, often skirted very narrowly the borders of Switzerland. But the confederates, in the consciousness of internal weakness and discord, had no desire, in addition to the evils which they already endured, to see the swords of foreigners in their valleys. They, therefore, prudently maintained the neutrality and territory of Switzerland inviolate. But so great was their disunion that they hindered each other in the protection of their common domains and allies. When the allied town of Mühlhausen came into peril by the incursions of the Swedish and imperial troops, Zurich and Berne sent forces for its protection; but when the Bernese would have marched through the passes of Soleure, the guards refused a passage, and sounded an alarm. The land-vogts of Soleure surrounded the troops of Berne, fired on them, cut them down, killed many of their number, and disarmed the rest. Soleure was, indeed, forced to give heavy compensation, and some of the offenders were condemned to death, others to banishment; but hatred and distrust were not to be mitigated by legal proceedings. Shortly afterwards, when the Swedish marshal Horn, in order to surprise the Austrian garrison of Constance, had forced a way for his troops through the town of Stein, in the Thurgau, belonging to Zurich, the catholic members of the confederacy upbraided the reformers with favouring Sweden to the prejudice of the emperor. Uri, Schwytz, Unterwalden, and Zug, by way of counterpoise, marched 3000 of their troops on the Lake of Constance. But this occasioned the instant arming of Zurich; and a menace on the part of that canton, that her forces should immediately combine with those of Sweden if the catholic confederates made common cause with Austria.

Soon afterwards the imperialists at Schaffhausen infringed on the Swiss territory, as the Swedes had done at Stein. The men of Schaffhausen, indeed, took up arms; and some troops of Zurich marched out of the

Thurgau to their assistance: but the measures taken were tardy, feeble, and isolated. The villages of Bargen, Altdorf, Begguigen, Barzheim, and Schleitheim were partly sacked and burnt by the imperialists. The peasants, however, banded themselves with good success against the invaders; while the panic-struck government of Schaffhausen only exchanged epistolary vollies with the imperial marshals.

Nevertheless, the troops of Austria made repeated incursions on the territory of Basle, and scoffed at the defensive preparations of the Helvetic body.

It was often, indeed, insisted upon at diets, that the holy and inviolable rights of the Swiss soil called loudly for a standing force on the frontiers. But the people of the interior cantons said that those on the frontiers might take care of themselves, and exclaimed against the expense of a standing army. Every one was willing to have the benefits of a federal union; but none would sacrifice any thing to preserve them. Moreover, the ambassadors of foreign powers interfered, as usual, either in an imperative style, or by means of secret intrigue and insidious counsel: and, even in minute and near concernments, the confederates had not always the spirit to counteract their influence.

At this time many strangers roamed into Switzerland from the seat of war in Italy and Germany. Adventurers and fugitives excited the people against the authorities, in order to take advantage of the public confusion. These unserviceable vagrants were so numerous, that in one day 100 of them were counted at Schwytz, and at least sixfold that number in the county of Baden. The land was rendered quite unsafe, until rigour was used against them. At Bremgarten, 236 malefactors were sentenced to death within a single year. Such severities struck a salutary terror into those birds of passage.

The country was, however, less relieved by the sword of justice than by the conclusion of the ge-

neral peace of Westphalia, after a thirty years' war,
between the principal European powers.   This treaty,
which restored the tranquillity of Europe, concerned
itself besides with the relations of the Helvetic body.
That body, which had once formed a portion of the
German empire, had for ages ceased to consider itself
dependent on the imperial government, to the support
of which it was neither called to contribute men nor
money.   The only remaining vestige of dependence was
the formal confirmation of their franchises, from time to
time renewed to the confederates by the emperor.   The
Swabian war, the design of which had been to reduce
the Swiss to their original subservience to the empire,
missed its aim ; but the claims of the empire were never
entirely abandoned.   Occasional encroachments on the
Helvetic body took place,—in particular through the
agency of the court of the imperial chamber.   But
now the Swiss ambassador succeeded in obtaining the
insertion of a clause into the treaty of Westphalia, which
formally, and for ever, declared the absolute independence
and separation of the lands of the confederacy from the
German empire.   So that Switzerland offers, perhaps, the
single example of a country, the political self-existence
of which had never been acknowledged till the energetic
epochs of that existence had been long past, and till it
no longer possessed strength to defend, without the aid
of foreigners, its tardily acknowledged independence.

The foreign relations of Switzerland at this period
enriched, as we have seen, individual families, but in
no degree conduced to the well-being of the country.
The councils of the Helvetic body were continually
occupied with regulations regarding the enlistments in
foreign services.   About this time nearly 25,000 Swiss
were in the pay of foreigners.

The distresses and embarrassments of various descriptions, incident to the warlike times of which we have
been treating, had unfavourable effects upon the culture
of science.   An artificial taste, as well in thought as in

style, became prevalent. Astrology, and faith in super-
natural signs, in general retained their hold almost universally. As men imagine easily enough that they see and
hear that which they desire should be imparted to them,
or that which they are at any time engrossed with, swords
and other appearances in the heavens were often visible.
How fragmentary and limited in those times was the
knowledge possessed even by distinguished men, may be
judged by the fact, that one of the most eminent Swiss
diplomatists, employed in the Westphalian negotiation,
was obliged to ask the French plenipotentiary, Longue-
ville, whether French troops could not go by land to
Portugal without being obliged to pass through Spain !

CHAP. XVI.

THE PEASANT WAR.

1653—1656.

INSURRECTION OF THE PEASANTRY IN BERNE, LUCERNE, SOLEURE, AND BASLE.

THERE was very little harmony in the sentiments with
which the declaration of Helvetic independence was
received in different parts of the confederacy. Many
viewed the matter with indifference, and regarded it,
though only recently recognised, as something which had
long been possessed. Political emancipation brought
about no respite of religious dissension ; and new matter of embroilment was now added to the old feud between catholics and protestants.

Much discontent prevailed at this time among the
country people of more than one of the cantons that
many valleys remained in feudal servitude, or at least
were still subject to feudal burdens. When these

people compared their own condition with that of Uri,
Schwytz, and Unterwalden, whose inhabitants were subject to no laws and no authority but such as they had
given themselves, and to no taxes but such as they
themselves had imposed, they felt the more deeply
their own condition as purchased bondsmen and subjects
of the towns, liable to taxes and imposts without their
own consent being asked, and loaded with laws and
duties without their wishes being consulted. But they
felt still more vexation on being forced to yield, in
all points, to proud land-vogts, and rapacious men in
office; when they were struck for mere trifles, ill-
treated, and incarcerated; or impoverished by exorbitant
and arbitrary fines. Complaints against influential and
official men were of little use, and had often fatal results to the complainant; as relations of the land-
vogts, for the most part, sat in the government. Nay,
even secretaries, sub-vogts, and inferior officers, acted as
if they might persecute and plague the boors with impunity. Yet, as the evil was not every where felt
equally, and many just and good functionaries still
were to be found in the land, every thing for a while
remained quiet.

It was not, however, only in the free bailiwicks that
the people had long complained of the oppressions and
extortions of many among the land-vogts and other
functionaries, particularly those from the democratic
cantons,—but even in the immediate domains of the
ruling towns an oppressive system of government was
introduced, which was rendered yet more burdensome
by arbitrary assumptions. Actual necessities, and the
example of larger states, had occasioned the imposition
of new taxes; and, since the recognition of Swiss independence, many men in office considered themselves
to stand in a more elevated position with regard to
those whom they looked upon as their subjects. Frequent complaints were made of severe corporal punishments, of exorbitant and arbitrary fines,—sometimes

even of actual snares being set for wealthy persons. An aristocratic government is tottering towards its fall, when those who preside in it have lost the power, or the will, to keep in check the malversations of the official tools under them.

When the government of Berne made an effort to improve its currency by excluding the small coins of other cantons from its territory, and lowered by one half the nominal value of its own batzen, discontent was spread throughout the whole canton; the more so as the poorer classes suffered most by the change. The people held assemblies in the villages; and every one brought his own particular wrong to swell the aggregate. One complained of the tyranny of the landvogt, another of the government salt-monopoly, a third of that of gunpowder, a fourth of the corporation restrictions, a fifth of the feudal burdens, — one and all of the contempt of justice. The more the people spoke, the more their heads became heated.

Such was the moment selected by the government of Lucerne to lower the value of its batzen in like manner. Upon this the commune of Entlibuch sent delegates to the town, and prayed that either the coin should be left at its original value, or that agricultural produce should be taken in payment instead of it. But their petition was so harshly received, that they returned home in a state of great discouragement. This heightened the existing discontent; and when the collectors made their appearance, they were driven back with insult. On this the avoyer Dulliker came to Entlibuch, accompanied by secular and spiritual dignitaries, to remonstrate with the elders of the communes. But the able-bodied men from all the villages now gathered together, armed with spears and clubs, bearing in their van a white banner, followed by three youths who blew alp-horns; and behind them three others in old Swiss costume, representing the men of Rutli; and, lastly, the whole body, 1400 strong. In this order the procession arrived at Dorf, where the delegates of the towns were assembled: and here was renewed the clamour about the calling in of the coinage, the raised interest of money, the fines imposed by the land-vogts, &c.; so that the delegates could effect nothing, but made their way back to the town. But the country people held assemblies, posted guards, searched all travellers, encouraged the neighbouring subjects of Berne to join them; and the ten bailiwicks of the district swore to a solemn league at Wollhausen.

When matters became thus serious, the six catholic cantons sent ambassadors to offer mediation. But when these met the delegates of the ten jurisdictions at Willisau, who had committed to writing seven and twenty articles of grievance, the tumults recommenced among the peasantry; the confederate envoys were arrested and placed under strict guard; the principal passes towards the town were occupied; and Lucerne itself was threatened with an inroad. But the lesser cantons speedily despatched 400 men to garrison and defend the town: Zurich and Berne likewise commenced warlike preparations. When this became known to the people of the ten jurisdictions, their courage fell; they liberated the captive envoys, and begged for their mediation: which was equitably afforded them in the shape of a written award, which smoothed over the principal grounds of dispute between the parties.

While all was now supposed to be settled, the storm broke out afresh in the canton of Berne, from Thun as far as the town of Brugg: for when the government here attempted to call the country people out against those of Lucerne, they answered, "No, we will not march against our brothers; for we have as many rights to reclaim, and wrongs to complain of, as they!" In all the villages, clamour and disorder had the upper hand. Every one would command — no one obey. Berne invoked the aid of the confederacy to quell this insurrection. Schaffhausen, Basle, and Mulhausen sent military aid instantly. Zurich and Lucerne, however, advised friendly arbitration; to which the government of

Berne at length acceded. Before they had come to any understanding, the forces of Schaffhausen had entered the Bernese territory at Brugg, those of Basle and Mulhausen at Aarau. This embittered the people in the Aargau; and a levy *en masse* was proclaimed throughout the whole county of Lentzburg.

The disturbance now took an aspect of importance. The peasants besieged the castles of the land-vogts; sent commissioners to the government of Berne; and even had recourse for foreign succours to Laberde, the French ambassador. This step did grievous injury to their cause; for the ambassador himself betrayed their overtures; and the hearts of many well-intentioned persons were now turned from them, since they had sought foreign arbitrement in the cause of their native country. Many persons, especially among the wealthier class, preserved their allegiance to the constituted authorities: these were nick-named *soft,* and the antagonist party *hard* ones. Many adherents of the governments had their beards, others their ears, cut off. In the district of Basle, a person of that description had his ear cut off and placed in his hand, with the remark, that he was now indeed an *ear-bearer* (tale-bearer). The heads of others were held close to grind-stones, which were then set in motion, so that hair and scalp came off together; in order, as it was said, to *harden them.*

In the mean time appeared delegates from the six reformed cantons in Berne, in order to bring to a friendly arbitration all disputes between the authorities and their subjects. The commissioners of the revolted communes co-operated for this purpose: and it was finally decided that the government should retain the salt-monopoly—the subject the right of freely purchasing salt for his private use wherever he chose; that corporate restrictions should be abolished; the batzen remain still at a depreciated value, &c. All this and more being satisfactorily settled, the commissioners of the communes sued for pardon on their knees before the

town-council of Berne, and all seemed peaceably adjusted.

But the peasantry in Lucerne now raised a new clamour, and said they could not acknowledge their league
of Wollhausen as punishable, as it was treated in the
recent declaration.   They also sent forth emissaries to
the subjects of the other cantons, who every where proclaimed that they would no longer be vassals of the
towns, but free people, as those of the lesser cantons
were.   The people in the Aargau and the Emmenthal
joined them; and upbraided the commissioners who had
prostrated themselves before the council of Berne, and
had accepted the agreement.   In the cantons of Soleure
and Basle, also, many country people rose and avowed
their adhesion to the men of Lucerne, Emmenthal, and
Aargau.   In the Sumiswald they held land-assemblies,
and elected Nicholas Leuenberger, a countryman of
Schönholz, to preside over the league of the four cantons of Lucerne, Berne, Basle, and Soleure.

As in the old times the counts and barons had freed
themselves from the power of the emperor, and had asserted their own hereditary jurisdiction in their domains; and as, at a later date, the large towns of Switzerland, favoured by fortune and by circumstances, had
purchased emancipation from the power of the old
counts and barons; so the subject peasants were now
in arms to vindicate a share of freedom equal to that of
the towns.   But their enterprise was calculated badly.
These furious mobs neither went to work with the pious
uprightness and strict union displayed of old by the
men of the forest cantons, nor with the prudence and
deliberate resolution of the towns.   They were rude
unknowing people, inexperienced in state affairs, mis-
trustful of each other, and each sharper set on his own
than on the general advantage.   They listened with
more willingness to ranting declaimers than to the
counsel of intelligent men; and they were very soon
found to be divided among themselves, and prepared for
every species of extravagance.

Meanwhile the towns prepared themselves to quell the revolters, while they continued to negotiate with them in order to gain time: yet Berne and the diet at Baden meant more fairly by the people. Many conferences were planned or held with the delegates of the insurgents; but no treaty could be brought to bear with furious hordes, on whose resolutions no sort of dependence could be placed from day to day.

All overtures being in vain, Zurich, then the principal canton, summoned the whole confederate forces into the field. Berne called out the troops of the Pays de Vaud, — which, by its language, had been held apart from the cause of the German subjects, — and nominated Sigismund of Erlach to the command. He had about 10,000 men under his orders. From the catholic cantons came about 5000, led by the colonel Zueyer; the rest of the confederates, to the number of 10,000, were commanded by the Zurich field-marshal Wertmüller. The free peasantry of the lesser cantons stoutly supported the towns in asserting their cause against the revolted populace; for they, too, were possessed of subject bailiwicks.

However, the revolters also were speedily under arms. But they had neither heavy artillery nor military stores, nor discipline, nor leaders of experience; since the posts of command had hitherto been exclusively held by burghers.

As soon as Leuenberger, the chief of the leagued burghers, Schybi, Ulli Galli, and the other heads of the insurrection, saw that the game would be played in earnest, they endeavoured to put the best face on their perilous enterprise, partly by airs of defiance, partly by renewed negotiations. From his camp at Ostermundigen, a league from Berne, where his troops robbed and plundered all around them, Leuenberger once more wrote to Berne to propose a peaceable settlement of the contest. The council at Berne, to avoid the shedding of blood, actually sent ambassadors to the insurgents; and offered a large subsidy of 15,000*l.* to the peasants: not, however, as an indemnity for their war expenses, but as succour and relief to their poverty. The insurgent delegates finally subscribed the very composition which had already once before been rejected by them; and again promised loyalty and allegiance. But they had hardly returned to their camp when all their labours were rendered null and void: for, as the confederates had taken up arms, the insurgents would not lay down theirs till their antagonists should have drawn off their troops likewise.

General Erlach marched from Berne on Langenthal, and in his way dispersed a body of 2000 peasants. On the plain before Herzogenbuchsee, he found a guard of six peasants armed with halberts. These assured him the rebels were all dispersed; but, as he rode with his followers towards the town, shot after shot saluted them. He now saw the insurgent bands suddenly before him who had occupied the neighbouring wood, and he charged them on three sides at once.

Now began a desperate conflict. The insurgents, soon overpowered, defended step by step their retreat to the village. While a part of it was burning at their backs, they fought in the houses, and then behind the walls of the church. Finally, they dispersed and fled through the woods.

Instead of the sounds of uproar and defiance, the silence of death, remorse, and terror now prevailed in all the villages. The districts were disarmed; the leaders imprisoned. At Zofingen the confederate council of war sat, and held courts martial. Schybi was transported thither from Entlibuch, and beheaded. Leuenberger, betrayed in his own house by his neighbours and comrades, was imprisoned at Berne, where he was shortly after executed, and his bloody head affixed to the gallows beside the insurgent covenant. His secretary, Brosmer, died in like manner; and Ulli Galli was hanged. At Basle, seven old men, with snow-white beards, were sentenced to death as having taken part in the insurrection. Of the others, some were sentenced to death, some to banishment, others to fines. Thus the free bailiwicks had to pay 10,000 guilders; the people of the county of Lentzburg, 20,000; the men of Soleure, 30,000; and others in proportion: and the emperor Ferdinand III. proclaimed a sentence of outlawry against the fugitive insurgents through the whole Roman empire.

All members of the Helvetic body might by this time have convinced themselves, that nothing but internal union could save them in times of threatened danger, whether from within or without. The most decisive experience of this truth had been afforded by the incidents of the recent insurrection. It had been seen with what facility the insurgents of both religions had agreed upon a common form of compact and conspiracy; an agreement which, for many generations, their rulers had been unable to bring to pass. This spectacle revived the wish to infuse renewed vigour into the league of the confederacy. The evangelical party gave utterance to this wish in 1654; and it was undertaken to mould the former alliances into one general instrument. But as, in politics, important matters are often treated slightly when once they have become things of habit, so slight matters are swelled into importance when any thing of a novel nature is brought under discussion. The older cantons would not give up the prerogatives which they enjoyed over those which had been received into the league at a later period. Moreover, it did not escape the penetration of the catholics that their close connections amongst themselves, and with foreign powers, must yield to the more comprehensive bond of the confederacy. Many popular leaders feared the loss of the most fruitful sources of gain in their vocation. And thus, for the present, no re-union was possible.

Meanwhile the foreign policy of the two religious parties took directions diametrically opposite. The

evangelicals allowed no nice scruples to deter them
from mixing in foreign interests to promote those of
protestantism.   The then English government (that of
Cromwell) paid extraordinary honours to the envoys of
the protestant cantons.   In 1654, they made, by word
and writing, the most urgent intercessions at the court
of Turin for the persecuted Waldenses; contributed
for them 18,000 florins; spoke at length of the
possibility of resorting to armed intervention: and
it was principally through their aid, with that of
England and Holland, that a treaty of toleration was
closed at Pignerol, when the French minister, Mazarin,
who had originally instigated these persecutions, ceased
to give his support to the cause of Savoy.

In the following year, the catholic cantons renewed
their league with the bishop of Basle.   The contracting
parties not only promised each other active assistance in
cases of religion, and in every other just cause, but also
equal division of all conquests made in common; a
clause which seemed to point at the domains of the
protestant cantons, as conquests over the neighbouring
great powers could not be dreamed of.   Still more dis-
quieting for the protestants was the renewal of the Borromean league by the catholic cantons.

CHAP. XVII.

RELIGIOUS WAR AND WAR OF TOGGENBURG.

1656—1718.

RELIGIOUS WAR. — BATTLE OF VILLMERGEN. — THE PLAGUE. — USURPATIONS OF THE ABBOT OF ST. GALL OVER THE PEOPLE OF TOGGENBURG. — CONDUCT OF SCHWYTZ AND GLARUS — OF BERNE. — WAR OF TOGGENBURG. — FLIGHT OF ABBOT LEODEGAR. — TOGGENBURGERS AIM AT INDEPENDENCE — WHICH IS REFUSED THEM. — SURPRISAL OF THE BERNESE TROOPS BY ACKERMANN OF UNTERWALDEN. — SECOND ACTION AT VILL-MERGEN. — PEACE OF AARAU. — HOSTILE INTERFERENCE OF THE POPE AND HIS NUNCIO. — REPRISALS OF THE HELVETIC BODY.

SCARCELY was the foregoing insurrection well disposed of, when a new dispute broke out among the cantons of the confederacy.

This was a fresh manifestation of that unchristian hatred which prevailed between protestants and catholics. The clergy on both sides, instead of extinguishing the flame of discord, blew it up by their preaching.

There never were wanting occasions of dispute among the governments, especially in the common or free baili-wicks, where each contended exclusively for its own creed and its own jurisdiction ; and none reposed confidence any longer in their colleagues, as none would believe any thing but evil of the rest. The catholics would not believe that Berne and Zurich built fortifi-cations, and entered into alliances with Holland and wito England, for nothing. The protestants com-plained of the catholics, for confirming the Borromean league, renewing their alliances with Savoy and the bishop of Basle, and keeping up relations of close amity with the court of Spain.

It happened that six families of Arth, in the canton of Schwytz, were obliged to fly for holding the evangelical persuasion, as their lives were hardly safe in their native village. They presented themselves with tears and prayers before the council of Zurich, and only begged that the free transport of their property might be procured for them. Upon this the council of Zurich addressed pressing intercessions to Schwytz in behalf of these persecuted people; but Schwytz refused to listen to their overtures, and demanded the surrender of the persons of the refugees. When upon this the reformed cantons appealed to the rights of the confederacy, Schwytz replied: "Within our own land we owe no account to any one, except to God and to ourselves." Moreover, they confiscated the goods of the emigrants, threw their relatives (as they also were of the protestant persuasion) into prison, put some of them to the torture, and condemned others to death.

Zurich now took up arms, as all admonition and mediation from the neutral cantons at diets had been useless. With equal celerity, Schwytz and the catholic cantons were in the field. Zurich, supported by Basle, Mulhausen, and Schaffhausen, marched troops towards the Rhine, occupied the Thurgau, and besieged Rapperswyl. But the catholics had already occupied Rapperswyl and the Albis, as well as Bremgarten, Mellingen, and Baden, and the Brunigberg, on the side of Berne. The Bernese sent detachments to the defence of Freyburg, Soleure, and Unterwalden, and marched to Lentzburg with forty banners to the succour of the Zurichers.

There was, however, nothing like discipline in the ranks of the reformers. They sacked and burned wherever they came, pillaged the monastery of Rheinau, plundered villages and churches, and drove off the cattle. So little order was preserved by the Bernese, that they encamped in the district of Villmergen, without troubling themselves at all about the enemy; sent out no scouts; and were not even provided with sufficient ammunition. And although some men of the Aargau had descried the enemy by the village of Wohlen, and gave the alarm to the Bernese; yet no attention was paid to them, as some young gentlemen of Berne had ridden out to reconnoitre and assured that all was safe.

More than 4000 men of Lucerne, in effect, lay in ambush on the heights of Wohlen. From a ridge in the hollow way, where they were covered up to the waist, they suddenly opened a fire on the Bernese lines. These fell into such panic and confusion that they could hardly be formed in order of battle. As powder and ball were deficient, they discharged only two rounds from their field pieces; the rout was general. Ten fresh squadrons, indeed, came to their aid; but those wheeled about and took to flight along with the rest. The general of Lucerne had in his pocket during the action a letter from his government containing an order not to fight, as a peaceable arrangement was in progress: but he put it up unopened, as he could guess at the contents, and pursued the flying Bernese, of whom a vast number were cut to pieces. They lost about 800 men, and eleven pieces of heavy artillery. A strong body of Bernese troops were posted in the neighbourhood, and saw the flight of their countrymen towards Lentzburg, but did not leave their position, not having orders.

Such was the fatal battle of Villmergen. The victors lay encamped, exulting, three days on the field of battle; they then marched homewards, loaded with plunder. A few weeks afterwards an armistice, and finally a peace, were concluded. For as, during warfare, the transport of the necessaries of life was suspended with regard to the lesser cantons, and as the government of Lucerne could as little as that of Berne repose confidence in its own discontented peasantry, it was the interest of all sides to put a speedy end to the war, which, though it lasted only nine weeks, had already cost the Zurichers above 414,000 florins. The pacification restored things to their previous situation. In matters of religion, and with regard to freedom of transit for goods between one canton and another, each canton retained the power of acting in its own domain at its own pleasure.

The catholics might have taken even greater advan-

tage of the wretched state of discipline in the protestant
cantons, if their own war department had been conducted
at all better. Peace was now restored without the spirit
of peace. Both sides were exhausted; but the damage
done reciprocally remained without compensation, and
the minds of both parties were embittered more than
ever. This was visible every where, and chiefly in
the common bailiwicks. In these, what hurt the one
pleased the others; and the populace exhibited their
unchristian zeal of doctrine according to the example
of their rulers. It lacked but a slight impulse to occasion a renewal of warfare.

An officer of Lucerne, who had levied troops for the service of Spain, marched them through the Thurgau, and
led them, with drawn sabres, into the protestant church of
Ripperswyl. From thence a woman pursued them with
curses and horrible cries to Wigoldingen, where the
population were speedily up in arms on the Spanish
soldiers, five of whom were slain, some wounded, and
others taken prisoners. This event called up the reformed and catholic cantons in arms. Troops were
levied; the five catholic cantons immediately occupied
Kaiserstuhl, Mellingen, and Bremgarten. Much debate
and negotiation followed. The catholic cantons were
not to be pacified save by blood. Two men of Wigoldingen were sentenced to death by the majority of the
cantons, which exercised sovereignty over the Thurgau,
notwithstanding Zurich's urgent solicitations for their
pardon. The commune of Wigoldingen being sentenced
to pay the whole expenses of the lengthened dispute,
collections were made in aid of that object in all the
churches of Zurich.

Similar disputes were very frequent in these times;
and persecutions on account of faith were practised
without mercy. Thus sorrow and distress were introduced into many households. Contagious sickness
next was added to all the other sources of misery, which
carried off numbers, especially in Basle and in the
Aargau. The season had been unhealthy, and warm

during almost the whole winter. Venomous worms and caterpillars covered trees, grass, and fruits; and water and field mice appeared in greater numbers than had before been known. This continued till the year came to an end, and a hard winter followed.

Many of the Swiss, though called free, were poor subjects, possessed of fewer rights than those of kings; nay, force and fraud were often used without scruple to extirpate, little by little, the few franchises of the people, that the power of their lords might luxuriate without limits.

The people had a special experience of this in the district of Toggenburg. In former times, through the favour of the old counts of Toggenburg, the communes had enjoyed important privileges in this district—participation in the appointment of the higher and lower courts of justice, and in general assemblies called to consult upon the military and civil administration. No land-vogt, moreover, could be imposed on them but by election from amongst the native inhabitants.

But the abbots of St. Gall having purchased of the barons of Raron the jurisdiction over the land which the latter had acquired by inheritance from the old counts of Toggenburg; the new possessors aimed in their turn at privileges, which, far from having purchased, they had formally acknowledged to belong to the people. And in like manner as the people of Toggenburg had set up, for the protection of their freedom, a common-law jurisdiction with the cantons of Schwytz and Glarus; so, in 1469, the abbot also established a defensive league with the same cantons, for the maintenance of his territorial rights. As his abbacy was connected with the confederacy, and he himself bore the title of prince of the holy Roman empire, he always knew how to take advantage of his twofold title. He opposed himself to the emperor, when it suited him, in his quality of confederate; to the confederates as prince of the empire, and delegate of imperial majesty; and thus he made his double character stand him in good stead.

He now began to speak of the freedom of Toggenburg in ambiguous terms, and went so far as to call the people his vassals, in order to accustom them to become such. At last he attacked their franchises openly, and much debate took place before the diets of the confederacy. These, however, seconded his pretensions. Thus he first obtained appellate jurisdiction from all tribunals in the country to his own court; then he assumed the right of choosing a foreigner for land-vogt, of holding the unchecked administration of church property, preserves, and fisheries; in addition to these, he set up a claim of appointing the priest in every church, and conferring the rights of citizenship at his pleasure. Lastly, the people were prohibited from holding assemblies; and the war administration of the country fell, in 1654, entirely into the abbot's hands. Now he domineered at pleasure, assented to compulsory enlistments in foreign services, filled all places with his creatures, and regarded with indifference the appropriation of the best lands to monasteries through methods the most fraudulent.

At length, the abbot Leodegar considered himself absolute lord in the land; he commanded the people to make, and to maintain, at their own cost, a new highway through the Hummelwald; and when the delegates of the people dared to remonstrate that this would be a burthen more oppressive than had formerly been the feudal services from which they had already bought themselves free, he condemned them to a heavy fine, to public recantation, and he declared them disarmed and dishonoured.

The oppressed Toggenburgers now brought their complaints before Schwytz and Glarus. Glarus took the distress of the poor peasantry to heart, as also did Schwytz, although the Toggenburgers professed the reformed faith. "And even though they were Turks and heathens," cried the Schwytzers in the general assembly, "they are nevertheless our countrymen and confederates, and we should help them to assert their rights." This incensed the abbot, who appealed to all the cantons in behalf of his confederate rights. Now came diet upon diet, from year to year. Many were well inclined towards the Toggenburgers, on account of their reformed and oppressed faith; many hostile to the abbot, for having shortly before closed a defensive alliance with Austria, and for appearing to regard the county of Toggenburg as a fief held of the emperor and the empire. The longer the quarrel lasted, the more perplexed, of course, became the matter out of which it arose. At length the old religious hatred threw in its venom; for so soon as Schwytz and the other catholic cantons perceived that Zurich and Berne afforded assistance to the Toggenburgers chiefly on the ground of their common faith, and encouraged them to stand fast for their old rights, Schwytz became better inclined to the abbot of St. Gall. This, however, did not deter Zurich and Berne from their purpose, or the citizens of Toggenburg from the exercise of their franchises. The imperial envoy now stepped in with a missive from his court, of which the purport was that the emperor would settle the affair, as the county of Toggenburg had indubitably, from time immemorial, been a fief of the empire; but Zurich and Berne replied, that Toggenburg lay within the Swiss frontier, and that the abbot of St. Gall had long acknowledged them as arbitrators. Moreover, the ambassadors of Holland and the kings of England and Prussia encouraged the men of Zurich and Berne in resistance to the emperor.

The matter of dispute became more and more indefinite, and tumult and violence now arose in Toggenburg itself. The abbot adhered stiffly to the maintenance of his usurped power. The Toggenburgers refused obedience, and drove away his functionaries; whereupon the abbot posted troops on all the bridges, roads, and passes in the district of St. Gall. Bailiff Dürler, in Lucerne, the most zealous friend of the abbot, called the catholic cantons out, to keep in check the rebels of Toggenburg. On the other hand, the mayor

of Berne, Willading, exhorted the reformed cantons to
appeal without delay to the sword, for the old rights of
the people of Toggenburg and the safety of the protestant
church.

So soon as the men of Toggenburg saw that Zurich
and Berne stood on their side, and that general Bodmer
was on his march from Zurich to their aid, with a
force of nearly 3000 men, they proclaimed war for the
maintenance of their rights against the abbot. Rabholz,
an eminent member of the government of Zurich, became
their leader, as he had before been their friend and counsellor, proclaimed a levy *en masse*, and engaged the
abbot's myrmidons as vigorously with the sword as he
had already done with the pen. The abbot's cloisters
and castles were besieged, and the troops of Zurich
ravaged the whole district of St. Gall without the slightest
restraint of order or discipline.

Now also Lucerne, Uri, Schwytz, Unterwalden, and
Zug took up arms, advanced on Toggenburg, and occupied the county of Baden. The nuncio gave them
26,000 thalers out of the papal treasury; and in Rome
prayers were offered up to the saints for their success.
Consecrated bullets and amulets were distributed by the
priests to the soldiers. Berne, on her part, raised 10,000
crowns from her own treasury, and brought 15,000 men
into the field. A Bernese force advanced against the
Stilli, crossed the Aar, and joined the forces of Zurich at
Würelingen: these, at the same time, had taken possession of the whole Thurgau.

Under these circumstances, Glarus and Soleure remained
neutral, as likewise did the bishop of Constance. Basle
and Freyburg lamented this civil contest between Swiss
and Swiss, and once more exhorted both sides to an
amicable agreement; but the admonition came too late.
The abbot of St. Gall transported his valuables to Lindau,
betook himself to Rosbach, and applied to the town of
St. Gall and to the territory of Appenzell and Glarus
for assistance; but they promised him nothing further
than their neutrality. The emperor, on the other hand,

summoned the circle of Swabia, as far as Presburg, in
Hungary, to the assistance of the abbot.

Meanwhile, the brave Rabholz had marched into the
old abbey-lands; the banners of Berne and Zurich went
victoriously through the whole Thurgau, as far as the
town of St. Gall: they there placed a garrison in the
abbey, and at Rosbach. The panic-struck abbot had
already taken refuge for himself and his valuables at
Augsburg.

The Toggenburgers, now that their cause was victorious, condemned those of the abbot's people to death
who had acted the part of betrayers towards them; they
threw off the abbot's dominion altogether, as well as the
connection with Schwytz and Glarus, and proposed to
the people of Gaster, Uznach, and others to found a
free and independent state, like the cantons of the confederacy; and they planned a new constitution, which
they brought before the diet at Aarau. But such language displeased the leaders of Berne and Zurich, as
they would rather have had the Toggenburgers for subjects than for fellow-confederates: even Rabholz, the
zealous champion of the Toggenburg cause, declined to
second the wishes of the people, although they offered
him large sums of money to do so.

Meanwhile infinite wrath and discord prevailed in the
catholic cantons. Some were for peace, others for war.
The French and Austrian ambassadors promised assistance; the pope sent money; Freyburg and Soleure
espoused their cause with the Valais, and the whole
catholic portion of the bailiwicks. But those reformed
districts, on the other hand, which had hitherto remained
quiet, threatened to take up arms; and all of that persuasion in the common bailiwicks actually did take up
arms in support of Zurich and Berne. Thus, at this time,
nearly 150,000 Swiss stood arrayed for mortal conflict
with each other: at no former period had the confederacy
taken the field in equal force against a foreign enemy.
And so it happened, that one sword kept another in the
scabbard.

While the envoys of the confederacy sat at Aarau
and treated of peace, the land-vogt and knight Ackermann of Unterwalden marched with 5000 men upon
the bridge of Sins, where the forces of Berne lay in
their encampment. The priest of Sins, on a previous
understanding with Ackermann, had given a banquet to
the leaders of the Bernese, in order to lull their vigilance.
They were thus taken by surprise, so that they saved
themselves with difficulty. Many of the Bernese were
slain. Their leader, Meunier, who, with 200 men, defended himself valiantly, first in the churchyard and
then in the church, was obliged at last to give himself
and his men up as prisoners : they would infallibly have
been cut down without mercy, had not Ackermann, with
generous boldness, curbed those blood-thirsty men. The
Schwytzers had moreover pressed forwards, in the direction of Hütten and Bellenschanz, towards the Lake of
Zurich. There, however, they came upon Hans Wertmüller, the vigilant commander of Zurich. Seven hours
long the Schwytzers fought — they lost 200 men ; but
they were finally compelled to yield to the Zurichers.
Among their slain were found consecrated tickets, with
numbers, and crosses, and assurances of victory.

Knight Ackermann drew catholic reinforcements
around him from all quarters. His troops were above
12,000 strong. He marched with vigour through the
land by Muri to Wohlen and Villmergen, where the
Bernese stood with 8000 men. Here, in the same
region where the Bernese once before had suffered a
bloody defeat from the catholic cantons, in 1656, the
turf was again to be reddened with Swiss blood shed by
Swiss hands. It was the 25th of July, 1712. The
Bernese had taken position near Meiengrün. The
thunder of artillery opened the conflict. Six long
hours the struggle was protracted. At length the
Bernese brought confusion and panic among the champions of the catholic cantons, broke their ranks and
put them to flight. The plain was strewed with the
corpses of above 2000 catholics.

The Toggenburgers now having gained possession of Uznach and Gaster, the town of Rapperswyl being surrendered to the Zurichers, and the conquerors having pressed from all sides into the catholic territory, their antagonists at length became intimidated, and begged for peace.

Already had the cantons of Lucerne and Uri subscribed to the terms of peace at the diet in Aarau; but the peasantry of the former canton, incited by the papal nuncio, as well as •by their own priests and monks, would not hear of peace, but had marched against the town to force the government into hostilities, and from thence against the Bernese at Villmergen. Here they had rushed on merited destruction.

The general peace of the country was at length concluded at Aarau, on terms of course advantageous to the victors. The five catholic cantons were not only compelled to cede their rights over Baden, Rapperswyl, and the lower bailiwicks, in favour of Zurich and Berne, but, besides, to take these two preponderant cantons into partnership of dominion over the Thurgau and the Rheinthal, where both religious parties from thenceforward exercised equal rights. Glarus remained exclusively in the possession of Berne and Zurich.

The humbled abbot Leodegar of St. Gall would not, however, accept the terms of pacification; and consequently remained, to the day of his death, in obstinate exile. Meanwhile the troops of Berne and Zurich occupied his lands. But when the new abbot, Joseph, in 1718, accepted the above mentioned terms of peace in Rosbach, his lands were restored, and the Toggenburgers placed once more in subjection to him; but with augmented rights and franchises, under the guarantee of Berne and Zurich. The pope and his nuncio only persisted in rejecting the peace of Aarau, declaring it altogether null and void. This, however, troubled the reconciled confederates but little: and when the people in some districts of the canton of Lucerne were incited by the clergy against the government, a garrison

from Entlibuch was taken into the town, a tax on monasteries demanded of the pope towards covering war
expenses, and at the same time the recall of the nuncio
Caracciolli was insisted on, who was denounced as the
principal promoter of all the mischief. The bitter effects
of this war were long felt by the catholic cantons, which,
in carrying it on, had incurred immense expenses.
Schwytz imposed on every household a tax of five thalers. Lucerne was compelled to use force in collecting
her imposts. Uri could only pacify her subjects in the
Val Levantina by conceding extensive franchises, and
by designating them thenceforwards as " well-beloved
and faithful countrymen."

CHAP. XVIII.

COURSE OF EVENTS DURING THE EIGHTEENTH CENTURY.

1702—1781.

FOREIGN RELATIONS AND POLICY OF THE HELVETIC BODY AT THE
BEGINNING OF THE EIGHTEENTH CENTURY. — JESUIT MISSIONS.
— CONDUCT OF DU LUC THE FRENCH AMBASSADOR. — CASE OF
THOMAS MASSNER OF COIRE. — CONSPIRACY OF HENZI AT
BERNE. — INSURRECTION OF CHENAUX AT FREYBURG. — NEW
ALLIANCE WITH FRANCE.

On the outbreaking of the war of the Spanish succession, the intrigues of foreign ambassadors in Switzerland occasioned partial ferments and divisions, but
the confederates kept carefully out of dangerous en-
tanglements. They aimed exclusively at securing their
neutrality; a point in which they succeeded but imper-
fectly, for the security of their frontiers and communications was subjected to frequent interruptions. The
belligerent powers harassed the Helvetic body with constant demands, and goaded them to inward dissension.
Such machinations were only too successful in a state
which was already making rapid approach to ruin, — in
which the common weal had ceased to be much regarded;

and every one held himself justified in pursuing his own interests in preference to those of his country.

The relations which subsisted between the Helvetic body and France were of a delicate and very peculiar nature. The latter power founded an especial claim to gratitude on the permanent employment of Swiss troops in her service : the French court thought fit to forget that the seeming profits of this connection were bought by the confederates at the price of streams of blood, of the decay of arts and agriculture, constantly increasing moral corruption, and utter extinction of patriotism and public spirit. But France only took account of the sums of money transmitted to Switzerland, regarded the latter country in the light of a sort of province, and treated all opposition to her wishes and proceedings as an overt act of treason against her majesty. In this spirit the French ambassador, count du Luc, expresses himself:—
" I had believed that, at least, families loaded by France with wealth and honours, must necessarily bear the fleur-de-lis traced in their inmost hearts : but I find that this nation retains no sense of received benefits ; that tokens of favour only weigh with those who enjoyed them personally ; and do not even influence the sentiments and actions of their nearest relations favourably to the interests of his majesty." He recommended, by way of remedy, to lavish constant good treatment exclusively on the pensioners of France, in order that their zeal and fidelity may frustrate the resistance of others. In like manner, he holds it indispensable that the friends of France should, at any expense, be promoted to the first official stations in the cantons. Du Luc goes on to advise that, in all military promotions, particular attention should be paid to the men of the Thirteen Cantons, and those of the Valais and the Grisons, who are accustomed to regard every step made by others as a robbery committed on themselves. For the rest, he says, the whole system of policy to be observed with Swiss statesmen may be expressed in two words:— these gentlemen must either be treated with great regard and honour; or fairly

crushed, and put out of the power of doing mischief.
The lengths which France was capable of going, in order
to strengthen her party in the confederacy, and to win,
fatigue, " or fairly crush" her opponents, may be judged
of from the following incident : —

Thomas Massner of Coire, a man of enormous wealth
and influence, and who was considered as the head of
the Austrian party in the Grisons, had made himself
obnoxious to France by his well-known political connections. The following plan was adopted by the French
ambassador, count du Luc, in order " to deprive him of
the power of doing mischief." Massner's son, a lad of
sixteen, a student at Geneva, was decoyed on a party of
pleasure into Savoy by the brother of the French agent
at Coire, kidnapped by the French, and carried off to
Fort l'Ecluse. The indignant father meditated active reprisals, and succeeded in obtaining possession of the person of the French agent at Coire himself, Merveilleux.
The French ambassador denounced the act as a breach
of the law of nations; while in the Grisons it passed for
an equitable, though extra-legal, retaliation. Massner's
friends compromised the matter, and engaged him to
liberate his captive, and ask pardon of the French ambassador, on condition that his son should likewise be
liberated : but Massner having honourably performed his
part of the treaty, and his son being still detained in
hopeless captivity, he fell upon new plans of revenge.
He took prisoner the duke de Vendôme, grand prior of
France, carried him to Feldkirch, and delivered him up
to the Austrians : this excusable act of vengeance proved
a seed of much misfortune to Massner. The government
of the Grisons did its utmost to negotiate the reciprocal
liberation of the captives. On the demand of France,
a tribunal was appointed at Ilanz for the trial of Massner,
who sought his safety in flight. In 1711, a sentence of
outlawry was passed against him ; his property was
confiscated, his house rased to the ground, and a monument of his ignominy erected on its site. Many of his
partisans were involved in his fall. A thousand ducats

were promised for him, if delivered alive into the hands
of justice ; and five hundred ducats for his dead body.
The outlaw lived for some time under the safeguard of the
emperor; but his services fell insensibly into oblivion at
the court of Vienna. Disgrace, disgust, or lingering love
of country, impelled him at length to quit the Austrian
territory ; and he wandered for awhile friendless and
helpless in the district of Glarus : here he was discovered, and the French ambassador claimed his surrender.
He lost his life in his flight by the oversetting of his
carriage. The conclusion of peace between France and
Austria, in 1714, brought about the liberation of young
Massner; who was received with exultation by his countrymen, and loaded with honours and dignities in return
for his protracted trials.

The years 1702, and 1705, exhibited a phenomenon
in Switzerland which our own times have reproduced
in the countries which adjoin it, with striking if not
permanent effect. In 1702, two jesuits made their appearance, accompanied by other monks as well as by
several laymen, at Chiavenna in the Swiss territory,
offering little devotional books and images for sale. They
pretended to the power of forgiving sins and working
miracles ; and were received with ready credulity in the
Valteline, though their pretensions had been laughed at
in France, in Italy, and even in Spain. They went
barefoot, slept for only three hours in the night, preached
and heard confessions in the day time; they took no salt
with their food, tasted neither flesh nor wine, began
their service at break of day with a procession out of
the town, and in the afternoon preached abundant ab-
surdities in the town itself, without text or arrangement,
to a concourse of people from all quarters : they thundered against vice with ludicrous gestures; and their
preachments were heard kneeling by the multitude.
After the close of their discourses, they frequently stripped
off their upper garments, and with blunt knives, which
they kept stuck in their girdles, cut their bare backs,
in such a manner that many sympathetic souls melted

into tears. All these exhibitions were performed in an
open place, as no church could contain such an assem-
blage. Their followers, especially those of the clerical
order, appeared barefoot, with ropes about their necks,
crowns of thorns upon their heads, some attired in black,
others in red or white and blue linen, others again with
their faces covered in coarse sacks which hung to the
ground. Nocturnal processions also were held, in which
the penitents carried lanterns on poles, and heavy crosses,
and flogged themselves with scourges armed with points.
The preachers declared absolutions and benedictions ineffectual with regard to those who did not follow their
discipline in all points. A large fire kept up beside the
station of the missionaries was fed, by the devotion of
their contrite hearers, with packs of cards, seductive
books, French head-dresses adorned with lace and ri-
bands, &c. &c. A little brook was blessed by these adventurers, that its waters might cure fever and flux,
which happened to be prevalent : for the same purpose,
consecrated tickets were distributed in the cathedral. One,
whose wife and children were sick, was commanded by
these jesuits, in order to effect their cure, to spend twelve
days and nights in a wood, without any other aliment
than herbs and roots. On returning half alive to his
home, he found his family cured — by death. The
people were persuaded, that those who contrived to get
nearest these missionaries during their processions obtained immediate entrance to heaven, without passing
through purgatory : accordingly, as every one was determined to be nearest, it came to *voies de fait;* and tumults took place which could hardly be stilled by the
influence of the spiritual mountebanks. On their departure, many followed them for eight or nine leagues
in sacks, in order to earn the absolution, promised to
extend to their posterity for twenty years after their
death. These holy doings lasted till the bishop of Como
came to take the waters at St. Moritz. This bishop, a
convivial and card-loving prelate, dispensed the contrite
sinners from their penitential practices, by virtue of his

spiritual authority and example; loose living became more universal than ever. " They imagined," observes Hottinger, " that they had fully atoned for their former sins, and lost no time in beginning a new score."

The farce was renewed in 1705. Two jesuit missionaries came into the democratical cantons from Italy; they preached repentance and remission of sins every where in the open air. Innumerable multitudes gathered around them. A mob of all ranks followed them about from place to place; and those of their hearers who set up for extraordinary devotion appeared in black garments, with robes and chains round their neck and loins: but the most devout of all enacted the scenes of the crucifixion. They went about barefoot, wearing crowns of thorns on their heads, and dragging heavy crosses, and allowed themselves to be struck, thrust about, and scourged by persons paid for it, misinterpreting, in a childish manner, the words of Jesus Christ, — " If any one will come after me, let him take up his cross and follow me." The missionaries left Switzerland loaded with wealth; and even flattered the pope with the agreeable anticipation that the protestant part of Switzerland might be led back to the lap of the church.

The outward peace enjoyed by the confederacy during the eighteenth century (the last of its existence in its primitive form) was contrasted by incessant inward disturbances. The first of these which claims our attention is the conspiracy of Henzi at Berne. Here, as in most towns of the confederacy, a more and more formal and regular aristocracy had grown up by degrees in the course of centuries. From time immemorial the powers of government had been held by the avoyer and council. For the protection of the burghers against the encroachments of the council, and of that body against the influence of the multitude, an assembly of 200 of the most respectable burghers was formed, the members of which were annually elected. The most important acts, which imposed duties on every burgher, not only for himself but for his posterity, were often

brought before the whole body of citizens, and even
country people; the more so as at that time a few villages constituted the whole domain of Berne.   The
continual aggrandisement of the state rendered obsolete
the fundamental laws of its constitution, which became
imperceptibly modified in proportion as political emergencies appeared to require alterations.   When the power
of Berne was doubled by the conquest of the Vaud, the
assembly of the burghers ceased to be thought of.   The
dignities of the state became hereditary in those families
which had once obtained a seat in the great council.   It
is true that the other burghers remained eligible to public
functions; but it was rarely indeed, and generally by
means of intermarriages, that a new family raised itself
to the rank of the rulers *de facto*.

The administration of these ruling families was, in
general, not devoid of wisdom and equity; and, in fact,
the principal subject of complaint was that participation
in state affairs had ceased to be open to all.   It was,
however, precisely this system of aristocratic exclusion
which was felt so insupportably by many of those who
were subjected to it, that so early as 1710 attempts were
made to break it up.   These were renewed with increased
vigour, in 1743, by six and twenty burghers, who combined to petition the council for the revival of a greater
equality of rights in favour of the general body of citizens.   These adventurous men incurred the censure of the
authorities, and were placed under arrest in their houses
or banished.   Amongst the exiles was Samuel Henzi, a
man of no ordinary talent and spirit.   He had fixed
on Neufchâtel as the place of his banishment; the term
of which was shortened by the favour of the authorities.
On his return, the embarrassed state in which he found
his domestic economy, and the ill-success of his efforts
to obtain a lucrative office, may have mingled with other
motives in inducing him to take the lead in a desperate
undertaking of a little band of malcontents, who, without
money, arms, or even unity of purpose, dreamed of
overturning a government strong in its own resources,

and sure of support from the whole Helvetic body, and of instituting equality of rights among all burghers, and appointment to all offices by lot. Yet, with all their root and branch work, the conspirators had no idea of remedying the real defects of the state, of satisfying the prevalent and increasing discontents of the Vaud, or of procuring an extension of political rights to the whole people: for, in the plan of a constitution annexed to their meditated manifesto, exclusive regard was paid to the burghers at Berne; and the rest of the people would hardly have been bettered by their accession to the dignities which had hitherto been engrossed by the ruling families. The 13th of July, 1749, was fixed for the execution of the plans of the conspirators; but many of their own number had opened their eyes by this time to the utter impossibility of success, produced by the disunion and imprudence of their colleagues — to the passion and cupidity of some, and the atrocious hopes of murder and plunder entertained by others. No man felt more sensibly the criminal views of his party than the only man of ability and public spirit among them, Henzi. He would not betray those with whom he had long pursued the same object; but he made an attempt to save himself by flight from farther participation in their plans and foreseen destiny. It was too late: a betrayer had already done his work. Henzi and other heads of the party were taken and beheaded during the first exasperation of the government. Sentence of death was also pronounced upon some who had made their escape; others were imprisoned or banished, but soon afterwards pardoned. On embarking with her two sons to quit the Helvetic territory, the wife of Henzi exclaimed, " I would rather see these children sink in the Rhine-stream than they should not one day learn to avenge the murder of their father." However, when the sons came to manhood, they displayed more magnanimity than their mother; and one of them, who rose to distinction in the service of the Netherlands, requited with good offices to the burghers of his native town the unmerited misfortunes which they had brought upon his family.

In Freyburg,—where, in old times, equality of rights for all burghers had been settled as a principle,—a no less close aristocracy had formed itself than in Berne, since the middle of the seventeenth century. A few houses, under the denomination of *secret families*, had contrived to exclude, not only the country people, but a large proportion likewise of the town burghers, from all participation in public affairs; and, in 1684, admission into the number of these secret families was rendered wholly impossible. From thenceforwards, constantly increasing discontent displayed itself both in town and country. Several very moderate proposals for alleviating the pressure of this oligarchy were rejected with such haughtiness by the government, that disaffection swelled into revolt. In 1781, Peter Nicolas Chenaux of la Tour de Trême, John Peter Raccaud, and an advocate of Gruyères, of the name of Castellaz, formed a league for the achievement of a higher degree of freedom. First they endeavoured to work upon the people by fair promises. Then Chenaux, at the head of a select band of fifty or sixty, undertook to terrify the government into a compromise. But the gates being closed on the party, and the walls manned with armed burghers, this undertaking ended in open revolt. The toll of alarm-bells summoned up the country people from every hill and valley in the canton to assist in the coercion of the domineering capital. A body of nearly three thousand men encamped before the walls of Freyburg, and farther aid was hourly expected. The terrified burghers instantly called for the armed intervention of Berne, and the latter town detached a part of its guard without delay. Three hundred dragoons marched upon Freyburg, and were to be followed by fourteen hundred foot. The burghers of Freyburg now thought themselves strong enough to meet force with force. The garrison made a sally from the town, and on the first sight of the Bernese flag, not to mention the heavy artillery, the malecontents solicited an armistice. The surrender of their arms and of their ringleaders was demanded as preliminary to all negotiation. The people refused the latter of these conditions, but fled panic-struck on the first attack, without making any resistance. The whole affair would have ended without bloodshed, had not the leader Chenaux been murdered in his flight by Henry Rosier, himself one of the popular party. The two remaining heads of the insurgents got clear off: Chenaux's corpse was delivered to the public executioner, and his head fixed on a spear above the Romont gate. Sentence of death was passed on Castellaz and Raccaud, the two fugitives. Several others were visited with less degrees of punishment: new reinforcements from Berne, Soleure, and Lucerne, secured the town from any recurrence of tumult, and their ambassadors strove to promote the restoration of tranquillity. It was ordered to be proclaimed, from all the pulpits, that the council was well disposed to protect the old and well attested rights of its loving subjects, as well as to hear, with its never-failing graciousness, every suitable and respectful representation. Three days were allotted to each commune to lay their complaints and wishes before the government, through delegates. But when months elapsed without the popular grievances having obtained a hearing, the loss of Chenaux began to be appreciated. Multitudes assembled round his tomb weeping and praying: pilgrimages, as if to the tomb of a saint, were made thither with banners, and with crucifixes. Vainly were these demonstrations of feeling stigmatised, by the government as crimes against the state, by the bishop as impious profanations. They were neither to be checked by posting sentinels, nor fulminating excommunications. They were the last sad consolation of the people,— the last substitute for hopes that were already given up.

In the disunited and feeble state of the Swiss confederation, it could not be matter of much surprise that foreigners began to treat it with very little respect. Instead of intrigue and corruption being now what

Philip de Comines had called them, the *only* means of
vanquishing the Swiss, naked menaces often proved a
very successful substitute.   Austria, and still more
France, perpetually encroached upon them.   A fertile
source of annoyance were the constant efforts of these
powers to jostle one another out of favour with the confederation, and in case of war to secure themselves an
exclusive supply of Swiss soldiers.   France in general
gained the upper hand in these competitions, and rewarded the land from which she drew whole hordes of
recruits by restraints on trade, prohibitions of export,
and all the frauds of national bankruptcy.   About the
middle of the eighteenth century, the confederates had
sunk into such contempt at the French court, that they
refrained from addressing even the most equitable
demands to it, in the certain anticipation of a refusal.
But all slights were compensated by such banquets as
that which the French ambassador gave at Soleure on
the 13th of September, 1751, in honour of the birth of
an heir to the throne.   On this occasion a large amount
of gold and silver coins was thrown to the crowd, to be
scrambled for at six different points of the town.   In
honour of the same happy event, gold medals of large
size were distributed to all the principal persons in the
cantons.   These were received with great pleasure
throughout the whole confederation; and the ambassador
had the address to reconcile Zurich and Berne with the
French court, after a long period of mutual alienation.
Finally, in 1777, a new alliance of the whole Helvetic
body with the crown of France was solemnly concluded
at Soleure.   But the confirmation of those commercial
privileges, which the confederates had looked for from
this alliance, were postponed by one of its clauses, which
set forth, " that both contracting parties, animated by
perfect reciprocal confidence, had been unwilling to
delay, by farther discussions, the conclusion of the
present alliance."

CHAP. XIX.

DISTURBANCES AT GENEVA, AND IN NEUFCHÂTEL.

1707—1789.

ARROGANCE OF "PATRICIANS" AT GENEVA. — POPULAR EBULLI-
TION AGAINST THEM IN 1707. — RENEWED IN 1714. —
AGAIN IN 1734. — DEFENSIVE MEASURES OF THE COUNCIL
BAFFLED BY THE POPULACE. — EDICT OF 1738. — BURNING
OF THE BOOKS OF ROUSSEAU. — REPRESENTATIVE AND NEGA-
TIVE PARTIES. — ARMED INTERVENTION OF FRANCE, ZURICH,
AND BERNE. — INTRIGUES OF THE FRENCH. — OF THE NEGA-
TIVES. — REVOLT OF THE REPRESENTATIVES, WHO ERECT A NEW
CONSTITUTION. — FRESH INTERFERENCE OF FRANCE, BERNE,
AND SAVOY. — ENTRANCE AND OCCUPATION OF GENEVA BY
THEIR TROOPS. — RÈGLEMENT OF 1782. — ITS CONSEQUENCES.
— DISCONTENTS IN NEUFCHÂTEL. — DEATH OF GAUDOT. — MAG-
NANIMITY OF FREDERICK II. OF PRUSSIA.

SHORTLY after the establishment of Genevan independence, it had been decreed by the general assembly, for
the better suppression of hostile attempts against their
hard-won freedom, that whoever should propose a change
in the government of Geneva should be considered to
deserve capital punishment.   This did not, however,
hinder alterations being made, at different times, in various
parts of the constitution.   So early as the middle of the
sixteenth century, the laws were revised and improved.
The advantageous situation of the town and the long
duration of peace promoted the increase of wealth in
Geneva, and the rise of many families to opulence.
These families aimed at separating themselves from their
fellow-citizens, even in their places of habitation, by
settling in the upper part of the town, near the council-
house, while the other burghers inhabited the lower town.
The principal families already regarded themselves as a
standing patriciate ; and even the name of patrician
came into use in the acts of council.   The *Régistres du*

Conseil de la République de Génève contain the following
sentence, dated 1690, on occasion of calumnious reports
upon a member of some privileged family: — *" Lesquels
bruits tendent à le priver de l'honneur auquel il estimait
être en droit de prétendre par son âge, ses services, et la
famille patricienne dont il descend."*   In the years preceding the breaking out of the tumults which we shall
have to relate, many examples of favouritism occur in
the elections of members of council; and a decree was
passed, on the 9th January, 1697, *" d'empêcher que l'on
donne aussi facilement le titre de madame aux femmes de
toutes conditions."*

The year 1707 witnessed an effort of the inferior
burghers to wrest from the principal families a part of
their usurped power, and to introduce amendments in
the constitution.   In this emergency, the council invoked
the mediation of Berne and Zurich, received a confederate garrison, and maintained itself by force of arms
and by execution of its principal antagonists.   A renewal
of the disturbances which had been quelled by such
violent measures, was produced, in 1714, by the imposition of an arbitrary tax by the council for the enlarge-
ment and completion of the fortifications of the town.
This stretch of power occasioned great discontent among
the burghers; bitter attacks and censures on the government appeared in print; and the more strictly these were
prohibited, they obtained the more eager perusal and
credence.   One of the arch-promoters of the rising storm
was Michael Ducrest, a Genevan burgher and noble,
an officer in the army, and a member of the great council.
This man opposed himself with extraordinary vehemence
to the building of the new fortifications, and heaped
offensive charges on the partisans of the measure.   The
government condemned him to recant, and, on his evading
compliance by flight, a penal sentence was pronounced
against him.   New attempts which he made to excite
disturbance were followed by a sentence of perpetual imprisonment.   This sentence could not be put in execution, as Ducrest had taken refuge under a foreign

jurisdiction, where he set at defiance the council of
Geneva, and provoked that body to such a degree by his
writings and intrigues against them, that sentences more
and more severe were heaped upon his head, until at
length the most offensive of his writings was torn by the
hangman, and his effigy was suspended from the gallows.
His person, however, enjoyed impunity till 1744, when
he was taken into custody in the territory of Berne. The
government of Geneva did not thirst for his blood, and
was content with his perpetual imprisonment. Even in
this situation he contrived to mix in Henzi's conspiracy,
was confined in the castle of Aarburg, and closed, in extreme old age, as a state prisoner, a life which he had
spent in incessant labours in the cause of democracy.

Meanwhile Geneva continued to be agitated by party
manœuvres and popular discontents. In the year 1734,
a body of 800 burghers addressed themselves to the heads
of the government, desiring the curtailment of the projected fortifications, and the repeal of the tax levied for
that object. The council only replied by preparations for
defence : fire arms were transported to the council hall ;
barricades erected in the approaches thither as well as in
those to the upper town, where the principal class of
burghers lived, and the garrison kept in readiness to act
on the first signal. All this apparatus was regarded with
mistrust by the burghers, who were still farther provoked
by reports of the approach of Bernese troops, and by the
removal of a part of the town artillery to the upper
regions, while two and twenty other pieces were spiked.
The multitude made themselves masters of the city guard,
pointed field-pieces on the road by which the troops from
Berne were expected, and tumultuously demanded the
convocation of the burgher assembly, the sovereign authority of Geneva. The council contrived to win over
the members of this body so far that they voted unanimously the completion of the fortifications and the
continuance of the tax for ten years. The declaration of
an amnesty and improvement of the criminal and judicial
administration formed the rest of their business. The

burghers laid down their arms and returned to their ordinary vocations; so that an embassy which arrived from Zurich and Berne found Geneva in a state of apparent tranquillity. Permanent ill will was fostered only against the syndic Trembley, commander of the garrison and conductor of the defensive preparations of the council. Whatever this person had done by the instructions of the council was laid to his individual account, and added to the mass of dark imputations which were heaped on him, as the head of an already obnoxious family. He plumed himself on the favour of the confederate ambassadors, and forfeited thus the last chance of retrieving himself in the public opinion. The remembrance of the armed intervention of Zurich and Berne, in 1707, was too recent to admit of their ambassadors doing any good to Trembley's cause through the medium of pacific intercession. The departure of these embassies removed the only screen of the syndic: he demanded his dismission, which was refused him, in order to deprive him of his functions more ignominiously. No resistance or artifice of a powerful connection could save him: the tumults were renewed with increased fury; and the question soon ceased to regard the person or party of Trembley, and became that of the triumph of the aristocratic or democratic principle at Geneva. In 1737, the council ventured several arrests, and the consequence was that the whole body of burghers rushed to arms, and the council was defeated, not without bloodshed. A garrison from Berne and Zurich was thrown into the town: the ambassadors of these cantons, in concert with the French ambassador, undertook the office of mediators, and in 1738 framed a constitution which set limits to the assumptions of the council and the principal families, and was gratefully and all but unanimously accepted as a fundamental law by the burghers.

After four and twenty years of repose and prosperity, occasion was given to new political movements at Geneva by a subject of a nature purely speculative. It pleased more than one government about this time to apply the doom of fire, which had been visited by inquisitors on the ill fated victims of their zealotry, to certain of the more remarkable works of the human intellect, — a proceeding highly calculated to draw the eyes of the reading public on productions which seemed worthy of such signal condemnation.   On the first appearance of that work of Rousseau which opened views so novel and so striking on the moral, and still more on the physical, education of man, the parliament of Paris had the work burnt by the hangman, and sentenced Rousseau to imprisonment, which he only escaped by flight.   Both of these decisions were immediately repeated by the council of Geneva, which improved on them by launching a like condemnatory sentence against the *Contrat Social* of the same author.   It was in vain that Rousseau's connections demanded a copy of the sentence against him : their reiterated demands, though supported by a large body of burghers, were rejected by the council.   The popular party, which vindicated the right of the burgher assembly to bring up representations or remonstrances against the council on any subject under discussion, distinguished themselves by the name of representatives. Their claims were met by asserting a *droit négatif*, or right of rejection, on the strength of which the council pretended that nothing that should not have been previously consented to by themselves could come before the general assembly.   The partisans of the council were called *negatives*.

The tranquillity of Geneva was once more disturbed to such a degree by passionate discourses, party writings, and manœuvres, that the ambassadors of Zurich, Berne, and France again interfered, and pronounced themselves in favour of the council.   The representatives rejected their decision, the ambassadors left Geneva, French troops advanced on the town, and all trade and intercourse were suspended.   But the French ministry speedily became lukewarm in the cause of the negatives. The latter, when they found themselves abandoned by all foreign aid, apprehending what might ensue, patched

up a peace with the representatives. By a compact
closed in March, 1768, the burghers acquired valuable
rights, and even a third party, that of the so-called
natifs or *habitans*, (old inhabitants, excluded by birth
from taking part in public affairs,) obtained extended
franchises, and was flattered with a prospect of participation in all the rights of citizenship. But on recovery from the first panic, reciprocal hatred soon
revived. The negatives were vexed at having made such
important sacrifices, and aimed at resuming all their
former ascendency. Moreover they found a favourable
hearing in the French court, which had long viewed
with an evil eye the trade and wealth of Geneva, desired to raise the neighbouring Versoix to a commercial
town, and hoped, by encouraging tumult and disorder
at Geneva, either to annihilate its industry and opulence,
or ultimately to bring it under the sovereignty of France.
French emissaries therefore aided the negatives in spi-
riting the *natifs* up against the representatives, by pro-
mising to confer on them the franchises withheld by
the latter. But the representatives flew to arms, took
possession of the gates, and speedily succeeded in disarming the unpractised and undisciplined mob of natifs.
Well aware by what manœuvres the natifs had been
led to revolt, they prudently abstained from taking any
vindictive measures against them; but, on the contrary,
imparted to them, in 1781, that equality of rights
which had been promised by the negatives, and endeavoured thus to win them over permanently to the
common cause. The council, on the other hand, impelled by French influence, declared the newly-conferred
rights illegally extorted, and invoked the mediation of
Berne and Zurich. But betwixt representative stub-
bornness and negative assumption, the ambassadors of
these towns could exert but limited influence. They
essayed to put an end to disputes by amicable arrangements, but were baffled by the intrigues of the French
court, which was resolved to recognise no democratical
system on its frontiers, and soon proceeded to open

force in support of its secret policy. . The first act of
aggression was to garrison Versoix; a measure which
gave just offence to Zurich and Berne, who thereupon
renounced all adhesion to the mediation of 1738, and
left the Genevans to their own discretion.   France also
declared she would mix no more in the affairs of Geneva—the government was overthrown—and a new
constitution established.

Zurich and Berne now declared formally and coldly
that they could not acknowledge a government erected
by revolt.   Still more indignation was exhibited by
France and Savoy, who entered into a league for the
coercion of the town.   Berne, too, joined this league in
1782, that the destiny of Geneva, that *point d'appui*
of her own dominion, might not be trusted altogether
to the caprice of foreign powers.   On the appearance
of the allied troops before the gates of Geneva, the
burghers, unaware of the bad state of their defences,
swore to bury themselves in the ruins of their native
town rather than yield.   But when the cannon of the
besiegers was advanced up to their walls, and the alternative of desperate resistance or surrender was offered,
the disunited city opened her gates without stroke of
sword, after the principal heads of the representative
party had taken to flight.   Mortal dread accompanied
the victorious troops as they entered Geneva.   Many
had reason to tremble for their lives, their liberty, and
possessions.   No punishments, however, were inflicted,
excepting only the banishment of the principal popular
leaders; but the rights of the burghers were almost entirely annihilated by the arbitrary arrangements of the
victors; the government was invested by them with
almost unlimited power, and proceeded under their
auspices to prohibit all secret societies, military exercises, books and pamphlets on recent events, and to reinforce the garrison by 1200 men under foreign leaders.
Thus the town was reduced to utter subjection, and depopulated by exile and emigration.   From thenceforwards commerce and enterprise fell into decay; and

for seven long years a forced, unnatural calm dwelt in
Geneva.*

During these years the government was conducted with
much mildness, the administration of justice was impartial, that of the public revenues incorrupt, art and
industry were encouraged to the utmost.   But nothing
could win the lost hearts of the people back to the
government.   The iniquity of the so-called *réglement*
of 1782, the destruction of their franchises, and the
disarming of their persons, had wounded irrecoverably
the feelings of the burghers.   The malecontents increased
daily in number; and even many former negatives now
disowned their party, which had gone greater lengths
than they had ever wished or expected.   At length, on
the death of Vergennes, the French minister, and arch
enemy of Genevan independence, the spirit of freedom
awoke with all its ancient strength in Geneva, and the
burghers arose to break their slavish fetters.   But the
recital of the subsequent occurrences must be postponed
until we come to notice the train of events fired by the
French revolution.

The little principality of Neufchâtel, the succession
of which had descended in the same line since the æra
of the second Burgundian monarchy, came, in 1707,
into the hands of the king of Prussia, as next heir to
the ancient house of Chalon.   In 1748, Frederick II.
displayed that love of economy which distinguished all
his measures, by farming out certain parts of the public
revenue arising from tithes, ground rents, and the
crown lands ; from the former administration of which
many of the inhabitants had enjoyed considerable profits.   The loss of these, of course, was felt as a grievance
by the losers ; but what was viewed with more concern
by the mass of the inhabitants was the prospect of still
farther innovations.   Accordingly five communes of the
Val de Travers transmitted their remonstrances through
a delegate to Berlin; and their example was soon afterwards followed throughout the principality.

* See the Appendix.

The arrival of two commissaries, despatched by the king to Neufchâtel, was viewed with discontent as an encroachment on its immunities. Shortly after their coming, an attempt was made to put in execution the proposed financial system, of which the only result was to provoke a tumultuous popular movement. On the 7th of January, 1767, the burgher assembly of Neufchâtel passed a resolution of exclusion from the rights of citizenship, against all who should farm or guarantee the farming of the revenues. On this the royal commissary, Von Derschau, brought a suit before the council of Berne, against the town of Neufchâtel; and the advocate-general, Gaudot, who had formerly been a popular favourite, much to the surprise of his fellow-citizens, seceded to the royal side, and thenceforwards gave his active assistance to the commissary.

The cause was decided at Berne (with some limitations) in the royal favour. With regard to the resolutions of the Neufchâtel burghers, already referred to, it was decreed that they should be cancelled in the presence of the burgher assembly, and a public apology made to the vice-governor. The costs of the whole process to be paid by the town. Gaudot, who had attacked the civic immunities both by word and writing, naturally became an object of popular indignation. By way of compensation, however, he received a lucrative government office, along with the functions of procurator-general, from which another man had been removed who possessed the popular favour. He returned to Neufchâtel from Berne with the royal plenipotentiaries. These and the vice-governor advised him to take up his residence in the castle; but, in spite of their recommendations, Gaudot thought fit to repair to his own residence. The same evening, clamour and disturbance took place around the house, which the magistrates were forced to protect by military force. The next morning the mob returned in increased numbers, and was still farther exasperated by missiles being thrown down upon them. A carriage, escorted by servants in the royal livery, which had been sent by the king's commissary for Gaudot, was knocked to pieces by the infuriated multitude. Gaudot and his nephew now imprudently fired from the windows, and their shots took effect, fatally for themselves. The exasperated populace forced its way into the house; Gaudot was killed by three shots, and the mob dispersed after the deed, with cries of " Long live the king!" The chief actors in this tragedy escaped, and could be executed only in effigy. The whole affair was ultimately compromised by the benevolent moderation of the great Frederick; and terms of pacification were accepted by the communes, which provided alike against arbitrary government and popular turbulence. On this occasion, Frederick displayed more generosity than would have been shown by any cantonal government; and his conduct seemed to justify the general reflection, which must often occur to the student of Swiss history, that when administrative abuses are introduced into a monarchy, it only requires a well-disposed and enlightened prince to crush the gang of official oppressors and extortioners; because such a prince is powerfully backed in such measures by the public opinion. Whereas, when the majority of the ruling class in misnamed republics is corrupted so far as to speculate on the profits of malversation, it generally takes care to recruit its ranks with new accomplices; or, at all events, only to promote to public offices such men as will at least shut their eyes to public abuses. The magnanimity of Frederick was but ill repaid to his successor by the tumults which ensued in Neufchâtel on the commencement of the French revolution; and we have lately seen the same misunderstandings, as in the last century, arise between the now *canton* of Neufchâtel and its Prussian sovereign.

CHAP. XX.

THE half century immediately preceding the French
revolution was the first in which the frontiers of the
Helvetic body had never been approached by foreign
warfare. The load of taxes which pressed on neighbouring nations was unknown in Switzerland; and most of
her governments, exclusively defended by their armed
populations, seemed as secure as military monarchies
fenced with bayonets. It is therefore that those years·
have been described by some contemporaries as a season
of halcyon calm, auspicious to every kind of improvement. Others, again, look back to them as a time
of deplorable slavery; during which monopolies and
corporation privileges had become acknowledged parts
of the public regimen. The country might be compared to a well-fed and carefully-tended child, every
one of whose movements, however, was kept under
minute control.

The democratical cantons, where the assembled population exercised the supreme power in their *landsgemeinde*,
held the lowest station, in almost every respect, amongst
the confederates. Narrowness of mind and ignorant
hatred of all innovation withstood every proposal of
improvement; while passion and prejudice, aided by
the artifices of demagogues, often occasioned acts of
crying injustice. Judicial proceedings were, in the
highest degree, arbitrary; confession of crimes was extracted by torture; which, indeed, was often employed,
when nothing more remained to confess. Capital
punishment, even for minor offences, was by no means
rare. Public offices, particularly that of bailiff or land-
vogt, were commonly conferred not on the worthiest,
but on the highest bidder; and the proceeds of this ig-

U

nominious traffic went to the public treasury. Was it to be wondered at if these functionaries in their turn set justice up to auction in their bailiwicks, and endeavoured to recover their advances to the government by every sort of oppression of its subjects? Mental cultivation was extremely neglected in these cantons, scientific establishments were rare, and those for education were, for the most part, in the hands of the capuchins; whose *esprit de corps* was at least on one occasion beneficial, by preventing the admission of the jesuits into the canton of Schwytz in 1758. Elsewhere, however, similar influences produced worse effects. In Glarus, so late as 1780, an unfortunate servant girl was executed as a witch, on the charge of having lamed the leg of a child by magic, and having caused it to vomit pins. Credulous souls were even found to believe the affirmation that the girl had administered pin-seed through the medium of a magical cake, which had afterwards borne its fruit within the body of the child. The political relations of these cantons, in the period now before us, were of little importance.

The constitutions of the aristocratical cantons had all of them this circumstance in common, that not only the capital towns assumed the rule of the whole canton, but the burghers of those towns themselves were divided into ruling and non-ruling families, of which the former monopolised admission to all places of honour. But the governments of these cantons deserve to be treated of more at length.*

Berne, which, in the first period after its foundation, had no domains of any importance outside its walls, possessed in that immediately preceding the French revolution a territory containing more than 400,000 inhabitants. This considerable tract of land was administered by 250 ruling families, of which, however, only about sixty were in actual possession of the government; and these again were divided into so-called great and small families, and did not easily suffer others to rise to

* See the statistical tables in the Appendix.

an equality with them. The sovereign power resided in 299 persons, of whom the great council was composed. A little council or senate of five-and-twenty formed the executive. The rural districts and the Pays de Vaud were governed by land-vogts or bailiffs. It was chiefly there that discontent prevailed against the Bernese government. The nobles of the Pays de Vaud were rendered wholly insensible to the real and solid advantages secured to them by that government, by resentment of their exclusion from all public employments. The peasants of that district, for the most part subjects or bondsmen of the nobles, sighed under the weight of feudal oppression and its accustomed offspring, poverty, neglected culture, mental and moral abortion. A singular attempt at revolt was made in 1723 by major Daniel Abraham Davel, a well-intentioned man, of excellent character, but a decided political and religious enthusiast, possessed with the idea that he was called by inspiration to emancipate the Vaud from Berne. He assembled the regiment of militia which he commanded, under the pretext of a review, and with these troops, who were altogether ignorant of his real design, and unprovided with stores or ammunition, he surprised the town of Lausanne at a point of time when all the Bernese land-vogts had gone to Berne for the annual installation. Davel offered his aid for the restoration of independence to the hastily assembled town council. He found, however, no kindred spirit in that body; and the cautious citizens put him off with fair words till a force was under arms sufficient to crush him. Meanwhile his troops had discovered the real object of their commander, and shrunk from him in surprise and consternation. He himself was arrested, cruelly tortured for the discovery of accomplices, of whom he had none, and lastly beheaded.

A certain contempt of scholastic acquirements seemed the prevailing tone at Berne; and school education naturally came to deserve the low esteem which it met with. Accordingly those patrician youths who did not serve in the army remained for the most part unem-

ployed until they obtained places under government.
The establishment of what was called the *exterior state*
afforded but a superficial substitute for more solid attain-
ments, and initiated youth only too early in the petty
intrigues and jealousies of faction. This institution,
which was also known by the name of the *shadow state*,
was intended to give the youth of the ruling families
opportunities for acquainting themselves with the forms
at least of public business, and of acquiring an unem-
barrassed address, so important for republicans. It
parodised the dignities and offices of the state, the election of avoyers, councillors, and senators, had its secretaries and functionaries of all ranks, and distributed by
lot 120 vogtships, which for the most part took their
names from ruined castles. Without any sufficient
evidence, some would refer to the æra of the Burgundian
war the origin of this institution, which received the
sanction of government in 1687, and for which a council-
house, far more splendid than that which belonged to
the actual government, was built in 1729. The seal of
this *exterior state* bore an ape astride on a lobster, and
looking at himself in a mirror. These and similar traits
of humour seem to owe their descent to an æra exceedingly remote from the measured formality of later times.

The government of Lucerne, which with Soleure and
Freyburg, formed the remaining pure Swiss aristocracies,
consisted of a little council of six-and-thirty members,
which, reinforced by sixty-four others, held the sovereign
authority. With regard to intellectual cultivation, the
most contradictory features were observable at Lucerne.
On the one hand, learning, enlightenment, and patriotism
were hereditary distinctions of some families; while, on
the other hand, the mass was imbued with ignorant fanaticism. On the one hand, the encroachments of the
papacy were resisted with inflexible firmness; while, on
the other hand, the clergy kept possession of a highly
mischievous influence in the state. On the one hand,
a series of saints' days and holidays was abolished, as
being dedicated to dissoluteness more than devotion;

while, on the other hand, we are horror-struck by the burning of a so-called heretic. In 1747, a court, consisting of four clergymen, sentenced Jacob Schmidli of the Sulzig, a man of blameless life, to be strangled, and then burnt with his books and writings, because he had not only read the Bible for his private edification, but had explained and recommended it to others as the sole true basis of religion. His wife, his six children, and seventy-one other persons, were banished, his house burnt to the ground by the hands of the public executioner, and a monument raised on its former site, to perpetuate the ignominy (query, of the victim or of his judges?).

The appearance of two pamphlets in 1769, on the question, " whether removal or restriction of the monastic orders might not be found beneficial to the catholic cantons?" excited terrible uproar at Lucerne, where certain classes were constantly scenting danger to church or state from some quarter. The town and country clergy, and the bigots in the council, were rejoiced to get so good an opportunity to persecute the holders of free principles, and raised a deplorable howl, as if the canton were on the verge of destruction. The whole population was plunged in consternation and astonishment, by thundering sermons and rigorous prohibitions of the obnoxious work. Free-thinkers were fulminated against by name from the pulpits; and Schinznacht, which had witnessed the formation of the Helvetic society, was denounced as the focus and head-quarters of heresy. This society, which aimed at the diffusion of useful knowledge, public spirit, and union throughout the Helvetic body, without reference to varieties of religion, rank, or political system, was founded by a knot of patriotic and instructed men, in the pious hope of arresting the decline of the confederation. At its commencement it consisted of no more than nine members, but added to its numbers with astonishing rapidity. The society was soon viewed with an evil eye by the cantonal governments, which dreaded all independence of feeling and action in the

people. At Berne, political dangers were anticipated
from it, as symptoms of refractoriness were exhibited
shortly after its formation by the nobles in the Vaud;
while at Lucerne it was regarded as a conspiracy for
shaking off the catholic religion, and assisting the supposed ambition of Berne to gain ascendency over the
whole confederation.

The aristo-democratical governments next come under
our notice, and in these, as in most of the purely aristocratical, the metropolis had obtained unlimited power
over the whole canton. In these, however, particular
families did not engross the sovereign power ; the collective body of citizens had maintained themselves by
means of the regulations of their guilds in the possession of considerable influence over the public affairs.
Accordingly the magistracy favoured the monopolies
which enriched the metropolitan traders, and imposed
restraints on the industry and invention of the surrounding country. Thence the subjects of these towns were
much more harshly administered than those of the aristocratical cantons. Their ancient charters fell into oblivion, and were withdrawn as far as possible from public
inspection ; they were not only excluded from civil and
military, but even from ecclesiastical functions; and
the exercise of many branches of industry, and the sale
of their productions in the towns, was wholly cut off
by corporation privileges. Moreover, since the commencement of the century of which we are treating, no
mode of acquiring the rights of burghers remained open;
they were only conferred on extremely rare occasions to
reward eminent merit; or when the times became trou-
blesome to conciliate influential burghers. Hence that
discontent and disaffection which broke out at the close
of the century found a principal focus in the heart of
the mixed aristocracies.

In the larger cantons the public administration was
for the most part incorrupt; and that of justice was
liable on the whole to fewer complaints than in many
other European countries. The pay of public servants,

with few exceptions, was extremely moderate. Men who had devoted their whole lives to public affairs, and who had filled the highest offices in the state, lost more than they gained by the bounty of their country. At Zurich, the expenses of the government were wholly defrayed without the imposition of taxes, properly so called, from the revenues and interests of the national lands and capital, from ground-rents, tithes, the salt monopoly, and the produce of the premium paid by the several guilds of traders in return for their exclusive privileges. The same description is applicable to the government of Berne, excepting that here the course of justice was tedious and expensive. The superior financial resources of the latter canton enabled her to execute more for public ends than Zurich. Berne invested considerable sums in foreign securities, particularly in the English funds ; and, besides, amassed a treasure amounting to some millions of dollars, which became, as we shall presently see, and as Mably had predicted, the booty of rapacious and powerful neighbours.

Very different was the condition of the *free* or common bailiwicks, particularly those of the democratical cantons; here most of the land-vogts sought by every species of extortion to indemnify themselves for the sums for which they had in fact *bought* their places from the general assemblies of their respective cantons. Many made an open traffic of justice; took presents from both parties; helped delinquents to evade deserved punishment who could pay for exemption, and exacted contributions from the wealthier class whenever and wherever they could. Even farther than in the German domains of Switzerland were abuses of this kind carried in the Italian bailiwicks, and most of all in those of the Grisons. The inevitable tendency of such treatment was to debase the popular character in those districts, and its effects have left unequivocal traces even to this day.

In those towns of which the constitution was grounded on corporate bodies, the privileges of the burghers and

their guilds received progressive extensions. Propositions were made which would hardly have been con-
ceivable in monarchical states, and could only, in fact,
take place where particular classes had to decide upon
the destiny of the rest of their fellow-countrymen. In
Basle it was several times proposed, under the pretext
of protection to agriculture, that the exercise of certain·
manufactures should be prohibited altogether in the
rural part of the canton.

Agriculture was advanced by the cultivation of clover
and of other artificial grasses, and by the consequent
increase of pasturage and manure. Many districts which
had formerly been regarded as unfruitful were thus rendered remarkable for fertility. The processes of ma-
nuring, and many others in Swiss cultivation, became
a model for foreign agriculturists. Arts and manufactures were extended more and more widely. In the
canton of Berne, in the Thurgau, and elsewhere, industry was employed on native materials in the linen-ma-
nufacture; in Zurich, St. Gall, and Appenzell, in working
up imported wool in spinning, weaving, and cotton
printing. Silk manufactures occupied Zurich and Basle,
and the latter town enriched itself by its riband manufacture. Trade in all its branches throve at Geneva;
where a wholesale watch manufacture was conducted,
and from whence watchmaking was soon spread through
the district of Neufchâtel, where it suggested many other
mechanical processes.

Intellectual culture and social refinements marched
abreast with commercial wealth. Not only the towns
were embellished with architectural structures, but in
the Emmenthal, and around the lakes of Zurich and
Geneva, arose new and splendid edifices which bespoke
increasing opulence. In Neufchâtel, which a century before had been inhabited by shepherds, the villages assumed the appearance of towns; and the wealthy marts
of England or the Netherlands were recalled to the mind
of the traveller by the principal street of Winterthur.
Intercourse with other states in trade or in foreign

services naturalised new wants and desires, yet many still adhered to the old usages and manners. In whole districts, especially in the democratic cantons, public opinion imperiously set limits to the advance of luxury. In other places sumptuary laws maintained a struggle with the various arts of invention and evasion; and a wholesome state of simplicity was preserved in Zurich, St. Gall, and Basle, in which celibacy became a sort of rarity.

Sciences and arts were diffused extensively in Switzerland. Albert von Haller, the labours of whose comprehensive mind were chiefly devoted to the sciences of botany and medicine, directed his attention also to politics and philosophy. Eloquence and daring imagination conferred European celebrity on Lavater. Rousseau promulgated truths in education and in politics, which will not be lost for future generations, whatever alloy of paradox or perverse misapplication they might suffer from himself or his followers. The merits of the Bernouillis, Eulers, Lamberts, Saussures, Bonnets, Tissots, Zimmermanns, and others, are still present to the memory of the literary public.

To render the war department of the confederacy more complete, and introduce into it some degree of unity, an association of military officers and magistrates was formed, which held its meetings at Aarau. More was done, however, for the military department by storing up munitions of war than by well adapted martial exercise. Instead of attempting to give precision of movement to the militia, the slower manœuvres of regular troops were objects of imitation. The formation of the Zurich corps of sharp-shooters, however, was more suitable to the real wants and nature of the country.

The bitterness of religious and political dissension which had long prevailed in so many odious forms began to decline, and the personal worth of men began to be estimated by less absurd criteria than their speculative opinions. Old prejudices vanished, or at all events were mitigated, and even if the recognition of principles

more enlightened was with many a matter of fashion
and imitation, still those may be deemed fortunate
whose existence falls on a period in which truth and
liberal sentiments find favour and adoption.

On the whole, the century was not worse than those
which had preceded it.   Even if the forms of government favoured many abuses, a more extended spirit of
activity prevailed amongst the people than in previous
generations; and though it is true that no extraordinarily
great actions were performed, it is also true that no
great occasion called for their performance.   It cannot
be denied that too much jealousy prevailed between the
cantons, and that more reliance was often placed on
strangers than on fellow-confederates.   But Germany,
which united might have given law to Europe, had been
even more distracted by like errors, reduced to a mere
battle-field for foreigner's, and robbed of its most valuable
dependencies.

CHAP. XXI.

FROM THE FIRST YEARS OF THE FRENCH REVOLUTION
TO THE PEACE OF AMIENS.

1789—1802.

FIRST EFFECTS OF THE FRENCH REVOLUTION IN SWITZERLAND.—
IMITATION OF ITS HORRORS AT GENEVA. — POLICY OF THE
FRENCH DIRECTORY. — CISALPINE REPUBLIC. — INSURRECTION
OF THE PEASANTRY OF BASLE. — DIFFUSION OF THE SPIRIT OF
REVOLT. — INSOLENCE OF COMMISSARY MENGAUD. — TROOPS
OF BRUNE AND SCHAUENBURG ENTER SWITZERLAND. — CAP-
TURE OF BERNE. — DEATH OF GENERAL ERLACH. — ERECTION
OF A "CONSTITUTION UNITAIRE." — STRUGGLE AND SUBJEC-
TION OF THE FOREST CANTONS. — FALL OF THE OLD HELVETIC
LEAGUE. — ANARCHY AND TYRANNY.

THE Swiss governments, as well as that large portion of
their subjects who were contented with their condition,

and desired no alteration in it, were startled out of a
state of perfect tranquillity by the first shock of the
French revolution.   The shifting of the whole political
scenery of Europe surrounded them with entirely new
embarrassments.   They resembled steersmen tolerably
capable of guiding their bark safely through the tempests
of their native lakes ; but who found themselves now on
unknown seas without chart or compass.   The situation
of the Swiss regiments engaged in the French service
afforded the first reason for disquietude : the next was
the apprehension of infection from the principles pre-
dominant in France.   Alarming political movements
soon began in the interior ; and the solution of the
problems which were set before Swiss politicians by the
progress of events in the neighbouring countries was the
more difficult the more various were the views, wants,
and relations of the cantons, and the lands which were
subject to them.

It was in the latter districts, as might have been expected, that the new ideas gained the greatest currency,
and that the first attempts were made for their realisation.   Educated and thinking men in the subject towns
and territories brooded resentfully on their exclusion
from all public posts and dignities.   In those cantons
where trade and manufactures were most cultivated, it
was regarded as an intolerable hardship by the enterprising and wealthy rural proprietor, that he was hindered by oppressive regulations from purchasing the
requisite raw materials, or from disposing of the pro-
ducts of his industry in any quarter except to a wholesale dealer of the capital.   Similar resentments were
excited by corporate privileges.   Nevertheless, in the
German regions of Switzerland, a longer time elapsed
before the new modes of thinking, and the comparisons
which they suggested, set the public mind in motion.
This took place much sooner in the west, where the
French language and neighbourhood made communication easier ; above all, in Geneva, where nothing but

an auspicious hour was waited for to burst asunder a yoke imposed by foreigners.

A rise in the price of bread, which was imputed to the government, gave occasion to the long prepared explosion. On the 26th of February, 1789, the burghers assailed the garrison with every thing which could be turned into a weapon of offence. Fire-engines with boiling water supplied the place of artillery: the garrison was put to the rout, and the power of the government overturned the more easily, as its foreign props had now ceased to support it. The ruling class was compelled to throw itself wholly on the citizens, to restore the ancient liberties of the town, and to recall the banished heads of the representatives. But the hour was come for the ruin of Genevan independence. The country people and *habitans* of the town now demanded an equality of rights with the burghers, on the model of republican France; and the latter power was induced to second their wishes, by the suggestions of the ex-representative Clavière. The malecontents were kept for a while in check by troops from Berne and Zurich; but, on the withdrawal of these in 1792, the country people, *habitans* and *natifs*, flew to arms, made themselves masters of the town, deposed the government, and established, on the model of France, a national convention, with committees of general safety and of public welfare.

A show of moderation and tranquillity lasted some time longer; but distrust and exasperation received continual new aliment, and the disinterested friends of peace could hardly prevent some furious outbreak. Many votes were gained to a proposed new constitution, by the hope of securing order and repose; and in the beginning of 1794 it was adopted by a large majority. In April, syndics and council were again installed in their former functions, and the event was announced to Zurich and Berne with expressions of hope and confidence. Berne, however, could not resolve, on the instant, to give the name of confederates to these newly re-established authorities; and what had been done had no effect in mitigating the violence of those who put themselves forwards as the organs of the multitude, which they first set in motion for their own purposes, and then were forced, in turn, to flatter its passions, in order to continue popular favourites. Meanwhile, the price of necessaries rose, while trade and industry stagnated; and the repeated demands for so-styled free-will offerings to the public were answered by supplies more and more sparing.

In order to crush, at a stroke, all resistance, and to furnish themselves with the necessary stores and ammunition, the party of terrorists made a nocturnal seizure of the arsenal in July, 1794, occupied all the posts in warlike array; and filled the prisons of the town,. and even the corn-magazine, with nearly six hundred men, whom they chose to designate as aristocrats; and amongst whom were a number of the most respectable members of the magistracy, merchants, and men of letters. Of eight of the prisoners first examined, a revolutionary tribunal contented itself with sentencing one to death; but the clamour and threats of the multitude worked on these unsteady judges to retract their verdict, and extend the same condemnation to all the others. The doom of four of these was commuted for banishment by the general assembly; but a band of wretches again collected, stormed the prisons, and the bloody tribunal now sentenced their victims to be shot; and afterwards endeavoured to excuse itself on the plea that this had only been done to prevent worse atrocities. More executions followed, which included several persons who had actively promoted revolution. Numbers were banished, in order to secure the ruling party a majority in the general assembly. The large sums required by a revolutionary government for the payment of public officers, and the armed force of the populace, were defrayed by imposing heavy contributions on the possessors of property; *indifferentists* being made to pay double, *aristocrats*, a treble amount.

Party spirit, however, cooled by degrees; approxi-

mations and concessions took place between all classes
of citizens, who felt, in common, the general ruin of
public and private happiness; and the disappointment
of all the hopes which had formerly found indulgence.
In 1796, a return to the old constitution was agreed
upon, on condition of equality of rights being conceded
to the old and new burghers, and the town and country
inhabitants. The exiles returned home, and all rejoiced
that they could again breathe freely. For two years
more, the little republic dragged on an infirm existence;
till it was finally united with France in 1798, and
forced to partake, for fifteen years, the destinies of that
country.

Of the men who had at different times been banished
for political offences from Switzerland, many had taken
refuge in the French metropolis, and endeavoured to
persuade the republican statesmen that their enemies
were equally those of France: their representations found
the easier audience, as Switzerland was already regarded
with greedy eyes by their hearers. " At an early period
of the revolution," observes an English writer *, " the
views of France were directed towards Switzerland, as
well from its importance as a barrier on her eastern
frontier, as from its central position between the German
empire and Italy. The reduction, therefore, of Switzerland, was a favourite object of the republican rulers,
and was only suspended by the dread of adding its people to the host of enemies who menaced France on all
sides; they accordingly temporised under the mask of
friendship, and succeeded in preserving the neutrality of
the Helvetic confederacy, by fomenting the national
antipathy to the house of Austria. Yet even during this
specious display of friendship, their agents industriously
spread disaffection, and prepared the mine which was
ready to explode on the first favourable opportunity:
such an opportunity presented itself at the conclusion of
the treaty of Campo Formio, which left the Swiss without an ally on the Continent. At this period the French

* Coxe.

republic had acquired a colossal strength. The king of
Sardinia, deprived of half his territory, was the vassal of
France; the pope, and the king of Naples, owed the
possession of a precarious sceptre to the forbearance of
the directory; Prussia pertinaciously maintained her
close connection with the new republic; and Austria,
vanquished by the genius of Bonaparte, had concluded
a dishonourable peace."

"But the French rulers were not content with planting
the tricoloured flag on the summit of Mont Blanc, on
the left bank of the Rhine, and at the mouth of the
Scheldt, and with establishing the limits of their empire
by the natural boundaries of the Pyrenees, the Alps, the
Mediterranean and the ocean. With a view to secure
their territories against the future aggressions of the
continental powers, they purposed to form a series of
dependent republics along the line of their frontiers, as
a kind of outwork, to remove the point of attack. At
the extremities of this line they had already established
the Ligurian and Batavian republics; the Cisalpine soon
followed. A connecting link of this chain was Switzerland, which covered the most vulnerable parts of the
French territory; and, from its natural strength and
central position, formed the citadel of Europe."*

Besides these motives, acknowledged by the French
themselves, their rapacity was stimulated by the treasures known to exist at Berne and elsewhere, the amount
of which, as usual, was enormously exaggerated. What
was required, in short, was not a motive but a pretext
for intermeddling with the internal regulations of the
Helvetic body. That body had avoided giving offence
with the utmost caution; had recognised every successive
form of government in France; and had turned out of
their territories the unfortunate French emigrants who
had fled thither for refuge from the rage of their own
countrymen.

The triumphs of Napoleon in Italy were concluded
by the construction of the Cisalpine republic. The Swiss

* See the Appendix.

subjects of the Valteline, Chiavenna, and Bormio, were
tempted to desire participation in the freedom thus established on their borders ; and Napoleon offered the
Grisons the alternative of conceding equal rights to these
districts, or of seeing them included in the new Cisalpine state. Parties ran so high on this proposal, that no
friendly understanding was possible ; and when the term
allowed for reply elapsed without any being given, Napoleon put his threat into effect, and confiscated all property belonging to the Grisons contained in the above-
mentioned districts.

Such was the first encroachment on the ancient limits
of Switzerland : shortly afterwards the bishopric of.
Basle was annexed to France. Great consternation was
caused by these proceedings in the confederation; but
still more serious evils were at hand. In the canton of
Basle the peasantry murmured loudly against the town :
in the Aargau several towns advanced tumultuous claims
against Berne, for the recovery of their old and chartered
rights ; and the Pays de Vaud reclaimed its freedom
with more impatience than ever. It was said besides,
that a French army was already marching on Switzerland; ostensibly to support the claims of the malcontents,
but really to make themselves masters of the land for
their own purposes. Berne and Freyburg hastily levied
forces for the coercion of their turbulent dependencies ;
and a diet of the confederacy was summoned at Aarau.
Much was said and nothing done at this meeting, as the
cantonal governments neither trusted each other nor
their subjects. The members of the diet renewed the
original league of the cantons, as if urged by the pre-
sentiment of its coming dissolution. The oath had hardly
been taken, when a messenger from Basle brought the
intelligence that the mansions of the land-vogts were in
flames ; that a large body of peasantry had entered the
town, and that all the subject districts had declared
themselves free.

The spectacle of feebleness and fear in the authorities,
combined with dogged resistance to the wishes of the

people, of course diffused, instead of quelling, the spirit
of revolt. As in the thirteenth and succeeding century,
the prerogatives of the nobles had been forced to yield to
the claims of a class of burghers and of shepherds, so soon
as the example of the Lombard towns, and the growth of
public prosperity, had excited independence of feeling ;
so likewise, in the times of which we are treating, it had
ceased to be within the power of a privileged class to contend with success against the claims of the so called *third
order*, encouraged as it was by the example of France.
Some districts, indeed, took no part in the prevalent
agitations, and pertinaciously adhered to the accustomed
order of things ; others, more distinguished for enlightenment and enterprise, demanded an equality of rights
in town and country ; others, again, required the restoration of ancient franchises : some regarded nothing
as attainable but by French interference ; while nobler
minds retained an insurmountable abhorrence for the
agency of strangers in the internal affairs of their country.

It became more and more evident, that the policy of
the French directory led them to foment intestine discord in Switzerland. For several years past it had been
observed, that foreign emissaries set themselves to work
upon the public opinion. A person of the name of Mengaud made his appearance at Basle, under the unusual
and equivocal title of *commissary,* and set his seal on
the papers of the French embassy : this individual not
only made no secret of his intelligence with the malcontents in Switzerland, but affected to display it osten-
tatiously. He went to Berne on the 10th of October,
1797, where he demanded, in a note addressed to the
government, the dismissal of the English ambassador,
Wickham, who had certainly exerted himself openly
against France, but had done so as the envoy of a power
at war with that country. Berne referred the demand
of Mengaud to the then directing canton, as a matter
which concerned the whole confederacy. Wickham relieved for the moment the embarrassment of the Helvetic

x

body, while he deprived the French directory of a present pretence for violence, by taking his departure on a
tour into Germany; but he left an able diplomatist
behind him in the person of his secretary Talbot. Mengaud was received at Zurich and Berne with undisguised
aversion, and no diplomatic visits were paid him at
either of these places. In the month of November, an
embassy from the latter town had been sent to Paris;
which, though admitted to an audience of the director
Barras, soon received a rude dismissal homewards.

Great were the hopes infused into the disaffected
party by the promises of Mengaud, and other subordinate agents of France; and proportional fears were
excited amongst the friends of the old system, including
the greater number of public functionaries. In order
to increase their uneasiness, Mengaud threatened the
diet of the confederation in January, 1798, with the
entrance of French troops into Switzerland, should
Austria be suffered to occupy the Grisons. He travelled
to the place of meeting at Aarau, with tricoloured flags
flying from his carriage; and, on his arrival there, hung
out an immense banner in front of his house. The
triumphant revolutionists of Basle had already formed a
tricoloured flag of their own, by the addition of green
to their former cantonal colours, black and white, and
their delegate at Paris, Ochs, had hastily sketched what
he called an Helvetic constitution, on the model of that
of the French republic. This document was printed in
Italian, French, and German, and distributed by Mengaud, not in official quarters only, but throughout the
whole population of the cantons.

In the mean time, a division of the French army,
under Menard, appeared on the western frontier; and
the Pays de Vaud, protected by it, declared its independence of Berne. The Bernese government saw the
necessity of trying the force of arms on its subjects; and
the command of the forces having been declined by
councillor Erlach of Spiez, who had hitherto been one
of the strongest assertors of aristocracy, it was con-

ferred on colonel Rudolf Weiss, who had, till then, sustained the character of a champion of the opposite
system; and had contributed, by a published work *, to
the favourable temper of the partisans of Robespierre
towards the Swiss confederation.   An unusual dele-
gation of full powers placed in his hands the whole
military government of the Vaud.   The new commander
held conferences with the leaders of the malcontents;
published a treatise intended to conciliate them †, but in-
termixed conciliation with menace.   Chillon was recovered by surprise from the insurgents, and the German
troops of Berne were moved on the frontiers of the
Vaud.   Meanwhile, general Menard was already on the
lake of Geneva, with 10,000 men of the conquering
army of Italy; and to him the insurgent leaders,
alarmed for their own safety, addressed themselves.
Menard replied, that he was instructed to give them aid
and protection; and threatened colonel Weiss that he
would repel force with force, if the former should persist in drawing troops around a territory already declared
independent, and in arming the communes against
each other.   Without taking any measures of defence,
—without even attempting to maintain himself on the
high grounds,—Weiss withdrew to the neighbourhood of
Yverdun.   It happened, accidentally, that two French
hussars were shot on the outposts of the Bernese army,
because they had not immediately answered the challenge
of the sentinels.   This incident was taken up by Menard, and afterwards by the directory, as an infringe-
ment of the law of nations, and commencement of hostilities.

The revolution of Basle, and the entrance of French
troops into the Pays de Vaud, rendered it impossible for
reflecting men any longer to doubt that sweeping social
changes were inevitable.   Yet the Swiss democracies
would not be persuaded that any one could shake their

* Coup-d'œil sur les rélations politiques entre la république Française et
le corps Helvétique. 1793.
† Réveillez-vous, Suisses, le danger approche.

x 2

constitutions, or force on them a new species of freedom.
The numerous friends of *things as they were* still hoped
to steer themselves through the crisis without any great
sacrifices, by mere dint of tenacity and delay.   Many,
moreover, flattered themselves with the notion that the
plans of France were levelled at no wider mark than
the Vaud; and were prompted by a petty feeling of
jealousy towards Berne, to see nothing in the affair but
a mortification to that envied canton.

It could hardly be conceived at Berne, that the
French should have advanced without meeting any resistance up to Yverdun, while the head quarters of
colonel Weiss were withdrawn behind Avenche.   He
was instantly dismissed from his command, which was
transferred to general Erlach of Hindelbank; but the
evil effects of exorbitant discretionary powers had
been so sensibly felt, that the opposite extreme was now
adopted.   Meanwhile, the leading statesmen of Berne
had, at length, become convinced that concessions must
be made to the people.   Fifty-two members were added
to the great council from amongst the burghers, citizens
of the minor towns, and rural inhabitants.   It was
resolved to introduce, within a year's time, a new constitution; in which admission to every public function
should be open to all, and due proportion should be observed in the emoluments of all public services. These resolutions were laid before the directory, together with a
demand for the withdrawal of the French troops. The
government also stooped to make a like communication
to Mengaud, to acquaint him with the actual political
system of Berne, and inform him of the wish of that
canton to preserve peace with France. Mengaud made
just such an answer as ought to have been expected from
him.   He demanded a prompt and complete change of
the old political system, declared that farther delays
could not be suffered by the *majesty* of the French republic; and designated the persevering defenders of the
existing order as a handful of inveterate tyrants.

Disregarding their own positive engagements, the

French, on the 8th of February, took possession of the town of Bienne. Yet the confederates still hoped to conciliate France, and were encouraged in this illusion by general Brune, who now commanded the French troops, reinforced by several thousand men, and fixed his head quarters at Payerne. This subtle leader, who, without having performed a lengthened public career, was, to borrow a diplomatic expression, *rompu dans les affaires*, proposed, with artful blandishments, and with hinted hopes of peaceful adjustment, an armistice of fourteen days ; during which the discipline and enthusiasm of the Bernese army had time to abate, indecision and distrust to increase, and recruits to join the French army.

Meanwhile, general Schauenburg had collected a division of troops on the frontiers of Soleure and Berne, equal in strength to that of Brune. The latter announced, on the 26th of February, that he had received full powers to treat from the executive directory. He proposed his ultimatum to the Swiss delegates, that without farther delay they should introduce a provisional government, take measures for the establishment of a new constitution, with securities for freedom and equality, liberate all prisoners for political offences, and withdraw their own troops, as well as those of the other cantons. On the due fulfilment of these conditions, the French troops should be drawn off likewise ; and should not again enter the Swiss territory, unless the government called for their assistance.

On the very day when Brune had given his insolent ultimatum, Erlach entered the great council at Berne, accompanied by eighty of his officers, who were members, like himself, of that body. In a moment of unusual resolution, he was invested with full powers to commence hostilities on the close of the armistice. However, two days afterwards, the delegates returned from Brune's encampment at Payerne. Erlach and his brothers in arms were no longer present in council ; the rest of that body were paralysed by the imminent and

x 3

gigantic danger.; and the full powers which had just
been given the general were taken away. The same
evening, Erlach received instructions *not* to attack the
French, which fired his troops with anger and suspicion,
and tended to confirm the belief in the treachery of
their leaders, already widely prevalent in the army.
Brune's ultimatum, in all its principal features, was
accepted. The delegates of Zurich, Wyss, and Tschar-
ner, sought a conference with him, when he renewed
his former offers in cold and peremptory language; but
now added a novel stipulation to them, namely, that, even
after the confederate troops were disbanded, his should
remain till the new constitution should be established. It
was affirmed, truly or otherwise, that he granted, without
difficulty, an extension of the truce for twenty-four hours;
notwithstanding which, the delegates, on their return, saw
his troops already in motion for the attack.   Orders for
the commencement of hostilities had also been forwarded
from the council of war at Berne to the army, and two
hours afterwards, retracted. In obedience to the first of
these contradictory instructions, the Bernese colonel Gross
had given notice to the French outposts that the truce
would come to an end at ten in the evening of the 1st
of March; but when he withdrew his former announcement on the arrival of counter-orders, Schauenburg
would admit no further parley. He had already attacked, without warning, the old castle of Dornach, in
the neighbourhood of Basle, which sustained a siege of
twenty-four hours. The attack of a Bernese division
near Vingels was repulsed with loss, and the French
surprised the Bernese posts at Lengnau, which they
carried after an obstinate resistance. The town of Soleure capitulated, on Schauenburg's appearance before
it. The passage across the Aar now lay open to the
French troops. Freyburg was attacked and taken, though
a stand was made by the Bernese garrison.

Erlach was now compelled to withdraw his troops
behind the Aar and the Sense; though it was not
without extreme reluctance that the men of Berne

abandoned Morat. On the 3d of March, Brune destroyed one of the finest monuments of Swiss courage
and union, the Ossuary of Morat; and the French,
among whom were many natives of Burgundy, honoured the bones of their ancestors with a grave, after
an interval of more than 300 years. Now at length
Berne, Soleure, and Freyburg proclaimed a levy *en
masse* of the able-bodied men within their territories. The Bernese army was in a dreadful state of
confusion; particularly that division which stood directly opposed to Brune, in which the distrust and exasperation of the soldiers were at their highest pitch.
Officers were dismissed by their soldiers, and others put
in their place. Colonels Stettler and Ryhiner were
bayonetted and shot before the very gates of Berne; and
colonels Crusez and Goumoens fell beneath the sabre-
strokes of their own dragoons. Nevertheless, the troops
were again assembled under command of Grafenried,
who was admirably supported by his officers, and repulsed the French in every attempt to charge them at
the point of the bayonet. Eighteen cannons were
taken from the enemy, and their loss in men besides was
very considerable.

The native troops had now fully recovered spirit and
confidence; but just as Grafenried prepared to cross
the Sense at Neueneck, the decisive intelligence arrived that Berne was in the hands of the enemy!
Early on the 5th, an attack had been made by Schauenburg on Soleure. His force was far numerically superior
to the Bernese; his horse artillery terrified the native
militia by its novelty, and his cavalry was nearly eight-
fold that of Berne in numbers. At Fraubrunnen, the
French turned the left flank of the Bernese: in the
Grauholz and at Breitenfeld their militia under Erlach offered a brave resistance, armed with scythes and
other agricultural implements. Men, women, and even
children mixed, and fell in the mortal struggle. On its
unsuccessful issue, ensued the capitulation of Berne.

All was lost:—the armed bands of the peasantry dispersed in every direction with loud accusations of treason against their officers, many of whom were slain by their own men. Amongst these was the general Erlach, an illustrious name in the annals of Berne. That unfortunate commander, and the avoyer Steiger, when the fortune of the day was decided, retreated towards the Oberland, whither they knew that arms and money had already been despatched by the government, and where they still hoped to offer an effective resistance. But Erlach was murdered in the way by the enraged fugitives, who breathed nothing but revenge for their imaginary betrayal, and it was only by chance that Steiger did not meet a similar fate.

Even public extremity could not restore public spirit. Every little canton treated, armed, and cared, 'for itself exclusively, totally regardless of the rest. Wherever the authorities had, till then, withheld freedom from their subjects, they no longer delayed to grant it; but bestowed emancipation with so ill a grace, as to indicate how gladly they would have refused it, had they dared.

France now assumed a tone of direct command, and proclaimed the dissolution of the Helvetic body, and the establishment of a *constitution unitaire*, embracing the whole of Switzerland under one uniform system of government. This system announced a perfect equality of rights between the inhabitants of the towns and of the villages, assigned the nomination of judges, magistrates, and legislators, to the people in their primary assemblies, and entrusted to the government the choice of executive functionaries. The founders of this new Helvetic republic next proceeded to the more material objects of their mission. They levied large contributions on the towns, appropriated the treasures amassed at Berne, Zurich, Soleure, and Freyburg, and carried off many members of council and other persons, as hostages for the further payments exacted from those places.

But the people of Uri, Nidwalden, Schwytz, and Glarus, were resolved not to deliver up their old independence so easily, and organised an heroic, though an useless, resistance under their brave leader Aloys Reding. The most brilliant and the most sanguinary struggle took place at Rothenthurm, in the neighbourhood of the battle-field of Morgarten. These Alpine shepherds combated with a spirit and success which showed them not unworthy of their forefathers. Thrice were the attacks of regular troops, four times their number, repulsed, with serious loss on the side of the enemy. But the vigour of this peasant militia was exhausted by their very successes, and they were, finally, compelled to accept terms from the invaders, and to bow beneath the yoke of the Helvetic republic. Thus ended the old Swiss confederation, after enduring for a term of nearly five centuries. " It fell," says an enlightened native historian*, "not exactly for want of strength in the bands which held it together; for, without any stronger bond of union the old confederates won their freedom, crushed or repelled the force of mighty antagonists, and rendered themselves powerful and formidable. The Swiss succumbed in the last unfortunate struggle, because the feeling of duty, the lofty faith in their country and its fortunes, had become chilled in the bosoms of the many, and because the democratical cantons thought of none but themselves."

While the well-instructed friends of their country regretted the rude violence with which every link in the system of society, from the Alps to the Jura, had been totally torn away from its ancient holdings, they could not fail to perceive the ultimate benefits educible from the general convulsion. The former aggregation of little states had been productive of estrangement and enmity; the cantons had been proved powerless, even for self-defence; separately too poor for public enterprises; collectively incapable of any combined action. But now an opportunity seemed to be given to the Swiss people of becoming one great family, enjoying equal rights. The mass of the people, however, was not penetrated by

* Ludwig Meyer.

such ideas, and only deplored the breach made in their old habits and usages. They had, indeed, demanded freedom and independence, but not this melting up into an uniform mass. They would have preferred that every petty district, nay, every single valley, should become a free and independent canton, ruling itself in its own assemblies, according to its own pleasure, and only connected by federal ties with the rest of the Swiss people. The whole subsequent march of events tended only to increase the desire for a subdivided federative system of this kind, and the aversion for the newly established order. The new general government, called an executive directory, after its prototype at Paris, resided at Aarau without inspiring either respect or confidence, dependent on its sole protectors, the French plenipotentiaries. In the senate and the great council, composed of delegates from all the cantons, the conflicting opinions of parties caused an incessant wordy warfare. Out of doors the same parties abandoned parliamentary weapons, and asserted their discordant creeds with arms in their hands. New and old laws and regulations were perpetually coming in collision. While the state was often without the most indispensable means for its maintenance, and even for the daily pay of its functionaries, the French plenipotentiaries, leaders, and subalterns, rioted in shameless superfluities at the cost of the country, and sent to France the surplus of their plunder.

The discontents of the people were considerably aggravated by the murmurs and manœuvres of the ci-devant authorities; of the monks who apprehended the abolition of all monasteries; of the priests who had suffered diminution of their stipends, and of the traders and artisans in the towns who no longer enjoyed the sweets of corporations and monopolies. They trusted to the approaching renewal of war between France and Austria, and prepared to support the emperor for the expulsion of the French. When the whole population was summoned, in July, 1798, to take the oath of allegiance to the newly formed constitution, disturbances and revolts

took place in the Rheinthal, Oberland, Appenzell, and
other districts. These were suppressed by military force,
the use of which in Nidwalden was accompanied by extraordinary circumstances of horror. Here Paul Styger,
a capuchin, with others of the clergy, had spirited the
people up to a desperate resistance, on the ground that
the French constitution was an immediate work of Satan.
They armed themselves against the overwhelming force
of Schauenburg, against which they made head for three
whole days, with a loss to the French of from 3000 to
4000 men. The enemy took a merciless revenge for
the resistance of this little band of shepherds by the
burning of Stans and Stans-stadt, and the massacre of
every living being which they found in these places.
The 9th day of September, 1798, witnessed the slaughter
of nearly 400 inhabitants of Nidwalden, with every
possible circumstance of atrocity.

War with France was at length renewed by the emperor of Austria, and a division of his army entered the
Grisons. A signal defeat sustained by the French troops
near Stockach, in Swabia, the victorious advance of the
Austrian army into Switzerland, and the removal of the
seat of the Helvetic government from Lucerne to Berne,
seemed to inspire the conflicting parties with renewed
animation and fury. Swiss fought against Swiss under
the banners of France and Austria; tumults and revolts
took place on account of the French conscription or in
favour of the Austrian invasion; battles were fought
between foreign armies in the vallies, on the Alps, and
on the banks of the lakes; and horse and man clambered
over heights which had formerly been only known to
the chamois hunter. The Grisons and the mountainous
lands as far as the St. Gothard, were alternately won and
lost by French and Germans. The victorious banners
of Austria were carried on the left as far as Zurich and
the St. Gothard, on the right up to the banks of the
Rhine, supported by the Russians under Suwarrow.
Switzerland had never sustained such desolating inroads

since the times of the Romans, Alemanni, and Burgundians.

Many of the old superseded members of the government now looked forward to the speedy restoration of
their authority, which they here and there attempted to
recover with the assistance of the Austrian bayonets:
even the new abbot of St. Gall resumed the exercise of
his feudal rights, such as they had existed before the
recent emancipation which had been granted to the
people. The effects of this iniquitous resumption did
not fail soon to be felt by the proud prelate himself;
Zurich and Schaffhausen, too, were soon forced to acknowledge that the people did not wish to be replaced
in its state of subjection. The decisive and brilliant
victory of Massena near Zurich, and the destruction of
Suwarrow's army, which had marched over the Alps
from Italy, restored the Helvetic constitution throughout
the whole country. Parties now supplanted and succeeded each other in quick succession, so that none could
remain long at the helm or consult for the public benefit.
First of all, the legislative councils dissolved the executive
directory, and substituted for it an executive committee;
then in its turn, this executive committee dissolved the
councils, convoked a new legislature, and styled itself
executive council. Twelve months afterwards a general
Helvetic diet was assembled at Berne for the formation
of a new and improved constitution: this, like the former
deliberative bodies, was arbitrarily deposed from its
functions, and a newest-of-all constitution established,
in October, 1801. Aloys Reding, the victor of Rothenthurm, as the foremost Swiss landamman, was placed
at the head of the senate; but as he neither possessed
the confidence of the French rulers, nor that of those
who detested all recurrence to the old state of things, a
new act of arbitrary power deposed him from the presidency of the council.

These continual changes of administration were looked
upon with absolute indifference by the Swiss people, who
only sighed at the total interruption of law and order,

the increase of taxes, and the lawless acts of the French
soldiery.   The Valais more particularly suffered by the
military tyranny to which it was subjected.   The object
of France was to separate it from Switzerland, in order
to keep a route open across the Alps into Italy.

In the same degree as popular consideration ceased
to attend the ever-changing, but equally odious, as-
pects of the new government, individual opinions and
wild fancies obtained prevalence.   Mystical views were
propagated in Appenzell ; and the anabaptists reared
their heads once more in Berne and Zurich.   The
quiet of the former town and its neighbourhood
was suddenly disturbed by a swarm of fanatics from
Amsoldingen.   Two years before, a quack doctor and
fanatic, by name Antony Unternerer, had fixed his abode
in that village.   A certain flow of language, combined
with prepossessing manners, and the profuse employment of benedictory formulas in human diseases, as well
as in those of cattle, had gained for this fellow the
confidence of the multitude.   He held meetings in
which particular parts of the New Testament were interpreted in a new and peculiar manner ; and his adherents ceased their attendance on the ordinary divine
service.   Unternerer addressed a summons in writing
to the supreme tribunal of Berne, to appear, with all its
prisoners and their keepers, in the cathedral church on
the morning of Good Friday, when the Saviour of the
world would ascend the pulpit, and hold his judgment.
He also summoned all his disciples to meet at Berne on
the same day.   Many of them had already remained
during several days assembled together; and, anticipating
the coming judgment, had transferred their worldly
possessions to others.   Curiosity drew a multitude together from all quarters.   Unternerer himself was announced as Saviour by his adherents ; and seditious
projects peeped out under the mantle of fanaticism.
However, such a wholesome effect was produced by
the arrest of the ringleader, the consignment of his
most conspicuous followers to the lunatic hospital, and

the billetting of dragoons in the houses of others, that the
poor enthusiasts soon came to their senses, lamented the
error of their ways, and the transfer of their properties.

The peace of Amiens, betwixt France and the other
belligerent powers, in consequence of which the French
garrisons were drawn home out of Switzerland, afforded opportunity to the party and provincial spirit
to show itself with new vigour. On the 12th of
July, Montrichard, the French resident in Switzerland, communicated in an extra-official note to the
Helvetic landamman, Dolder, that he had received
commands from the minister of war to hold himself,
with the troops under his orders, in readiness for
instant return to France. The landamman laid tnis
note before the then executive council, who were considerably embarrassed by its import, and addressed
themselves to Montrichard and to the Swiss ambassador
at Paris, to petition for a postponement of the measure.
But shortly afterwards, Boizot, secretary of the Helvetic
embassy, arrived from Paris with Talleyrand's note,
which fixed for the approaching 20th of July the complete evacuation of Switzerland. It was now out of the
question for the heads of the Helvetic government to
oppose themselves to a measure invoked by the wishes
of a large majority. Accordingly the executive council
did its best to assume an unconstrained and easy attitude;
and with all expedition voted its liveliest thanks to the
first consul for his purpose of withdrawing his troops
from Switzerland, which they hailed as the highest
proof of his benevolence and respect for the independence of the Helvetic nation. The reply of the French
minister was couched in terms of disinterested delicacy,
which almost seemed ironical. He talked of the French
troops as the battalions which the first consul had consented to leave in Switzerland on the conclusion of peace.
He based the proposed measure on the confidence entertained by the first consul in the virtues of the Helvetic people, who were now better agreed, as he said,
on the principles of political organisation, and in whose

attachment the government would find sufficient securities for the maintenance of order and tranquillity. " The Helvetic government could not but regard this resolution as a pledge of the consul's confidence in its friendly intentions and policy, and of his disinclination to meddle with the internal affairs of other nations."

It is impossible to assign with any certainty the motives by which this ambiguous language and conduct were dictated. The first consul may have meant to give a popular example of moderation and respect for the faith of treaties ; or he may have designed a covert chastisement for the feeble attempts at independence made by the Helvetic government, and its refusal of unconditional acquiescence in the projected separation of the Valais; or he may have wished to extort an express prayer for the stay of his troops, or to revive the struggle of parties, and compel the Helvetic government to throw itself into the arms of France, and urge him, as though against his will, to assume the part of arbiter and ruler ; or, finally, perhaps, the best solution of his conduct may be found by supposing the combination of all or most of these motives.

Conformably with the system thus enforced upon them, the executive council made known to the Swiss people the departure of the French troops, as a gracious boon, the offer of which they had eagerly accepted. In effect, the removal of these troops was performed with such celerity, that none were left behind but the sick in the hospitals, and a handful of men here and there to guard whatever French property was not of a moveable description.

The news of the retreat of the French troops, and the ill-concealed uneasiness of the government, flew through the country with wonderful rapidity, and every where roused the concealed but numerous enemies of the existing order, who had hitherto lurked inactively, as it were in scattered cantonments. The Valais declared itself independent. Uri, Schwytz and Unterwalden took up arms against the Helvetic government. The town of Zurich, likewise, threw off allegiance to it; an example which was speedily followed by Schaffhausen and Basle. A general levy took place in the Aargau against Berne: the helpless Helvetic government fled for refuge to Lausanne, while a diet was held in Schwytz for the restoration of the old league. The feeble body of troops in the pay of the government were driven from the interior of the country, and followed their employers into the Vaud: every where the opposite factions prepared for active hostilities; the towns planned the destruction of the general government; the peasants armed for their freedom against the pretensions of the towns; and the Pays de Vaud arrayed itself in defence of Helvetic unity. Blood had already flowed, and civil war appeared inevitable, when Napoleon turned his eyes again upon Switzerland, and commanded peace in a tone which was not apt to meet with resistance.

" Inhabitants of Switzerland !" (such were the terms of a declaration addressed by him through general Rapp to the cantons of the Helvetic republic,) " you have presented, during two years, a melancholy spectacle. Sovereign power has alternately been seized by opposite factions, whose transitory and partial sway has only served to illustrate their own incapacity and weakness. If you are left to yourselves any longer, you will cut one another to pieces for years, without any prospect of coming to a rational understanding. Your intestine discord never could be terminated without the effective interposition of France. I had resolved not to mix in your affairs; but I cannot and will not view with indifference those calamities to which I now perceive you exposed. I retract my former resolution. I offer myself as your mediator, and will exert my mediation with that energy which becomes the powerful nation in whose name I speak. Five days after reception of the present declaration, the senate shall assemble at Berne, to nominate three deputies to be sent to Paris, and each canton will also be admitted to send delegates thither. All citizens who have held public employments during the last three years may also appear at Paris to deliberate by what means may best be effected the restoration of concord and the reconciliation of parties. Every rational man must perceive that my purposed mediation is a blessing conferred on Switzerland by that Providence, which, amidst so many concurring causes of social dissolution, has always preserved your national existence and independence. It would be painful to think that destiny had singled out this epoch, which has called to life so many new republics, as the hour of destruction to one of the oldest commonwealths in Europe."

The Helvetic senate instantly replied to this announcement, by declaring that it received, with lively gratitude, this new proof of the friendly dispositions of the first consul, and would conduct itself in all points in conformity with his wishes. In a proclamation, addressed to the Helvetic people, after some allusion to the mighty and uplifted arm of the mediator, it recommended union, tranquillity, and calm expectation. The cantonal diets met to elect deputies to Paris. The several communes also were permitted to despatch delegates thither at their own expense. The mandate of Napoleon, and the presence of his soldiers, induced conflicting parties to suspend their hostilities, and tacitly, at least, to acquiesce in his mediation, as they could come to no agreement with each other.

CHAP. XXII.

FROM THE ACT OF MEDIATION TO THE PRESENT TIMES.

ACT OF MEDIATION. — ITS EFFECTS. — FALL OF NAPOLEON. —
DECLARATION OF NEUTRALITY BY THE SWISS DIET. — PRO-
CLAMATION OF PRINCE SCHWARTZENBERG. — AUSTRIAN INVA-
SION. — CONGRESS OF VIENNA. — RECOGNITION OF THE XXII
CANTONS. — SWITZERLAND A PARTY TO THE HOLY ALLIANCE.
— FOREIGN POLICE. — SURVEILLANCE OF THE PRESS. — RE-
VIVAL OF THE JESUITS. — EDUCATION, ETC. — CONCLUSION.

On the 10th of December, 1803, Swiss delegates were
received in the office of foreign affairs at Paris, to hear
a note of Bonaparte read, in which he addressed them
as president of the French and Cisalpine republics, and
laid down the basis of his intended mediation. "A
federal constitution," he said, "is a point of prime necessity for you. Nature herself has adapted Switzerland
for it. What you want is an equality of rights among
the cantons, a renunciation of all family privileges, and
the independent federative organisation of each canton.
The central constitution may be easily arranged afterwards. The main points for your people are neutrality,
promotion of trade, and frugal administration: this is
what I have always said to your delegates when they
asked my advice; but the very men who seemed to be
the best aware of its truth, turned out to be the most
obstinately wedded to their privileges. They attached
themselves, and looked for support, to the enemies of
France. The first acts of your insurgents were to appeal
to the privileged orders, annihilate equality, and insult
the French people. No party shall triumph; no counter-
revolution take place. In case of violation of neutrality,
your government must decide upon making common
cause with France."

On the 12th, Bonaparte received a select number
of the Swiss deputation, to whom he farther addressed
himself as follows: — " The only constitution fit for

Switzerland, considering its small extent and its poverty, is such a one as shall not involve an oppressive load of taxation. Federalism weakens larger states by splitting their forces, while it strengthens small ones by leaving a free range to individual energies." He added, with an openness peculiar to great characters, and unequivocally indicative of good will, " When I make any demand of an individual, he does not often dare to refuse it; but if I am forced to apply myself to a crowd of cantonal governments, each of them may declare itself incompetent to answer. A diet is called : a few months time is gained; and the storm blows over."

Almost every word of the first consul during these negotiations has historical value. Most of his expressions wear a character of greatness; all of them afford a clue to the system on which he acted. One or two passages, taken at random here and there, will suffice for a specimen. " It is the democratic cantons which distinguish you, and draw on you the eyes of the world. It is they which do not allow the thought of melting you up with other states to gain any coherence or consistency. The permission to settle wherever they please, in pursuit of their vocation, must be extended to all natives of Switzerland. The small cantons are said to be averse to this principle; but who on earth would ever think of troubling *them* by settling amongst them ? France will re-open a source of profit in favour of these poorer cantons, by taking additional regiments into her pay. France will do this, not because she needs additional troops, but because she feels an interest in attaching these democracies."

The *Act of Mediation*, which resulted from these conferences, restored the old federative system; but not without introducing very considerable improvements. The amnesty announced by it precluded all persecutions, and the new agitations necessarily arising from them. All servitude and all privilege were abolished; while equality of rights and freedom of industry were established. The mischievous freedom formerly enjoyed

by the several cantons of entering into hostilities or
alliances against each other was quite put an end to. In
future, they could only use their arms against the common enemy; and the objects of the whole league could
no longer be frustrated by the humours of its individual
members.

The dissolution of the Helvetic general government
followed naturally on the completion of the above-mentioned arrangements; and soon afterwards Napoleon recalled his troops from Switzerland. The people, in
almost every part of the country, returned quietly to
their usual occupations, and tendered their allegiance to
the new order of things. In the canton of Zurich alone,
several communes refused the oaths; complaining of
the difficulties newly thrown in the way of the redemption of tithes, ground-rent, and other burdens. They
would listen to no friendly representations; but committed acts of violence on unoffending functionaries;
set fire to the castle of Wädenschwyl; and finally took to
arms. The prolonged disorders of former years had
accustomed them to lawless self-defence; but the insurrection was soon suppressed by the aid of the neighbouring cantons, combined with the well-affected part of the
Zurichers. The ringleader, John James Willi, a shoemaker in the village of Horgen, and others of his more
conspicuous comrades, were punished with death. The
less distinguished rioters suffered imprisonment, and
forty-two offending communes were visited with a war-
tax of above 200,000 florins. It was well that the
first flame of revolt was speedily extinguished, before it
had time to spread itself through the country. Parties
remained every where unreconciled; and each imagined nothing to be required for their predominance
but the fall of the new order of things. The friends of
Helvetic unity still murmured at the cantonal partition
of the country. The monasteries murmured as they
felt their existence threatened; and Pankratius, the
ci-devant abbot of St. Gall, openly stigmatised the inhabitants of that district as contumacious vassals of the

empire. Many of the country people murmured, who
wished for *landsgemeinde*, on the model of the original
cantons. Many patrician and city families murmured
that their privileges were swept away, and the peasantry
no longer their subjects. The majority of the people,
however, wished for nothing but peace and quiet, and
decidedly adhered to the existing order of things, and
the rights which they had acquired under that order.

Thus the peace of the country remained for the most
part undisturbed; and a series of comparatively pros-
perous years followed. The energies of the Swiss had
been awakened by the years of revolution and of civil
war, and displayed themselves in a hitherto unprecedented degree. They no longer stood apart from each
other as formerly, like strangers; but had been made
better acquainted by the storms of social collision. The
concerns of each canton were now interesting to all.
Journals and newspapers, which had formerly been
suppressed by timid governments, instructed the people
in useful knowledge, and drew its attention to public
affairs. The Swiss of all cantons formed societies for
the furtherance of objects of common utility; for the
encouragement of various arts and sciences, and for the
maintenance of concord and patriotism. The canal of
the Linth formed a lasting monument of this newly re-
awakened public spirit.

Since the people had ceased to be viewed as in a state
of perpetual infancy, a new impulse was given to trade
and industry, which were now no longer cramped and
confined, as formerly, by corporate restrictions and monopolies. The participation in public affairs allowed to
all free citizens enforced a mild and equitable conduct on the governments. Schools were increased and
improved throughout the country; the military force
was newly organised; and, on the whole, a greater
number of laudable objects were provided for in the
space of ten years, than had been thought of in the previous century.

When the throne of Napoleon sunk under the power

of the allies, the public-spirited part of the Swiss nation fondly imagined that the hour was come in which their country's honour and independence might be established on a firmer footing than ever. To preserve the benefits gained to the land by his act of mediation was the wish of a large majority of the people. If the Swiss had sometimes felt, along with others, the iron arm of that formidable despot, (who had, however, spared them more than any neighbouring population,) yet his gift of a constitution had become deservedly dear to them. It had dried up innumerable sources of discord.   Under it a fellow-feeling, never before experienced, had been diffused in the same degree as individual pride had been humbled. The cessation of a state of subjection, wherever it had before existed, had decupled the number of confederates, and all restraints on free communication betwixt one canton and another had been removed.

The cantons sent their contingents for the protection of the frontiers, voted extraordinary imposts for their maintenance, and a diet was assembled at Zurich with unanimous instructions from its constituents. This body declared with one voice its resolution " to observe a conscientious and impartial neutrality with regard to all the high belligerent powers," expressing, at the same time, its full anticipation that " the same would be acknowledged upon their part."   It addressed itself as follows to the confederates:—" The great and only end of all our endeavours is to maintain this neutrality by every means in our power ; to protect our country's freedom and independence; to preserve its soil inviolate, and to defend its constitution."   The senate of Berne expressed itself as follows :—" Our object is to guard the pacific borders of our country inviolate from the march of foreign armies; we are unanimously resolved, however, at all events, to maintain tranquillity, order, and security in our canton by all the means which stand in our power."

Such was the general sense of the Swiss people. Not such, however, was the sense of the great families in the once dominant towns of the confederation. Many of these wished to see their country invaded by foreign armies, by aid of which they hoped to restore the old league of the thirteen cantons, with all its hated appendages of sovereignty and servitude, which had vanished from the face of the land in 1798.

The Swiss delegates were received in a friendly manner by the emperor of Austria and the king of Prussia; but no direct recognition of their neutrality was vouchsafed to them. The satellites of these monarchs gave them distinctly to understand that Switzerland was regarded and would be treated as nothing else than as a limb of the French system. A large Austrian force was collected on the frontiers, particularly in the neighbourhood of Basle; yet many still believed that a determined vindication of neutrality would not be put down by violence. In the mean time, the Swiss delegates were stopped at Freyburg in Brisgau on their return homewards from Frankfort, and their letters were intercepted. A general enervation seemed to have spread itself over the conduct of the affairs of the confederation at this crisis. There is no ground for supposing that the men who led their forces, and presided in their governments, acted the part of secret conspirators against the order of things which they professed to defend. But when the overwhelming powers of the allies came pouring in upon them; when these were joined by kings who owed their crowns to Napoleon; when even the French ambassador dissuaded reinforcement of the frontier cordon; when, in short, the ancient state of things renewed its sway on every side; while a decided popular will showed itself nowhere; opposition was in a manner overwhelmed by the force of circumstances.

A proclamation, couched in terms of mildness and of amity, was issued by prince Schwartzenberg, the Austrian commander-in-chief; and at the same time count Capo d'Istria declared on his arrival in Zurich, that "the monarchs could not recognise a neutrality which, in the existing situation of Switzerland, must be nothing more than nominal. The armies of the allied powers hoped to find none but friends there. Their majesties pledged themselves solemnly not to lay down their arms until they should have secured the restoration to Switzerland of the territories wrested from her by France —(a pledge which we shall presently see was adhered to but indifferently). · They disclaimed all wish of meddling with her internal constitution ; but at the same time could not allow her to remain under foreign influence. They would recognise her neutrality from that day forth in which she became free and independent."

The Austrian army marched over the Rhine on the 21st of December, 1813, through the territories of Basle, Aargau, Soleure, and Berne, into France. During the first months of the following year the burdens, and even the dangers of war, were felt very severely in the northern and western parts of Switzerland, particularly in Basle, which received much annoyance from the obstinate defence of Huningen, and the hostile disposition of the commander of that place. Geneva, too, while she welcomed in anticipation the new birth of her ancient independence, saw herself suddenly surrounded with the actual horrors of warfare, and threatened with a regular siege. The continual passage of large bodies of troops brought malignant fevers and maladies in their train, and it became more and more difficult to supply them with provisions.

On the entrance of the Austrian troops, Berne set the example of abolishing the act of mediation, and reclaimed the restoration of the predominance which she had previously enjoyed in the Helvetic body. The example was followed first by Soleure and Freyburg, and then by Lucerne. In Zurich, too, the diet declared the act of mediation, by virtue of which it was sitting, null and void, and drew up a plan for a new confederation of the nineteen cantons. But this was not enough for some of the men in power at that time, who demanded nothing short of the restoration of the old league of the thirteen cantons, and had already summoned the Pays de Vaud

and the Aargau to return under the government of Berne.
These cantons, however, resolutely rejected the proposal.

The diet, which was again convoked at Zurich, and
consisted of delegates newly elected by all the nineteen
cantons, was now the only feeble bond which kept the
Helvetic body together. Interested voices were raised
on every side for annihilating or mutilating the last
constructed cantons, which for sixteen years had enjoyed
the boon of freedom and independence. Zug demanded
a part of its former subject lands from the Aargau; Uri
the Val Levantina from the canton of Tessin; Glarus
the district of Sargans from the canton of St. Gall; the
prince abbot Pancrace his former domains and sove-
reignties in the Thurgau; Schwytz and Glarus combined to demand compensation for their privileges over
the districts of Uznach, Gaster, Wesen, and Ersatz;
Unterwalden, Uri, and Schwytz, united in a similar
demand for compensation for the sovereign rights which
had formerly been possessed by them in Aargau, Thurgau, St. Gall, and on the Tessin.

In these cabals and commotions Zurich, Basle, and
Schaffhausen displayed the least of prejudice or passion;
while the Aargau and the Vaud showed themselves
worthy of their freedom by the spirited resolution of
their people. In the lands and towns of Basle, Soleure,
and Zurich, it was proposed to espouse the cause and
rally round the standard of the Aargau. Berne, however, avoided open hostilities, and even offered to recognise the independence of the Vaud on certain conditions,
which were rejected by the latter. Aargau now made
menacing demonstrations, and a dangerous ferment
showed itself in the Oberland. Here, as in many
other places, the jealousy and suspicion of the various
parties came into play, in proportion as discussion was
broached on the limits to be assigned to the rights of the
people and their governments. News were daily received
of scattered plots and insurrections, of imprisonments
and banishments, in various places. The town of Soleure called for the protection of a Bernese garrison

against the threatened attacks of its own people. Swiss
troops were precipitately despatched to the banks of the
Tessin to prevent the breaking out of civil war; while
other troops were sent into the canton of St. Gall to put
an end to a scene of absolute confusion.

While Switzerland was thus given up to a state of such
disquietude, that blood had already flowed in more than
one district, and the gaols of several towns were filled
with prisoners, the plenipotentiaries of the great powers
were sitting in congress at Vienna, to establish the peace
of Europe on a durable foundation. The allies had
already allowed the addition to the Helvetic body of
Geneva, as well as of the Valais, and the Prussian principality of Neufchâtel. Swiss delegates made their appearance with equal promptitude in the imperial metropolis on the Danube, as they had done eleven years
before in the capital of France. But the politics of
Europe moved no faster at Vienna than those of Switzerland did at the diet of Zurich. No settlement of
Swiss affairs had been made, when the sudden news of
Napoleon's landing from Elba, and his triumphal march
through France, awakened European diplomacy once
more from its slumbers. The diet called to arms the
half contingent of 15,000 men for the defence of the
frontiers. Two battalions of the Vaud were detached
hastily to Geneva, and the same canton received as friends
and comrades the troops of Berne, against which it had
taken up arms a month before. The most important
elements of discord seemed to have disappeared — the
most inveterate enemies to be reconciled.

On the 20th of March, 1815, the definitive arrangements of the allied powers were promulgated. The
existing nineteen cantons were recognised, and the
increase of their number to two-and-twenty confirmed,
by the accession of Geneva, Neufchâtel, and the Valais.
The canton of Vaud received back the Dappenthal,
which had been taken from it by France. Bienne and
the bishopric of Basle were given to Berne by way of
compensation for its former sovereign rights over the

Vaud. One moiety of the customs received in the Val Levantina was assigned to Uri; the prince abbot Pancrace, and his *ci-devant* functionaries, were indemnified with 8000 florins yearly. A decision was also given on the indemnification of those Bernese who had possessed jurisdictions in the Pays de Vaud, and on many other points in dispute. The complaints of the Grisons alone were disregarded—Chiavenna, the Valteline, and Bormio, which had now become the property of Austria, were neither restored, nor any compensation for them given, notwithstanding the clause to the contrary in prince Schwartzenberg's proclamation.

The cantons now remodelled their respective constitutions in the midst of agitations of all kinds. Those in which the supreme power is assigned to the *landsgemeinde* for the most part removed the restrictions on the popular prerogative, which had been introduced by the act of mediation, and approximated anew to pure democracy. In the city cantons, the capitals recovered, though in various modifications and proportions, a preponderance in the system of representation. Even in these privileged places, however, many friends of the public weal remained true to the conviction tried and proved by past experience (and about to receive after no long period additional confirmation from the march of events), that participation of the lesser towns and rural districts in public functions was a requisite condition for the permanence of tranquillity; and that the members introduced from these remoter parts of the country would form vigorous roots of the slender stem of authority, and fix them wide and deep in a republican soil.

From 1815 till 1830 no political movements of any extent or importance disturbed the outward semblance of repose in the Helvetic body. In 1817, the confederates were led by the invitation of the emperor Alexander into a signal deviation from the policy of their forefathers. They entered into a close alliance with Austria, Russia, and Prussia; and allowed themselves to be mixed up with the system of the great powers, by giving their adhesion to the Holy Alliance, unmindful of the lessons left by the Swiss of old times, whom the whole force of the empire could not frighten into the *petticoat league.* But the new alliance held itself destined to higher ends than that of Swabia, although in both perhaps the high contracting parties went to work with equal singleness of purpose. The holy alliance aimed at nothing less than the attainment of the loftiest ends of the purest cosmopolitism!—the realisation of that perpetual peace which had hitherto been regarded as a fugitive thought of Henry IV., or as a philanthropic vision of the abbé St. Pierre.

On the conclusion of the war of liberation from Napoleon, an opinion which the allied powers had encouraged by their promises became prevalent through great part of Germany—that the efforts of the people should be requited by the grant of representative constitutions. The realisation of this object was pursued by open and secret means, which soon aroused attention and mistrust on the part of the governments. Investigations were set on foot, which were followed up by penal inflictions; and many of the accused parties made their escape into Switzerland. A similar course was taken by some Italians, on the suppression of the Piedmontese revolts, and the abortive revolution of Naples. Natives of France, moreover, who had given offence to their government, either by republican principles, or by adherence to the cause of Napoleon, in like manner sought a place of refuge in Switzerland. These occurrences did not fail to give umbrage to several cabinets, which was increased by the friendly welcome and assistance afforded to the fugitives from Greece. It never seemed to occur to foreign potentates, what a blessing in the vicissitudes of European affairs were the existence of a land to which political victims of all parties might resort as an inviolable sanctuary.

The year 1823, which, it will be remembered, was that of the French invasion of Spain under Louis XVIII.

seemed an epoch of especially unfriendly dispositions in
more than one European court against Switzerland.
There were personages who would willingly have used
these dispositions to effect some limitation of Helvetic
independence; but their influence was either insufficient
for that purpose in the cabinets to which they belonged,
or Europe seemed *as yet* not ripe for success in such an
experiment. Meanwhile the remonstrances and demands
of continental powers afforded matter of anxious consultation to the Helvetic diet; and their usual subjects
of discussion were increased by two new topics,—*foreign
police*, and *surveillance of the press.**

It was resolved that both these points touched the
prerogatives of the separate cantons, and therefore did
not admit of decision at any general diet. An invitation was accordingly issued to the governments of all
the cantons, exhorting them to adopt vigorous measures,
in order that nothing might find its way into newspapers and journals inconsistent with proper respect to
friendly governments. With regard to *foreign police*
it was proposed to take measures for preventing the
entrance or residence of such strangers as had left their
country on account of crimes, or efforts at disturbance
of the public repose; and for providing that no foreigners should be admitted except such as could show
certificates or passports from their respective governments.

In many of the cantons these demands were met by
a ready alacrity, not only to urge their execution in their
full extent, but even to improve on them by subjecting
discussion of *domestic* as well as of foreign affairs to
strict surveillance. On the other hand, in more enlightened parts of the confederacy, it was thought that
public discussion and the old right of sanctuary should
be guarded from every species of encroachment. The
diets continued to busy themselves with deliberations
on both subjects. Returning tranquillity diminished
the uneasiness of the cabinets; and, by consequence,

* See the Appendix.

their inquisitive and minute attention to Switzerland.
Individuals lost the importance which had formerly
been ascribed to them, and the sojourn of strangers in
Switzerland again became freer.   The press occasioned
more prolonged discussions at the diets and in several
of the councils; but in the midst of these it obtained
more and more freedom, and in some districts shook
off all its former restrictions.

During these years an interest in church affairs diffused itself amongst laymen, as well as amongst theo-
logians by profession.   In the educated classes religious
indifferentism became less frequent; while the genuine
spirit of tolerance made progress.   This tendency, like
every other widely extended mental movement, had its
questionable as well as its pleasing features.   Shocking
ebullitions of fanaticism are reported to have taken place
in Zurich, Berne, and other cantons.   A footing was
gained in Freyburg and the Valais by the revived order
of jesuits; and the friends of human improvement
could not regard, without anxiety, their influence in
ecclesiastical matters, and in education.

In the latter department much has been done in every
part of Switzerland, though much still remains to be
desired.   Those restrictions of the chairs in universities
and academies to the natives of particular localities,
which formed so complete a counterpart to the old corporation privileges, have come to an end in almost all
the principal towns of Switzerland; where foreigners, or
Swiss of other cantons, hold a distinguished place at the
head of learned establishments.   Many branches of
knowledge, once neglected, have been diffused and per-
fected.   The name of Pestalozzi has obtained deserved
celebrity throughout all Europe, and even beyond its
limits, as well on account of the practical improvements
which he made in particular parts of elementary instruction, as of the impulse which he gave to the cause of
general education.   The culture of the mind and the soil
are both indebted to Fellenberg, whose agricultural establishments, besides their direct utility, have been above

all efficacious, by attracting the attention of the educated
classes, and giving a scientific direction to husbandry,
which is equally distinct from that of mere routine as
of mere theory. The removal of former restrictions has
encouraged the progress of industry, and the spirit of
invention and enterprise.

Such was the course of affairs up to the memorable
year 1830, when the mere vibration of those mighty
explosions, which shook the social atmosphere from Paris
to Warsaw, brought the popular masses in Switzerland
down on her half-renewed aristocracies, like the avalanche, which the slightest sound precipitates on her
valleys. The constitutional changes introduced in the
cantons have not yet acquired sufficient consistence to
come within the province of history; nor is a Swiss revolution now an event of European interest.* The fate
of empires no longer waits the arbitrement of Alpine
shepherds ; and the masses of modern warfare laugh to
scorn individual heroism. But the triumphs of peace
are yet reserved for Switzerland : *her* standard shows
the *trois couleurs* of EDUCATION, ECONOMY, INDUSTRY ;

" AND OF THAT EMPIRE THERE SHALL BE NO END."

---

* See the Appendix.

APPENDIX.

PAGE 46.

THE dignity of history, it is hoped, will not be offended by the insertion here of a ballad, entitled " *The Count of Haps-burg*," translated from the German of Schiller, as it affords a pleasing version of the legendary ornaments with which popular tradition loved to grace the rise of its hero. Tschudi, who has furnished the foundation for it, further relates, that the priest, to whom this incident with Rudolph occurred, afterwards became chaplain to the archbishop of Mentz; and, at the first imperial election which followed the interregnum, contributed not a little to turn that prelate's thoughts on the count of Hapsburg:—

> 'Twas at his crowning festival,
>   Rob'd in imperial state,
> In Aix-la-Chapelle's ancient hall
>   The good king Rudolph sate.
> His viands bore the Palatine,
> Bohemia serv'd the sparkling wine,
>   And all th' Elective Seven *
> Lowly the lord of earth surround,
> As the glorious sun is girt around
>   With his starry choir of heaven.
>
> Crowds from the high balcony gaze
>   In joy tumultuous pressing,
> And mix with the mounting hymns of praise
>   Full many a murmur'd blessing:
> For ended at last are the crownless years,
> With their harvest of ruin, of blood and tears,

---

* The seven princes who exercised the right of giving, or *selling*, the empire, were the archbishops of Mentz, Trier, and Cologne, the elector palatine, Branderburg, Bohemia, and Saxony.

Earth owns a judge once more.
Ended at last is the reign of steel;
No more the feeble dread to feel
   The gauntlet-grasp of power.

And the Kaiser uplifts his goblet bright,
   As he speaks with blithesome voice: —
" Fair is the feast, and proud the sight;
   Mine heart might well rejoice:
Yet miss I the minstrel, the bringer of pleasure,
The soother of hearts with his magic measure,
   The teacher of lore divine.
So I have held in my youthful prime,
And the lessons I learn'd in my knightly time
   As Kaiser shall still be mine."

In long-flowing robe, through the courtly crew,
   The Minstrel's form appears;
His locks are bleach'd with a silver hue,
   With the fulness of wasting years.
" Sweet melody sleeps in the golden strings;
The minstrel of love and its guerdon sings,
   He sings of the Highest, the Best,
Of all ye can covet with heart or eye;
But say what may sort with the majesty
   Of my Kaiser's crowning feast."

" I rule not the singer," was Rudolph's word,
   " Nor recks he of earthly power;
He stands in the right of a greater Lord,
   And obeys the inspiring hour.
As the storm-wind sweeps through the midnight air,
One knows not from whence it is borne, or where;
   As the springs from a soundless deep;
So the minstrel's song from his bosom swells,
Our feelings to wake, where in inmost cells
   Of the heart they strangely sleep."

Sudden and strong the Minstrel plays,
    And rapidly flows his strain :—
" A valiant knight to the chamois chase
    Rode forth across the plain,
Him follow'd his squire with his hunting-gear;
When a tinkling sound accosts his ear
    On a meadow's gentle marge:
'Twas the sacring bell that moved before,
And a priest, who the Saviour's body bore,
    Came next with his hallow'd charge.

And the Count to earth has bow'd him low,
    His head all humbly bare,
The faith of a Christian man to show
    In him our sins who bare.
But a brooklet brawl'd o'er the meadow-side,
High swell'd by the Giessbach's rushing tide,
    The wanderer's path it stay'd;
And softly he laid the host adown,
And swiftly he doff'd his sandal-shoon,
    The brawling brook to wade.

" Now whither away? " the Count began,
    And he cast a wondering glance.
" Sir knight, I haste to a dying man,
    For heavenly food who pants:
And here, as I sought my wonted way,
The stepping-stones all have been torn away
    By the Giessbach's whirling force.
Thus, lest a soul salvation miss,
The brook with naked foot, I wis,
    Behoves me now to cross."

But the Count set him up on his knightly steed,
    And reach'd him the bridle gay,
That he fail not to solace a sinner's need,
    Nor the holy rite delay.
Himself rode forth on the horse of his squire,
To share in the chase at his heart's desire.

The other his way pursued,
And thankfully came with morning red,
And humbly back by the bridle led
    To the knight his courser good.

" Now saints forfend," said that noble knight,
" I should e'er bestride him more,
In reckless chase, or heady fight,
    My Saviour's self that bore !
Mayst thou not make the good steed thine own,
I freely devote him to God alone ;
    I give it to Him who gives
To man, his bond-slave, breath and blood,
And earthly honour, and earthly good ;
    In whom he moves and lives."

" O, then, high Heaven, whose watchful ear
    Inclines to the poor man's vow,
To thee give honour above and here,
    As Him thou hast honour'd now !
Thou noble count, whose knightly brand
Widely hath waved in Switzerland,
    Seven daughters fair are thine :
Each shall enrich thine ancient stem
With the dower of a kingly diadem,
    Sent down to the latest line."

The brow of the Kaiser is bent in thought,
    As he dream'd of distant years,
Till the eye of that aged bard he caught,
    And the sense of his song appears.
He recalls the face, so long unseen,
And veils his tears with his mantle sheen :
    'Tis the priest himself is here !
All eyes are turn'd on their silent lord,
All know the knight of the Giessbach's ford,
    And the hand of Heaven revere.

PAGE 56.

A STORY very similar to the Swiss legend of Tell is related in the Danish annals by Saxo Grammaticus; in which Harold king of Denmark supplies the place of the land-vogt Gessler, Toko that of William Tell; and this event, which is said to have happened in 965, is attended also with nearly the same incidents as those recorded in the Swiss accounts. It is far from being a necessary consequence (as is very justly observed in Coxe's Travels), that because the authenticity of the story concerning the apple is liable to some doubts, *therefore* the whole tradition relating to Tell is fabulous. Neither is it a proof against the reality of a fact, that it is not mentioned by contemporary historians. The general history of William Tell is repeatedly celebrated in old German songs, so remarkable for their ancient dialect and simplicity, as almost to raise the deeds they celebrate above all reasonable suspicion : to this may be added the constant tradition of the country, together with two chapels erected some centuries ago in memory of his exploits. The following is the passage from Saxo Grammaticus : —

" Nec silentio implicandum quod sequitur. Toko quidam aliquandiu, regis (*i. e.* Haraldi Blaatand) stipendia meritus officiis quibus commilitones superabat complures virtutum suarum hostes effecerat. Hic forte sermone inter convivas temulentius habito tam copioso se sagittandi usu callere jacti-tabat, ut pomum quantumcunque exiguum baculo e distantiâ superpositum primâ spiculi directione feriret. Quæ vox pri-mum obtrectantium auribus excepta regis etiam auditum at-tigit. Sed mox principis improbitas patris fiduciam ad filii periculum transtulit, dulcissimum vitæ ejus pignus baculi loco statui imperans. Cui nisi promissionis auctor primo sagittæ conatu pomum impositum excussisset, proprio capite inanis jactantiæ pœnas lueret. Urgebat imperium regis militem majora promissis edere, alienæ obtrectationis insidiis parum sobriæ vocis jactum carpentibus.

" Exhibitum Toko adolescentem attentius monuit, ut æquis auribus, capiteque indeflexo quam patientissime strepitum jaculi venientis exciperet, ne lævi corporis motu efficacissimæ

z 3

artis experientiam frustraretur. Præterea demendæ formidinis
consilium circumspiciens, vultum ejus, ne viso telo terreretur,
avertit. Tribus deinde sagittis pharetrâ expositis prima quam
nervo inseruit proposito obstaculo incidit.

"Interrogatus autem a rege Toko cur plura pharetræ spicula
detraxisset, cum fortunam arcus semel duntaxat experimento
prosequi debuisset. ' Ut in te,' inquit, ' primi errorem reli-
quorum acumine vindicarem, ne mea forte innocentia pœnam
tui impunitatem experiretur violentia.' Quo tam libero dicto
et sibi fortitudinis titulum deberi docuit, et regis imperium
pœnâ dignum ostendit."

PAGE 282.

THE following passage, on the Règlement of 1782, is
translated from "*Meiners' Briefe über die Schweitz,*" an interesting series of letters on Switzerland, published shortly
before the French revolution : —

" Even if the edict of 1782 had produced much greater
advantages than it actually did produce, yet still we cannot
blame the representative party for regarding it as the offspring and the instrument of despotism : it was not left to
the free choice of the citizens whether they would or would not
accept a legislation which was to bind themselves and their
posterity for ever, but the ambassadors of the guaranteeing
powers excluded, as a preliminary step, from the conseil général,
to which the edict was to be submitted, all those who had
taken up arms on the 8th of April, or in the sequel; and thus,
in that general assembly in which the new edict was confirmed
hardly a third of the burghers were present who had the right
of voting on the validity or invalidity of new laws. In the
edict itself the most important rights were withdrawn from the
people, or, at all events, subjected to restriction. What,
however, gave the burghers greater pain than all these losses
was their total disarming, the abolition of the circles of the
burgher militia, and all the civic exercises which had hitherto
been the most joyous popular festivals. Finally, in order to
enchain the mind as well as the body, all speaking and writing
on public affairs was forbidden, and a garrison of 1000 men

was introduced, which, instead of being billeted on the burghers, was to live in separate barracks, as in fortresses. All the *useful* rights of the burghers were extended to the natives, and the senate was allowed the freedom of giving strangers, under the name of domiciliés, allowance to settle for a year in Geneva, and to carry on mechanical trades, and other private vocations."

PAGE 284.

General view of the Thirteen Cantons, Subject Bailiwicks, and Confederated States, as they existed from the Peace of Aarau up to the French Revolution.

I. *The Cantons.*

	Square Miles.	Population.	Contingent of Troops.	Form of Government.	Religion.	Language.
1. Zurich	676	175,000	1,400	Aristo-democratic	Protestant	German
2. Berne	3,840	374,000	2,000	Aristocratic	Protestant	German & French
3. Lucerne	544	100,000	1,200	Aristocratic	Catholic	German
4. Uri - -	550	26,000	400	Democratic	Catholic	German & Italian
5. Schwytz	326	23,000	600	Democratic	Catholic	German
6. Unterwalden	179	23,500	400	Democratic	Catholic	German
7. Zug - -	102	20,000	400	Democratic	Catholic	German
8. Glarus -	336	16,000	400	Democratic	Mixed	German
9. Basle - -	160	40,000	400	Aristo-democratic	Protestant	German
10. Freyburg	467	73,000	800	Aristocratic	Catholic	German & French
11. Soleure -	288	45,000	600	Aristocratic	Catholic	German
12. Schaffhausen	128	30,000	400	Aristo-democratic	Protestant	German
13. Appenzell	256	51,000	600	Democratic	Mixed	German
Totals - -	7,852	996,500	9,600			

The greatest part of the materials for compiling these tables have been collected from Durand's Statistique Elémentaire de la Suisse. The measures of extent which, in foreign authors, are generally given in German miles, 15 to a degree, are here reduced to geographical miles, 60 to a degree. — V. Planta, Hist. Switz. iii. 117.

II. *The Subject Bailiwicks.*

	Square Miles.	Population.	Contingent of Troops.	Sovereigns.	Religion.	Language.
1. Thurgau	266	60,000	500	VIII. Old Cantons	Mixed	German·
2. Rheinthal	84	13,000	200	Ditto with Appenzell	Mixed	German
3. Sargans -	148	12,000	300	VIII. Old Cantons	Mixed	German
4. Gaster 5. Uznach 6. Gambs	149	9000	—	Schwytz and Glarus	Catholic	German
7. Rapperswyl - -	8	5000	—	Zurich and Berne	Catholic	German
8. Baden -	188	24,000	200	Zurich, Berne, and Glarus	Mixed	German
9. Upper free Bailiwicks 10. Lower free Bailiwicks - -	85	20,000	300	VIII. Old Cantons, Zurich, Berne, and Glarus	Catholic	German
11. Bremgarten - - 12. Mellingen - -	—	5,000	—	Zurich, Berne, and Glarus	Catholic	German
13. Schwartzenberg - 14. Morat - 15. Granson 16. Orbe and Echallens	150	40,000	—	Berne and Freyburg	Catholic Protestant Protestant Mixed	German German & French German & French French
17. Bellinzona - 18. Riviera, or Polese 19. Val di Blenzo -	110	38,000	—	Uri, Schwytz, and Unterwalden	Catholic	Italian
20. Lugano	205	53,000	400	All the cantons, except Appenzell	Catholic	Italian
21. Locarno	263	30,000	200			
22. Val Maggia - -	158	24,000	100			
23. Mendrisio -	67	16,000	100			
Totals - -	1831	344,000	2400			

III. *Confederated States.*						
	Square Miles.	Population.	Contingent of Troops.	Form of Government.	Religion.	Language.
I. Associates.						
Abbey of St. Gall.						
a. Alte Landschaft - -	124	45,000	1000	Monarchic limited monarchy	Catholic	German
b. Tockenburg	188	46,000			Mixed	German
2. City of St. Gall - -	—	8,300	200	Aristo-democratic	Protestant	German
3. Town and territory of Bienne -	144	5,500	200	Mono-aristocratic	Protestant	German
4. Mühlhausen	—	8,000	—	Democratic	Protestant	German
II. Allies.						
1. Grison leagues	2,304	150,000	—	Democratic	Mixed	German and Romaunsch
Their subject provinces	960	100,000	—	Monarchical	Catholic	Italian
2. The Valais	1,280	100,000	—	Six dixaines democratic One dixaine aristocratic	Catholic	French and German
3. Neufchâtel and Valengin - -	240	40,500	—	Mono-aristocratic	Protestant	French and German
4. Geneva -	88	34,000	—	Aristo-democratic	Protestant	French
5. Part of the bishopric of Basle allied to the cantons - -	106	24,000	—	Mono-aristocratic	Protestant	French
III. Sovereignties under the Protection of the Forest Cantons.						
1. Abbey of Engelberg -	28	4,500	—	Monarchical	Catholic	German
2. Gersau -	—	1,000	—	Democratic	Catholic	German
Totals - -	5,462	566,800	1,400			
Totals in the whole confederation	15,145	1,907,300	13,400			

PAGE 295.

M. Thiers, in his History of the French Revolution, has criticised the opinion which prevailed in 1799, and which attached extreme importance to the occupation of Switzerland in warlike operations on a grand scale: —

" On pensait alors," he says, "que la clef de la plaine était dans les montagnes. La Suisse, plaçée au milieu de la ligne immense sur laquelle on allait combattre, paroissait la clef de tout le Continent. La France, qui occupait la Suisse, semblait avoir un avantage décisif. Il semblait qu'en ayant les sources du Rhin, du Danube, du Pô, elle en commandât tout le cours. C'était là une erreur: on conçoit que deux armées qui appuient immédiatement une aile à des montagnes, comme les Autrichiens et les Français, quand ils se battaient aux environs de Vérone, ou aux environs de Rastadt, tiennent à la possession de ces montagnes, parceque celle des deux qui en est maîtresse peut déborder l'ennemi par les hauteurs. Mais quand on se bat à cinquante ou cent lieues des montagnes, elles cessent d'avoir la même influence. Tandis qu'on s'épuiserait pour la possession du St. Gothard, les armées qui seraient sur le Rhin, ou sur le Bas Pô auraient le temps de décider du sort de l'Europe. Mais on concluait du petit au grand ; de ce que les hauteurs sont importantes sur un champ de bataille de quelques lieues, on en concluait que la puissance maîtresse des Alpes, devait l'être du Continent. La Suisse n'a qu'un avantage réel ; c'est d'ouvrir des débouchés directs à la France sur l'Autriche, et à l'Autriche sur la France. On conçoit dèslors que pour le repos des deux puissances et de l'Europe, la clôture de ces débouchés soit un bienfait. Plus on peut empêcher les points de contact et les moyens d'invasion, mieux on fait ; surtout entre deux états qui ne peuvent se heurter sans que le Continent en soit ébranlé. C'est en ce sens que la neutralité intéresse toute l'Europe, et qu'on a toujours bien fait d'en faire un principe de sureté générale."

PAGE 333.

The following were the definitive measures adopted with respect to foreigners: —

" Art. 1. No foreigner shall fix his legal residence in any canton, unless he have previously obtained permission.

" 2. Every foreigner is obliged to give notice to the police, within twenty-four hours after his arrival in the canton.

" 3. Foreigners who after their arrival in the canton shall desire to remain more than three weeks, shall apply to the director-general of police, at the Alien-office.

" 4. Foreigners who shall reside in the canton without being authorised shall be sentenced to pay a fine of 500 florins, and to two months' imprisonment.

" 5. Keepers of furnished hotels, innkeepers, and householders, who shall have lodged foreigners without permission, shall be liable to a fine of 1000 florins, and to three months, imprisonment; in case of a repetition of the offence, the penalty shall be doubled."

The decree on the printing of political writings comprises the following articles: —

" Art. 1. No person shall sell, or cause to be printed, without the previous licence of the council of state, works relative to foreign policy.

" 2. This licence shall not be given, till the MS. has been examined, to see if it contains any thing reprehensible. In both cases, it must be signed by the author and the printer, and deposited in the chancery.

" 3. The author, printer, or bookseller, who shall transgress this order shall be brought before the tribunal, where they may be condemned to a fine of 1000 florins, and a year's imprisonment. The penalty may be increased, according to the contents of the writing, as the seriousness of the circumstances may require."

PAGE 335.

It has not entered into our plan to particularise every petty rising which has recently taken place in the towns or rural districts of Switzerland, and the recital of which would not even possess the sanguinary interest which distinguishes the peasant insurrection of the seventeenth century. It may, however, conduce to the purposes of historical instruction, to mark the leading points of view in one or two of those districts, the fortunes of which have chiefly claimed our attention in the past, and in which the continuance, or interruption, of former modes of being forms the most interesting, as well as instructive, feature in the present.

Geneva, during nearly the whole course of the eighteenth century, has been already described as labouring under incessant agitation; occasioned by the arrogance of a class of monied oligarchs, confronted with the growing force of an active and turbulent commonalty; and terminated only towards the close of that century in the agonies of social dissolution. All the evils exhibited on more conspicuous theatres, arising from an obstinate monopoly of political power, broke forth within the narrow bounds of this Lilliputian commonwealth, with all the aggravations of those evils which are wont to result from hostile and external interference. Hence the insulting *règlement* of 1782, when the grasping spirit of native aristocracy was encouraged in its all engrossing claims by foreign bayonets. Hence also the reign of terror in 1794, when French support, which had previously been given to the oligarchs, was transferred to the scale of the democratic party. It is some consolation to those who would fain believe in the progress of their species, that the crash of those enormous fortunes which, previously to the first revolution, were chiefly invested in French public securities, and the fall of that ' patrician' dynasty, solely maintained by French influence, have been attended by the total disappearance of their concomitant ostentation and assumption; while the terrible experience of all parties has effectually softened their irrational embitterment. In the recent revolutionary changes which have occurred in Switzerland, Geneva has been amongst the places wholly exempt from disturbance. The constituted authorities there wisely took the initiative of such constitutional changes as the temper of the times required, by voluntarily conceding an extension of the elective franchise, and an abridgment of the tenure of public offices.

The comparison of Geneva with Berne affords a striking instance of the difference between overweening oligarchy and pure aristocracy. In the former state, what was more revolting than any practical grievance was aristocratic *morgue*, combined with purse-proud ostentation. In the latter, that systematic repression of popular developement, inherent in the nature of aristocracy, was accompanied at least with much of the dignified and paternal aspect with which philosophical minds have often invested that austere domination. Of such a government Montesquieu might truly have called moderation *the soul* — such might have found an approver in Dion, an eulogist in Plato. In Berne, at least equally with Venice, economy, prudence, and self-dependence held paramount sway; pauperism, and consequent vice, were extirpated with unwearied care; and the popular respect was secured by forbearing to swell the public burthens. In Berne alone could a law have been regarded as *truly aristocratic* *, which enforced equal division of the paternal estate amongst the children.

Not unrewarded by long esteem and permanence was the upright aristocracy of Berne; and truly has it been stated by an eminent burgher of that canton †, with regard to its first overthrow in 1798, that the revolution did not find developement *from within.* " Without the aggression of hostile armies," (we still translate from the same authority), " the sound block of the old building would long have remained standing, and would have kept its decayed outworks standing along with it. It is true that fermentation pervaded the Vaud, as well as several districts in the interior; but matters would not have gone so far without French intervention. The German subjects of Berne, unmoved by the insinuations of French emis-

* " Ein wahrhaftig aristokratisches Gesetz." — *Meiners, Briefe über die Schweitz.* 1er Theil.
† See Schlosser's Archiv für Geschichte und Litteratur, 2er Band, p. 324.

saries, fought resolutely, not to say furiously.   They deemed themselves invincible, as of old, confiding in the protection of God and their own personal strength, unfortunately of too little account in modern warfare.   Incendiary suggestions found no entrance, so long as their authors stuck to preaching freedom and equality; but so soon as it occurred to them to ascribe the errors of government, and such military evolutions as to common men were inexplicable, to a secret understanding of their rulers and officers with the French, the popular rage instantly took a new direction against their leaders, as supposed secret adherents of the new-fangled notions of freedom; and horrible scenes ensued, which hastened the hour of dissolution."

INDEX.

A.

AARAU, the peace of, 267.

Ackermann, of Unterwalden, marches with 5000 men against the Bernese, and surprises their troops, 266.

Adolphus, count of Nassau, elected emperor, his character and death, 53.

Agnadello, the battle of, 182.

Agnes, queen of Hungary, 60.

Albert of Hapsburg, 49. His character; seizes on the imperial insignia, 52. Aims at erecting a new dukedom in Helvetia, 53. Forbids his subjects on the frontiers all intercourse with the forest cantons, 58. Death of, 59.

Albert, duke of Austria, demands from the Zurichers satisfaction for the burning of Rappersweil, 74. Besieges Zurich, 75. Endeavours to compel the people of Zug to renounce their connection with the Swiss league, 77. Concludes a treaty with the confederates, commonly known by the name of the Peace of Thorberg, 79.

Albigenses, 106.

Alemanni, the, 13.

Amberg, the Swiss land-vogt, 210.

Amiens, the peace of, 318.

Anabaptists, the, 209. Excesses of, 213.

Angoulême, duke d', 152.

Appenzell, revolt of, 99. Independence of, 103.

Arbedo, the battle of, 114.

Arnold of Cervola, 89.

Arnold of Winkelried, a knight of Unterwalden, killed in the battle of Sempach, 94.

Arnold, of Brescia, 199.

Augusta Rauracorum, the colony founded by Munatius Plancus, 8.

Austria forms an alliance with Zurich, 97. Vanquished by the genius of Bonaparte; concludes a peace, 303.

B.

Baden, a disputation held at, 212. The catholic majority of the meeting declare themselves to have triumphed in the controversy; and prohibit the works of Luther and Zwingli, 213.

Bailli of Dijon, the French agent in Switzerland; his threats to the Bernese, 168. Levies a force of 24,000 Swiss, 179.

Barras, the French director, 306.

Basle, the bishop of, 46.

Basle, the university of, founded in 1460, 125.

Beaume, Peter de la, 219.

Berchthold of Rheinfelden; death of, 33.

Berchthold II., duke of Zæringen, 33. Appears in the presence of the emperor at the diet of Mentz, in 1097; surrenders the ducal office and dignity into the hands of Frederick of Hohenstaufen, 34.

Berchthold IV., duke of Zæringen, 37.

Berchthold V., duke of Zæringen, 38. Lays the foundation of Berne; places it as a free town of the empire under the immediate protection of the emperor, 39. Refuses the imperial crown; receives compensation from Philip, son of the late emperor; his death, 40.

Berchthold, abbot of St. Gall, 46.

Berenger of Landenberg, his cruelty and tyranny, 54.

Berne erected into a free town of the empire by Berchthold V. duke of Zæringen, 39. Becomes obnoxious to the bordering nobility, 81. Renews her league with the forest cantons, 84. Her plans of aggrandisement, 86. Empowered by the confederates to close a treaty with France, in which they engage to give no aid to the duke of Burgundy, 135. Declares war with Burgundy, 141. The cause

THE END.

LONDON:
Printed by A. & R. Spottiswoode,
New-Street-Square.

COSIMO is a specialty publisher of books and publications that inspire, inform and engage readers. Our mission is to offer unique books to niche audiences around the world.

COSIMO CLASSICS offers a collection of distinctive titles by the great authors and thinkers throughout the ages. At COSIMO CLASSICS timeless classics find a new life as affordable books, covering a variety of subjects including: *Biographies, Business, History, Mythology, Personal Development, Philosophy, Religion and Spirituality,* and much more!

COSIMO-on-DEMAND publishes books and publications for innovative authors, non-profit organizations and businesses. COSIMO-on-DEMAND specializes in bringing books back into print, publishing new books quickly and effectively, and making these publications available to readers around the world.

COSIMO REPORTS publishes public reports that affect your world: from global trends to the economy, and from health to geo-politics.

FOR MORE INFORMATION CONTACT US AT
INFO@COSIMOBOOKS.COM

If you are a book-lover interested in our current catalog of books.

If you are an author who wants to get published

If you represent an organization or business seeking to reach your members, donors or customers with your own books and publications

COSIMO BOOKS ARE ALWAYS
AVAILABLE AT ONLINE BOOKSTORES

VISIT COSIMOBOOKS.COM
BE INSPIRED, BE INFORMED

Printed in the United States
90906LV00002B/273/A

9 781602 061170